STATISTICS
FOR PEOPLE
WHO *(Think They)*
HATE
STATISTICS

This is dedicated to the one I love.
In memory of Doris Kenner-Jackson and the Shirelles

STATISTICS FOR PEOPLE WHO *(Think They)* HATE STATISTICS

NEIL J. SALKIND

Sage Publications, Inc.
International Educational and Professional Publisher
Thousand Oaks ▪ London ▪ New Delhi

For information:

Sage Publications, Inc.
2455 Teller Road
Thousand Oaks, California 91320
E-mail: order@sagepub.com

Sage Publications Ltd.
6 Bonhill Street
London EC2A 4PU
United Kingdom

Sage Publications India Pvt. Ltd.
M-32 Market
Greater Kailash I
New Delhi 110 048 India

Printed in the United States of America

Library of Congress Cataloging-in-Publication Data

Salkind, Neil J.
   Statistics for people who (think they) hate statistics / by Neil J. Salkind.
      p.   cm.
   Includes index.
      ISBN 0-7619-1621-0 (cloth: alk. paper)
      ISBN 0-7619-1622-9 (pbk.: alk. paper)
      1. Statistics. I. Title
   HA29.S2365   2000
   519.5—dc21   99-050472

This book is printed on acid-free paper.

00 01 02 03 04 05 10 9 8 7 6 5 4 3 2

Acquiring Editor:	C. Deborah Laughton
Editorial Assistant:	Eileen Carr
Production Editor:	Diana Axelsen
Editorial Assistant:	Nevair Kabakian
Designer/Typesetter:	Janelle LeMaster
Cover Designer:	Candice Harman

BRIEF CONTENTS

PART I

PART II

PART III

PART IV

PART V

DETAILED CONTENTS

PART II

PART III

PART IV

PART V

A NOTE TO THE STUDENT: WHY I WROTE THIS BOOK

I have been fortunate enough in my 26 years at the University of Kansas to teach the basics of statistics to thousands of students. What many of them have in common (at least at the beginning of the course) is a relatively high level of anxiety, the origin of which is, more often than not, what they've *heard* from their fellow students. Often, a small part of what they have heard is true—learning statistics takes an investment of time and effort (and there's the occasional monster for a teacher). But most of what they've heard (and where most of the anxiety comes from)—that statistics is unbearably difficult—is just not true. Thousands of fear-struck students have succeeded where they thought they would fail. They did it by taking one thing at a time, pacing themselves, seeing illustrations of basic principles as they are applied to real-life settings, and even having some fun along the way.

After a great deal of trial and error and some successful and many unsuccessful attempts, I have learned to teach statistics in a way that I (and many of my students) think is unintimidating and informative.

What you will learn from this book is the information you need to understand what the field and study of basic statistics is about. You'll learn about the fundamental ideas and the most commonly used techniques to organize and make sense out of data. There's very little theory (but some), and there are few mathematical proofs or discussion of the rationale for certain mathematical routines.

Why isn't this material in *Statistics for People Who (Think They) Hate Statistics*? It's not that I don't think it is important. Rather, at this point and time in your studies, I want to offer you material at a level I think you can understand and learn with some reasonable amount of effort—while at the same time, not be scared off from taking future courses.

So if you are looking for a detailed unraveling of the derivation of the analysis of variance F ratio, go find another good book from Sage Publications (I'll be glad to refer you to one). But if you want to learn why and how statistics can work for you, you're in the right place. This book will help you understand the material you read in journal articles, explain what the results of many statistical analyses mean, and teach you how to perform basic statistical work.

Good luck and let me know how I can improve this book to even better meet the needs of the beginning statistics student.

–Neil J. Salkind
University of Kansas
njs@ukans.edu

ACKNOWLEDGMENTS

The best books result from the combined efforts of good editors and competent writers. If this book does what it should, it's because of C. Deborah Laughton's guidance, insight, and hard work; Eileen Carr's excellent assistance; and others at Sage who still think that authors deserve to be treated fairly and with respect: Kate Peterson, copy editor; Nevair Kabakian, editoral assistant; Diana Axelsen, production editor; Janelle LeMaster, interior designer/typesetter; Kristi White, graphics; Jason Love, cartoonist; and Candice Harman, cover designer. Thanks also to the following reviewers for their suggestions: Lewis Margolis, James Craig, Ron Fisher, Amanda Blackmore, and Craig L. Frisby.

PART I

Yippee! I'm in Statistics

SNAPSHOTS

N ot much to shout about you might say? Let me take a minute and show you how some very accomplished scientists use this widely used set of tools we call statistics.

- Michelle Lampl is a pediatrician and an anthropologist at the University of Pennsylvania. She was having coffee with a friend, who commented on how quickly her young infant was growing. In fact, the new mother spoke as if her son was "growing like a weed." Being a curious scientist (as all scientists should be), Dr. Lampl thought she might actually examine how rapid this child's growth, and others, is during infancy. She proceeded to measure a group of children's growth on a daily basis and found, much to her surprise, that some infants grew as much as one inch overnight! Some growth spurt.

Want to know more? Why not read the original work? You can find it in Lampl, M., Veldhuis, J. D., and Johnson, M. L. (1992). Saltation and stasis: A model of human growth. *Science, 258,* 801-803.

- Sue Kemper is a professor of psychology at the University of Kansas and has been working on the most interesting of projects. She and several other researchers are studying a group of nuns and examining how their early experiences, activities, personality characteristics, and other information relates to their health during their late adult years. Most notably, this diverse group of scientists (including psychologists, linguists, neurologists, and others) wants to know how well all this information predicts the occurrence of Alzheimer's disease. She's found that the complexity of the nuns' writing during their early 20s is related to the nuns' risk for Alzheimer's 50, 60, and 70 years later.

Want to know more? Why not read the original work? You can find more about this in Snowdon, D. A., Kemper, S. J., Mortimer, J. A., Greiner, L. H., Wekstein, D. R., and Markesbery, W. R. (1996). Linguistic ability in early life and cognitive function and Alzheimer's disease in late life: Findings from the nun study. *Journal of the American Medical Association, 275,* 528-532.

- John Wright and Aletha Huston are researchers and teachers at the University of Texas in Austin and have devoted a good deal of their professional lives to understanding what effects television watching has on young children's psychological development. Among other things, they specifically investigated the impact that the amount of educational television programs watched during the early preschool years might have on outcomes in the later school years. They found convincing evidence that children who watch educational programs such as *Mr. Rogers* and *Sesame Street* do better in school than those who do not.

Want to know more? Why not read the original work? You can find more about this in Collins, P. A., Wright, J. C., Anderson, D. R., Huston, A. C., Schmitt, K., and McElroy, E. (1997). *Effects of early childhood media use on adolescent achievement.* Paper presented at the biennial meeting of the Society for Research in Child Development, Albuquerque, NM.

All these researchers had a specific question they found interesting and used their intuition, curiosity, and excellent training to answer it. As part of their investigations, they used this set of tools we call statistics to make sense out of all the information they collected. Without these tools, all this information would have been just a collection of unrelated outcomes. The outcomes would be nothing that Lampl could have used to reach a conclusion about children's growth or Kemper could have used to better understand Alzheimer's disease or Huston and Wright could have used to better understand the impact of watching television on young children's achievement and social development.

Statistics, the science of organizing and analyzing information to make the information more easily understood, made the task doable.

The reason why any of the results from such studies are useful is because we can use statistics to make sense out of them. And that's exactly the goal of this book—to provide you with an understanding of these basic tools and how they are used.

In this first part of *Statistics for People Who (Think They) Hate Statistics,* you will be introduced to what the study of statistics is about and why it's well worth your efforts to master the basics, the important terminology and ideas that are central to the field. It's all in preparation for the rest of the book.

Statistics or Sadistics?

It's Up to You

Difficulty Scale ☺☺☺☺☺ (really easy)

What you'll learn about in this chapter

- What statistics is all about
- Why you should take statistics
- How to succeed in this course

WHY STATISTICS?

You've heard it all before, right? "Statistics is difficult," "The math involved is impossible," "I don't know how to use a computer," "What do I need this stuff for?", "What do I do next?", and the famous cry of the introductory statistics student, "I don't get it!"

Well, relax. Students who study introductory statistics find themselves, at one time or another, thinking about at least one of the above, if not actually sharing it with another student, their spouse, a colleague, or a friend.

And all kidding aside, there are some statistics courses that can easily be described as *sadistics*. That's because the books are repetitiously boring, and the authors have no imagination. That's not the case for you. The fact that you or your instructor has selected *Statistics for People Who (Think They) Hate Statistics* shows that you're ready to take the right approach: one that is unintim-

5

idating, informative, and applied (and even a little fun) and that tries to teach you what you need to know about using statistics as the valuable tool that it is.

If you're using this book in a class, it also means that your instructor is clearly on your side—he or she knows that statistics can be intimidating but has taken steps to see that it is not intimidating for you. As a matter of fact, we'll bet there's a good chance (as hard as it may be to believe) that you'll be enjoying this class in just a few short weeks.

A FIVE-MINUTE HISTORY OF STATISTICS

Before you read any further, it would be useful to have some historical perspective about this topic called statistics. After all, almost every undergraduate in the social, behavioral, and biological sciences and every graduate student in education, nursing, psychology, and anthropology (you get the picture) is required to take this course. Wouldn't it be nice to have some idea from whence the topic it covers came? Of course it would.

Way, way back, as soon as humans realized that counting was a good idea (as in "How many of these do you need to trade for one of those?"), collecting information also became a useful skill. If counting counted, then one would know how many times the sun would rise in one season, how much food was needed to last the winter, and what amount of resources belonged to whom.

That was just the beginning. Once numbers became part of language, it seemed like the next step was to attach these numbers to outcomes. That started in earnest during the 17th century when the first set of data pertaining to populations was collected. From that point on, scientists (mostly mathematicians, but then physical and biological scientists) needed to develop specific tools to answer specific questions. For example, Francis Galton (a cousin of Charles Darwin), who lived from 1822 to 1911, was very interested in the nature of human intelligence. To explore one of his primary questions regarding the similarity of intelligence among family members, he used a specific statistical tool called the correlation coefficient (first developed by mathematicians), and then he popularized its use in the behavioral and social sciences. You'll learn all about this tool in Chapter 5.

In fact, most of the basic statistical procedures that you will learn about were first developed and used in the fields of agriculture, astronomy, and even politics. Their application to human behavior came much later.

The past 100 years have seen great strides in the invention of new ways to use old ideas. The simplest test for examining the differences between the averages of two groups was first advanced during the early 20th century. Techniques that build on this idea were offered decades later and have been greatly refined. And the introduction of personal computers and such programs as the SPSS® products (see Appendix A) has opened up the use of sophisticated techniques to anyone who wants to explore these fascinating topics.

The introduction of these powerful personal computers has been both good and bad. It's good because most statistical analyses no longer require access to a huge and expensive mainframe computer. Instead, a simple personal computer costing less than $1,000 can do 95% of what 95% of the people need. On the other hand, less than adequately educated students (such as your fellow students who passed on taking this course!) will take any old data they have and think that by running them through some sophisticated SPSS analysis, they will have reliable, trustworthy, and meaningful outcomes—not true. What your professor would say is, "Garbage in, garbage out"—if you don't start with reliable and trustworthy data, what you'll have after your data are analyzed are unreliable and untrustworthy results.

Today, statisticians in all different areas from criminal justice to geophysics to psychology find themselves using basically the same techniques to answer different questions. There are, of course, important differences in how data are collected, but for the most part, the analyses (the plural of analysis) that are done following the collection of data (the plural of datum) tend to be very similar even if called something different. The moral here? This class will provide you with the tools to understand how statistics are used in almost any discipline. Pretty neat, and all for just three or four credits.

If you want to learn more about the history of statistics, a great place to start is Jan de Leeuw's Internet site located at http://www.anselm.edu/homepage/jpitocch/biostatshist.html.

STATISTICS: WHAT IT IS (AND ISN'T)

Statistics for People Who (Think They) Hate Statistics is a book about basic statistics and how to apply them to a variety of different situations including the analysis and understanding of information.

In the most general sense, **statistics** describes a set of tools and techniques that is used for describing, organizing, and interpreting information or data. Those data might be the scores on a test taken by students participating in a special math curriculum, the speed with which problems are solved, the number of patient complaints when using one type of drug rather than another, the number of errors in each inning of a World Series game, or the average price of a dinner in an upscale restaurant in Sante Fe.

In all these examples, and the million more we could think of, data are collected, organized, summarized, and then interpreted. In this book, you'll learn about collecting, organizing, and summarizing data as part of descriptive statistics. And then you'll learn about interpreting data when you learn about the usefulness of inferential statistics.

What Is Descriptive Statistics?

Descriptive statistics is used to organize and describe the characteristics of a collection of data. The collection is sometimes called a **data set** or just **data**.

For example, the following list shows you the names of 22 college students, their major areas of study, and their ages. If you needed to describe what the most popular college major is, you could use a descriptive statistic that summarizes their choice (called the mode). In this case, the most common major is psychology. And if you wanted to know the average age, you could easily compute another descriptive statistic that identifies this variable (that one's called the mean). Both of these simple descriptive statistics are used to describe data. They do a fine job allowing us to represent the characteristics of a large collection of data such as the 22 cases in our example.

Name	Major	Age	Name	Major	Age
Richard	Education	19	Elizabeth	English	21
Sara	Psychology	18	Bill	Psychology	22
Andrea	Education	19	Hadley	Psychology	23
Steven	Psychology	21	Buffy	Education	21
Jordan	Education	20	Chip	Education	19
Pam	Education	24	Homer	Psychology	18
Michael	Psychology	21	Margaret	English	22
Liz	Psychology	19	Courtney	Psychology	24
Nicole	Chemistry	19	Leonard	Psychology	21
Mike	Nursing	20	Jeffrey	Chemistry	18
Kent	History	18	Emily	Spanish	19

So watch how simple this is. To find the most frequently selected major, just find the one that occurs most often. And to find the average age, just add up all the age values and divide by 22. You're right—the most often occurring major is psychology (9 times) and the average age is 20.3. Look Ma! No hands—you're a statistician.

What Is Inferential Statistics?

Inferential statistics is often (but not always) the next step after you have collected and summarized data. Inferential statistics is used to make inferences from a smaller group of data (such as our group of 22 students) to a possibly larger one (such as all the undergraduate students in the College of Arts and Sciences).

This smaller group of data is often called a **sample,** which is a portion, or a subset, of a **population.** For example, all the fifth graders in Newark, NJ would be a population (it's all the occurrences with certain characteristics—being in fifth grade and living in Newark), while a selection of 150 of them would be a sample.

Let's look at another example. Your marketing agency asks you (a newly hired researcher) to determine which of several different names is most appealing for a new brand of potato chip. Will it be Chipsters? FunChips? or Crunchies? As a statistics pro (we know we're moving a bit ahead of ourselves, but keep the faith), you need to find a small group of potato chip eaters that is representative of all potato chip fans and ask them to tell you which one of the three names they like the most. Then, if you did things right, you can easily infer the findings to the huge group of potato chip eaters.

Or, let's say you're interested in the best treatment for a particular type of disease. Perhaps you'll try a new drug as one alternative, a placebo (or a substance that is known not to have any effect) as another alternative, and even nothing as the third alternative to see what happens. Well, you find out that a larger number of patients get better when no action is taken and nature just takes its course! The drug does not have any effect. Then, with that information, you infer to the larger group of patients who suffer from the disease, given the results of your experiment.

In Other Words . . .

Statistics is a tool that helps us understand the world around us. It does so by organizing information we've collected and then letting us make certain statements about how characteristics of those data are applicable to new settings. Descriptive and inferential statistics work hand in hand, and which one you use and when depends on the question you want answered.

WHAT AM I DOING IN A STATISTICS CLASS?

There are probably many reasons why you find yourself using this book. You might be enrolled in an introductory statistics class. Or you might be reviewing for your comprehensive exams. Or you might even be reading this on vacation (summer horrors!) in preparation and review for a more advanced class.

In any case, you're a statistics student whether you have to take a final exam at the end of a formal course or whether you're just in it on your own accord. But there are plenty of good reasons to be studying this material—some fun, some serious, and some both. Here's the list of some of the things that my students hear at the beginning of our introductory statistics course.

1. Statistics 101 or Statistics 1 or whatever it's called at your school looks great listed on your transcript. Kidding aside, this may be a required course for you to complete your major. But even if it is not, having these skills is definitely a big plus when it comes time to apply for a job or for further schooling. And with more advanced courses, your résumé will be even more impressive.

2. If this is not a required course, taking basic statistics sets you apart from those who do not. It shows that you are willing to undertake a course that is above average in regard to difficulty and commitment.

3. Basic statistics is an intellectual challenge of a kind that you might not be used to. There's a good deal of thinking that's required, a bit of math, and some integration of ideas and application. The bottom line is that all this activity adds up to what can be an invigorating intellectual experience since you learn about a whole new area or discipline.

4. There's no question that having some background in statistics makes you a better student in the social or behavioral sciences since you will have a better understanding not only of what you read in journals but also what your professors and colleagues may be discussing and doing in and out of class. You will be amazed the first time you say to yourself, "Wow, I actually understand what they're talking about." And it will happen over and over again since you will have the basic tools necessary to understand exactly how scientists reach the conclusions they do.

5. If you plan to pursue a graduate degree in education, anthropology, economics, sociology, or any one of many other social, behavior, and biological pursuits, this course will give you the foundation you need to move on further.

6. Finally, you can brag that you completed a course that everyone thinks is the equivalent of building and running a nuclear reactor.

Ten Ways to Use This Book (and Learn Statistics at the Same Time!)

Yep. Just what the world needs—another statistics book. But this one is different. It's directed at the student, is not condescending, is informative, and is as basic as possible in its presentation. It makes no presumptions about what you should know before you start and proceeds in slow, small steps, letting you pace yourself.

However, there has always been a general aura surrounding the study of statistics that it's a difficult subject to master. And we don't say otherwise, because parts of it are challenging. On the other hand, millions and millions of students have mastered this topic, and you can too. Here are a few hints to close this introductory chapter before we move to our first topic.

1. **You're not dumb.** That's true. If you were, you would not have gotten this far in school. So treat statistics like any other new course. Attend the lectures, study the material, and do the exercises in the book and from class, and you'll do fine. Rocket scientists know statistics, but you don't have to be a rocket scientist to succeed in statistics.

2. **How do you know statistics is hard?** Is statistics difficult? Yes and no. If you listen to friends who have taken the course and didn't work hard and didn't do well, they'll surely volunteer to tell you how hard it was and how much of a disaster it made of their entire semester, if not their life. And let's not forget—we always tend to hear from complainers. So we'd suggest that you start this course with the attitude that you'll wait and see how it is and judge the experience for yourself. Better yet, talk to several people who have had the class and get a good general idea of what they think. Just don't base it on one spoilsport's experience.

3. **Don't skip lessons—work through the chapters in sequence.** *Statistics for People* is written so that each chapter provides a foundation for the next one in the book. When you are all done with the course, you will (we hope) refer back to this book and use it as a reference. So if you need a particular value from a table, you might consult Appendix B. Or if you need to remember how to compute the standard deviation, you might turn to Chapter 3. But for now, read each chapter in the sequence that it appears. It's OK to skip around and see what's offered down the road. Just don't study later chapters before you master earlier ones.

4. **Form a study group.** This is one of the most basic ways to ensure some success in this course. Early in the semester, arrange to study with friends. If you don't have any who are in the same class as you, then make some new ones or offer to study with someone who looks to be as happy about being there as you are. Studying with others allows you to help them if you know the material better, or to benefit from others who know that material better than you. Set a specific time each week to get together for an hour and go over the exercises at the end of the chapter or ask questions of one another. Take as much time as you need. Studying with others is an invaluable way to help you understand and master the material in this course.

5. **Ask your teacher questions and then ask a friend.** If you do not understand what you are being taught in class, ask your professor to clarify it. Have no doubt—if you don't understand the material, then you can be sure that others do not as well. More often than not, instructors welcome questions. And especially since you've read the material before class, your questions should be well informed and help everyone in class to better understand the material.

6. **Do the exercises at the end of a chapter.** The exercises are based on the material and the examples in the chapter they follow. They are there to help you apply the concepts that were taught in the chapter and build your confidence at the same time. How do the exercises do that? An explanation for how each exercise is solved accompanies the problem. If you can answer these

end-of-chapter exercises, then you are well on your way to mastering the content of the chapter.

7. **Practice, practice, practice.** Yes, it's a very old joke:

> Q. How do you get to Carnegie Hall?
> A. Practice, practice, practice.

Well, it's no different with basic statistics. You have to use what you learn and use it frequently to master the different ideas and techniques. This means doing the exercises in the back of Chapters 1-14 as well as taking advantage of any other opportunities you have to understand what you have learned.

8. **Look for applications to make it more real.** In your other classes, you probably have occasion to read journal articles, talk about the results of research, and generally discuss the importance of the scientific method in your own area of study. These are all opportunities to look and see how your study of statistics can help you better understand the topics under class discussion as well as the area of beginning statistics. The more you apply these new ideas, the better and more full your understanding will be.

9. **Browse.** Read the assigned chapter over first, then go back and read it with more intention. Take a nice leisurely tour of *Statistics for People* to see what's contained in the various chapters. Don't rush yourself. It's always good to know what topics lie ahead as well as to familiarize yourself with the content that will be covered in your current statistics class.

10. **Have fun.** This indeed might seem like a strange thing to say, but it all boils down to you mastering this topic rather than letting the course and its demands master you. Set up a study schedule and follow it, ask questions in class, and consider this intellectual exercise to be one of growth. Mastering new material is always exciting and satisfying—it's part of the human spirit. You can experience the same satisfaction here—just keep your eye on the ball and make the necessary commitment to stay current with the assignments and work hard.

ABOUT THOSE ICONS

An icon is a symbol. Throughout *Statistics for People . . .* you'll see a variety of different icons. Here's what each one is and what each represents:

This icon represents information that goes beyond the regular text. We might find it necessary to elaborate on a particular point, and we can do that more easily outside of the flow of the usual material.

Here, we select some more technical ideas and tips to discuss and to inform you about what's beyond the scope of this course. You might find these interesting and useful.

Throughout *Statistics for People . . .* , you'll find a small stepladder icon like the one you see here. This indicates that there is a set of steps coming up that will direct you through a particular process. These steps have been tested and approved by whatever Federal agency approves these things.

That finger with the bow is a cute icon, but its primary purpose is to help reinforce important points about the topic that you just read about. Try to emphasize these points in your studying, since they are usually central to the topic.

Most of the chapters in *Statistics for People . . .* provide detailed information about one or more particular statistical procedures and the computation that accompanies them. The computer icon is used to identify the "Using the Computer to . . ." section of the chapter.

These chapters also contain instructions for using Version 10 of SPSS to complete the same procedures, so that you can have both "hands-on" experience and experience using one of the most powerful statistical analysis packages available today. Appendix A contains an introduction to SPSS. Working through this appendix is all you really need to do to be ready to use SPSS. If you have an earlier version of SPSS (such as Version 7 or Version 8), you will still find this material to be very helpful.

When you get to each section titled "Using the Computer to . . . ," you'll find reference to a data set (such as "Chapter 2 Data Set 1"). Each of these sets is shown in Appendix C, and you will use these data to successfully complete the "Using the Computer to . . ." sections if you want to follow along. You can either enter the data manually or download it from the book's Internet site (see page 345 of this volume). Just follow the instructions to download and you're set to go.

KEY TO DIFFICULTY INDEX

1 very hard	☺
2 hard	☺☺
3 not too hard, but not easy either	☺☺☺
4 easy	☺☺☺☺
5 very easy	☺☺☺☺☺

GLOSSARY

Bolded terms in the text are included in the glossary at the back of the book.

SUMMARY

That couldn't have been that bad, right? We want to encourage you to continue reading and not worry about what's difficult or time-consuming or too complex for you to understand and apply. Just take one chapter at a time, as you did this one.

TIME TO PRACTICE

Since there's no substitute for the real thing, Chapters 1-14 end with a set of exercises that will help you review the material that was covered in the chapter. And so you don't have to go hunting, the answers to these exercises can be found at the very end of those chapters as well.

For example, here is the first set of exercises.

1. Interview someone who uses statistics in his or her everyday work. It might be your adviser, an instructor, a researcher who lives on your block, a market analyst for a company, or even a city planner. Ask them what their first statistics course was like. Find out what they liked and what they didn't. See if they have any suggestions to help you succeed. And most important, ask the person about the ways he or she uses these new-to-you tools at work.

2. Search through your local newspaper and find the results of a survey or interview about any topic. Summarize what the results are and do the best job you can describing how the researchers who were involved, or the authors of the survey, came to the conclusions they did. It may or may not be apparent. Once you have some idea what they did, try to speculate as to what other ways the same information might be collected, organized, and summarized.

3. Go to the library and copy a journal article in your own discipline. Then go through the article with one of those fancy highlighters and highlight the section (usually the "Results" section) where statistical procedures were used to organize and analyze the data. You don't know much about the specifics of this yet, but how many of these different procedures (such as t test, mean, and calculation of the standard deviation) can you identify? Can you take the next step and tell your instructor how the results relate to the research question or the primary topic of the research study?

PART II

Σigma Freud and Descriptive Statistics

SNAPSHOTS

And you thought *your* statistics professor
was tough...

One of the things that Sigmund Freud, the founder of psychoanalysis, did quite well was to observe and describe the nature of his patients' conditions. He was an astute observer and used his skills to develop what was the first systematic and comprehensive theory of personality. Regardless of what you may think about the validity of his ideas, he was a good scientist.

Back in the early 20th century, courses in statistics (like the one you are taking) were not offered as part of undergraduate or graduate curricula. The field was relatively new, and the nature of scientific explorations did not demand the precision that this set of tools brings to the scientific arena.

But things have changed. Now, in almost any endeavor, numbers count. This section of *Statistics for People (Who Think) They Hate Statistics* is devoted to understanding how we can use statistics to describe an outcome and better understand it, once the information about the outcome is organized.

Chapter 2 discusses measures of central tendency and how computing one of several different types of averages gives you the one best data point that represents a set of scores. Chapter 3 completes the coverage of tools we need to fully describe a set of data points in its discussion of variability including the standard deviation and variance. When you get to Chapter 4, you will be ready to learn how distributions, or sets of scores, differ from one another and what this difference means. Chapters 5 and 6 both deal with the nature of relationships between variables, namely, correlations. The special case of correlation called regression is the focus of Chapter 6, the last chapter in this part.

When you finish Part II, you'll be in excellent shape to start understanding the role that probability and inference plays in the social and behavioral sciences.

Means to an End

Computing and Understanding Averages

Difficulty Scale ☺☺☺☺ (moderately easy)

What you'll learn about in this chapter

- Understanding measures of central tendency
- Computing the mean for a set of scores
- Computing the mean and the median for a set of scores
- Selecting a measure of central tendency

Y ou've been very patient, and now it's finally time to get started working with some real, live data. That's exactly what you'll do in this chapter. Once data are collected, a usual first step is to organize the information using simple indexes to describe the data. The easiest way to do this is through computing an average, of which there are several different types.

An **average** is the one value that best represents an entire group of scores. It doesn't matter whether the group of scores is the number correct on a spelling test for 30 fifth graders or the batting percentage of each of the New York Yankees or the number of people who registered as Democrats or Republicans in the last election. In all these examples, groups of data can be summarized using an average. Averages, also called **measures of central tendency,** come in three flavors: the mean, the median, and the mode. Each provides you with a different type of information

21

about a distribution of scores and is simple to compute and interpret.

COMPUTING THE MEAN

The **mean** is the most common type of average that is computed. It is simply the sum of all the values in a group, divided by the number of values in that group. So if you had the spelling scores for 30 fifth graders, you would simply add up all the scores and get a total and then divide by the number of students, which is 30.

The formula for computing the mean is shown in Formula 2.1.

$$\overline{X} = \frac{\Sigma X}{n} \tag{2.1}$$

where

- The letter X with a line above it (also called "X bar") is the mean value of the group of scores or the mean.
- The Σ, or the Greek letter sigma, is the summation sign, which tells you to add together whatever follows it.
- The X is each individual score in the group of scores.
- Finally, the n is the size of the sample from which you are computing the mean.

To compute the mean, follow these steps.

1 List the entire set of values in one or more columns. These are all the Xs.

2 Compute the sum or total of all the values.

3 Divide the total or sum by the number of values.

For example, if you needed to compute the average number of shoppers at three different locations, you would compute a mean for that value.

Location	Number of Annual Customers
Lanham Park store	2,150
Williamsburg store	1,534
Downtown store	3,564

The mean or average number of shoppers in each store is 2,416. Formula 2.2 shows how it was computed using the formula you saw in Formula 2.1.

$$\overline{X} = \frac{\Sigma X}{n} = \frac{2{,}150 + 1{,}534 + 3{,}564}{3} = \frac{7{,}248}{3} = 2{,}416 \qquad (2.2)$$

See, we told you it was easy. No big deal.

THINGS TO REMEMBER

The mean is sometimes represented by the letter M and is also called the typical, average, or most central score. If you are reading another statistics book or a research report, and you see something like $M = 45.87$, it probably means that the mean is equal to 45.87.

- In the formula, a small n represents the sample size for which the mean is being computed. A large N (like this) would represent the population size. In some books and in some journal articles, no distinction is made between the two.
- The sample mean is the measure of central tendency that most accurately reflects the population mean.
- The mean is like the fulcrum on a seesaw. It's the centermost point where all the values on one side of the mean are equal in weight to all the values on the other side of the mean.
- Finally, for better or worse, the mean is very sensitive to extreme scores. An extreme score can pull the mean in one or the

other direction and make it less representative of the set of scores and less useful as a measure of central tendency. This, of course, all depends on the values for which the mean is being computed. More about this later.

TECH TALK

The mean is also referred to as the **arithmetic mean,** and there are other types of means that you may read about such as the harmonic mean. Those are used in special circumstances but need not concern you here. And if you want to be technical about it, the arithmetic mean (which is the one that we have discussed up to now) is also defined as the point at which the sum of the deviations from the mean is equal to zero (whew!). So if you have scores like 3, 4, and 5 (where the mean is 4), the sum of the deviations (–1, 0, and +1) is 0.

Remember that the word average means only the one measure that best represents a set of scores and that there are many different types of averages. Which type of average you use best depends on the question that you are asking and the type of data you are trying to summarize.

Computing a Weighted Mean

You've just seen an example of how to compute a simple mean. But there may be situations where you have the occurrence of more than one value and you want to compute a weighted mean. A weighted mean can be easily computed by multiplying the value by the frequency of its occurrence, adding the total of all the occurrences, and then dividing by the total number of occurrences.

To compute a weighted mean, follow these steps.

1 List all the values in the sample for which the mean is being computed such as those shown in the column labeled Value (the value of X) in the following table.

2 List the frequency with which each value occurs.

3 Multiply the value by the frequency as shown in the third column.

4 Sum all the values in the Value × Frequency column.

5 Divide by the total number of values.

For example, here's a table that organizes the values and frequencies in a flying-proficiency test for 100 airline pilots.

Value	Frequency	Value × Frequency
97	4	388
94	11	1,034
92	12	1,104
91	21	1,911
90	30	2,700
89	12	1,068
78	9	702
60 (don't fly with this guy)	1	60
Total	100	8,967

The weighted mean is 8,967/100, or 89.67. Computing the mean this way is much easier than entering 100 different scores into your calculator or computer program.

TECH TALK

In basic statistics, an important distinction is made between those values associated with samples (a part of a population) and those associated with populations. To do this, statisticians use the following conventions.

For a sample statistic (such as the mean of a sample), Roman letters are used. For a population parameter (such as the mean of a population), Greek letters are used. So the mean for the spelling score for a sample of 100 fifth graders is represented as $\overline{X}_s$, while the mean for the spelling score for the entire population of fifth graders is represented as μ_s, using the Greek letter mu, or μ.

COMPUTING THE MEDIAN

The median is also an average, but of a very different kind. The **median** is defined as the midpoint in a set of scores. It's the point at which one-half, or 50%, of the scores fall above and one-half, or 50%, fall below. It's got some special qualities that we will talk about later in this section, but for now, let's concentrate on how it is computed. There's no standard formula for computing the median.

To compute the median, follow these steps.

1 List the values in order, either from highest to lowest or lowest to highest.

2 Find the middle-most score. That's the median.

For example, here are the incomes from five different households.

> $135,456
> $ 25,500
> $ 32,456
> $ 54,365
> $ 37,668

Here is the list ordered from highest to lowest.

> $135,456
> $ 54,365
> $ 37,668
> $ 32,456
> $ 25,500

There are five values. The middle-most value is $37,668, and that's the median.

Now, what if the number of values is even? Let's add a value ($34,500) to the list so there are six income levels. Here they are.

$135,456
$ 54,365
$ 37,668
$ 34,500
$ 32,456
$ 25,500

When there is an even number of values, the median is simply the average between the two middle values. In this case, the middle two cases are $34,500 and $37,668. The average of those two values is $36,084. That's the median for that set of six values.

What if the two middle-most values are the same, such as the following set of data?

$45,678
$25,567
$25,567
$13,234

Then the median is same as both of those middle-most values. In this case, it's $25,567.

**TECH
TALK**

If you know about medians, you should know about **percentile points.** Percentile points are used to define the percentage of cases equal to and below a certain point in a distribution or set of scores. For example, if a score is "at the 75th percentile" it means that the score is at or above 75% of the other scores in the distribution. The median is also known as the 50th percentile, since it's the point below which 50% of the cases in the distribution fall. Other percentiles are useful as well such as the 25th percentile, often called Q_1, and the 75th percentile, referred to as Q_3. So what's Q_2? The median, of course.

Here comes the answer to the question you've probably had in the back of your mind since we started talking about the median. Why use the median instead of the mean? For one very good reason. The median is insensitive to extreme scores where the mean is not.

When you have a set of scores where one or more score is extreme, the median better represents the centermost value of that set of scores than any other measure of central tendency. Yes, even better than the mean.

What do we mean by extreme? It's probably easiest to think of an extreme score as one that is very different from the group to which it belongs. For example, in our list of five incomes that we worked earlier (shown again here):

$$\$135,456$$
$$\$\ 54,365$$
$$\$\ 37,668$$
$$\$\ 32,456$$
$$\$\ 25,500$$

the value $135,456 is more different from the other five than any other value in the set. We would consider that an extreme score.

The best way to illustrate how useful the median is as a measure of central tendency is to compute both the mean and the median for set of data that contains one or more extreme scores and then compare them to see which one best represents the group. Here goes.

The average or mean of the set of five scores you see above is the sum of the set of five divided by five, which turns out to be $57,089. On the other hand, the median for this set of five scores is $37,668. Which is more representative of the group? The value $37,668, since it clearly lies more in the "middle" of the group and we like to think about the average as being representative or assuming a central position. In fact, the mean value of $57,089 falls above the fourth highest value ($54,365) and is not very central or representative of the distribution.

It's for this reason that certain social and economic indicators (mostly involving income) are reported using a median as a measure of central tendency, such as "The median income of the average American family is . . . ," rather than using the mean to summarize the values. There are just too many extreme scores that would **skew,** or significantly distort, what is actually a central point in the set or distribution of scores.

You learned earlier that sometimes the mean is represented by the capital letter M instead of $\overline{X}$. Well, other symbols are used for the median as well. We like the letter M, but some people confuse it with the mean so they use Med for median or Mdn. Don't let that throw you—just remember what the median is and what it represents and you'll have no trouble adapting to different symbols.

THINGS TO REMEMBER

Here are some interesting and important things to remember about the median.

- The mean is the middle point of a set of values and the median is the middle point of set of cases.
- Since the median cares about how many cases, and not the values of those cases, extreme scores (sometimes called **outliers**) don't count.

COMPUTING THE MODE

The third and last measure of central tendency that we'll cover, the mode, is the most general and least precise measure of central tendency but plays a very important part in understanding the characteristics of a special set of scores. The **mode** is the value that occurs most frequently. There is no formula for computing the mode.

To compute the mode, follow these steps.

1 List all the values in a distribution, but list each only once.

2 Tally the number of times that each value occurs.

3 The value that occurs most often is the mode.

For example, an examination of the political party affiliation of 300 people might result in the following distribution of scores.

Party Affiliation	Number or Frequency
Democrats	90
Republicans	70
Independents	140

The mode is the value that occurs most frequently, which in the above example is Independents. That's the mode for this distribution.

Want to know what the easiest and most commonly made mistake is when computing the mode? It's selecting the number of times a category occurs, rather than the label of the category itself. Instead of the mode being Independents, it's easy for someone to conclude the mode is 140. Why? Because they are looking at the number of times the value occurred, and not the value that occurred most often! This is a simple mistake to make so be on your toes when you are asked about these things.

Apple Pie à la Bimodal

If every value in a distribution contains the same number of occurrences, then there eally isn't a mode. But if more than one value appears with equal frequency, the distribution is multi-modal. The set of scores can be bimodal (with two modes) such as the following set of data using hair color illustrates.

Hair Color	Number or Frequency
Red	7
Blond	12
Black	45
Brown	45

In the above example, the distribution is bimodal since the frequency of the values of black and brown hair occurs equally. You can even have a bimodal distribution when the modes are relatively close together, but not exactly the same, such as 45 people with black hair and 44 with brown hair. The question becomes, how much does once class of occurrences stand apart from another? Can you have a trimodal distribution? Sure—where three values have the same frequency. It's unlikely, especially when you are dealing with a large group of data points, but certainly possible.

WHEN TO USE WHAT

OK, we've defined three different measures of central tendency and given you fairly clear examples of each. But the most important question remains unanswered. That is, "When do you use which measure?"

In general, which measure of central tendency you use depends on the type of data that you are describing. Unquestionably, a measure of central tendency for qualitative, categorical, or nominal data (such as racial group, eye color, income bracket, voting preference, and neighborhood location) can be described only using the mode.

For example, you can't be looking at the most central measure that describes which political affiliation is most predominant in a group and use the mean—what in the world could you conclude, that everyone is half-Republican? Rather, that out of 300 people, most (140) are Independent seems to be the best way of describing the value of this variable. In general, the median and mean are best used with quantitative data such as height, income level in dollars (not categories), age, test score, reaction, and number of hours completed for a degree.

It's also fair to say that the mean is a more precise measure than the median, and the median is a more precise measure than the mode. This means that all other things being equal, use the mean, and indeed, the mean is the most often used measure of central tendency. However, we do have occasions where the mean would not be appropriate as a measure of central tendency such as when we have categorical or nominal data such as hair color, right? Then we use the mode. So here is a set of three guidelines that may be of some help. And remember, there can always be exceptions.

1. Use the mode when the data are categorical in nature and values can fit only into one class, such as hair color, political affiliation, neighborhood location, and religion. When this is the case, these categories are called mutually exclusive.

2. Use the median when you have extreme scores and you don't want to distort the average such as income.

3. And, finally, use the mean when you have data that do not have extreme scores and are not categorical such as the numerical score on a test or the number of seconds it takes to swim 50 yards.

USING THE COMPUTER AND COMPUTING DESCRIPTIVE STATISTICS

If you haven't already, now would be a good time to turn to Appendix A so you can become familiar with the basics of using SPSS. Then come back here.

Let's use SPSS to compute some descriptive statistics. The data set we are using is named Chapter 2 Data Set 1, which is available in Appendix C and from the Sage Internet site. There is one variable in this data set:

Variable	Definition
Prej	The value on a test of prejudice as measured on a scale from 1 to 10

Here are the steps to compute the measures of central tendency that we discussed in this chapter. Follow along and do it yourself. With this and all exercises including data you enter or download, we'll assume that the data set is already open in SPSS.

1. Click Analyze → Descriptive Statistics → Frequencies.

2. Double-click on the variable named prej to move it to the Variable(s) box.

3. Click Statistics and you will see the Frequencies: Statistics dialog box shown in Figure 2.1.

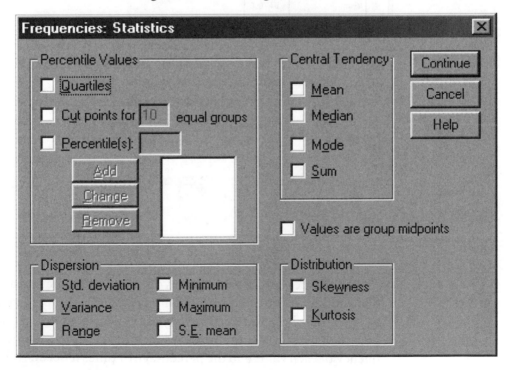

Figure 2.1. Frequencies: Statistics Dialog Box

4. Under Central Tendency, click the Mean, Median, and Mode boxes.

5. Click Continue.

6. Click OK.

The SPSS Output

Figure 2.2 shows you selected output from the SPSS procedure for the variable named prej.

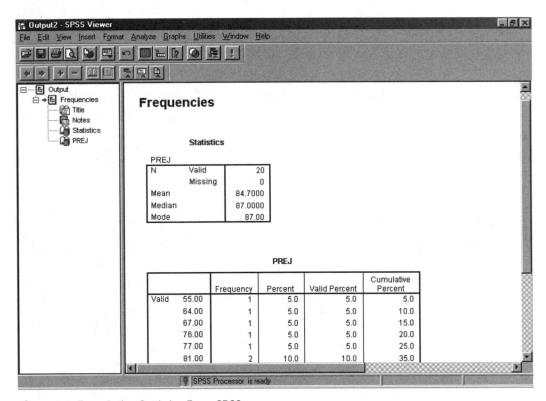

Figure 2.2. Descriptive Statistics From SPSS

In the Statistics part of the output, you can see how the mean, median, and mode are all computed along with the sample size and the fact that there were no missing data. SPSS does not use symbols such as $\overline{X}$ in its output. Also listed in the output is the frequency of each value and the percentage of times it occurs, all useful descriptive information.

It's a bit strange, but if you select Analyze → Descriptive Statistics → Descriptives in SPSS and then click Options, there's no option to select the median or the mode, which you might expect since they are basic descriptive statistics. The lesson here? Statistical analysis programs are usually quite different from one another, use different names for the same things, and make different assumptions about what's where. If you can't find what you want, it's probably there. Just keep hunting. Also, be sure to use the Help feature to help navigate through all this new information until you find what you need.

SUMMARY

No matter how fancy schmancy your statistical techniques are, you will still almost always start by simply describing what's there—hence the importance of understanding the simple notion of central tendency. From here, we go to another important descriptive construct: variability, or how different scores are from one another.

TIME TO PRACTICE

1. Compute the mean, median, and mode for the following three sets of scores saved as Chapter 2 Data Set 2. Do it by hand or use a computer program such as SPSS. Show your work, and if you use SPSS, print out a copy of the output.

Score 1	Score 2	Score 3
3	34	154
7	54	167
5	17	132
4	26	145
5	34	154
6	25	145
7	14	113
8	24	156
6	25	154
5	23	123

2. You are the manager of a fast food store. Part of your job is to report to the boss at the end of each day what special is selling best. Use your vast knowledge of descriptive statistics and write one paragraph to let the boss know what happened today. Here are the data. Don't use SPSS to compute important values; rather, do it by hand. Be sure to include a copy of your worksheet.

Special	Number Sold	Cost
Huge Burger	20	$2.95
Baby Burger	18	$1.49
Chicken Littles	25	$3.50
Porker Burger	19	$2.95
Yummy Burger	17	$1.99
Coney Dog	20	$1.99
Total specials sold	119	

3. Under what conditions would you use the median rather than the mean as a measure of central tendency? Why? Provide an example of two situations where the median might be more useful than the mean as a measure of central tendency.

ANSWERS TO PRACTICE QUESTIONS

1.

	Score 1	Score 2	Score 3
Mean	5.6	27.6	144.3
Median	5.5	25.0	149.5
Mode	5	25, 34	154

2. Here's what your one paragraph might look like.

> As usual, the Chicken Littles [the mode] led the way in sales. The total amount of food sold was $303, for an average of $2.55 for each special.

3. You use the median when you have extreme scores, which would dispropor- tionately bias the mean. One situation where the median is preferable to the mean is where income is reported. Since it varies so much, you want a measure of central tendency that is insensitive to extreme scores. Another example is where you have an extreme score or an outlier, such as the speed with which a group of adolescents can run 100 yards, where there are one or two exception- ally fast individuals.

Vive la Différence
Understanding Variability

Difficulty Scale ☺☺☺☺ (moderately easy, but not a cinch)

What you'll learn about in this chapter

- Why variability is valuable as a descriptive tool
- How to compute the range, standard deviation, and variance
- How the standard deviation and variance are alike—and how they are different

WHY UNDERSTANDING VARIABILITY IS IMPORTANT

In Chapter 2, you learned about different types of averages, what they mean, how they are computed, and when to use them. But when it comes to descriptive statistics and describing the characteristics of a distribution, averages are only half the story. The other half is measures of variability.

In the most simple of terms, **variability** reflects how scores differ from one another. For example, the following set of scores shows some variability.

7, 6, 3, 3, 1

The following set of scores has the same mean (4) and has less variability.

3, 4, 4, 5, 4

The next set has no variability at all—the scores do not differ from one another—but it also has the same mean as the other two sets we showed you.

4, 4, 4, 4, 4

Variability (also called spread or dispersion) can be thought of as a measure of how different scores are from one another. It's even more accurate (and maybe even easier) to think of variability as how different scores are from one particular score. And what "score" do you think that might be? Well, instead of comparing each score to every other score in a distribution, the one score that could be used as a comparison is—that's right—the mean. So variability becomes a measure of how much each score in a group of scores differs from the mean. More about this in a moment.

Remember what you already know about computing averages—that an average (whether it is the mean, the median, or the mode) is a representative score in a set of scores. Now, add your new knowledge about variability—that it reflects how different scores are from one another. Each is an important descriptive statistic. Together, these two (average and variability) can be used to describe the characteristics of a distribution and show how distributions differ from one another.

Three measures of variability are commonly used to reflect the degree of variability, spread, or dispersion in a group of scores. These are the range, the standard deviation, and the variance. Let's take a closer look at each one and how each one is used.

COMPUTING THE RANGE

The range is the most general measure of variability. It gives you an idea of how far apart scores are from one another. The **range** is computed simply by subtracting the lowest score in a distribution from the highest score in the distribution.

In general, the formula for the range is

$$r = h - l \qquad\qquad (3.1)$$

Where

r is the range

h is the highest score in the data set

l is the lowest score in the data set

Take the following set of scores, for example (shown here in descending order).

$$98, 86, 77, 56, 48$$

In this example, $98 - 48 = 50$. The range is 50.

**TECH
TALK**

There really are two kinds of ranges. One is the **exclusive range,** which is the highest score minus the lowest score (or $h - l$), the one we just defined. The second kind of range is the **inclusive range,** which is the highest score minus the lowest score plus 1 (or $h - l + 1$). You most commonly see the exclusive range reported in research articles, but the inclusive range is also used on occasion.

The range is used almost exclusively to get a very *general* estimate of how wide or different scores are from one another—that is, the range shows how much spread there is from the lowest to the highest point in a distribution.

So although the range is fine as a general indicator of variability, it should not be used to reach any conclusions regarding how individual scores differ from one another.

COMPUTING THE STANDARD DEVIATION

Now we get to the most frequently used measure of variability, the standard deviation. Just think about what the term implies; it's a deviation from something (guess what?) that is standard. Actually, the **standard deviation** (abbreviated as *s* or *SD*) represents the average amount of variability in a set of scores. In practical terms, it's the average distance from the mean. The larger the standard deviation, the larger the average distance each data point is from the mean of the distribution.

So what's the logic behind computing the standard deviation? Your initial thoughts may be to compute the mean of a set of scores and then subtract each individual score from the mean. Then, compute the average of that distance.

That's a good idea—you'll end up with the average distance of each score from the mean. But it won't work (see if you know why even though we'll show you why in a moment).

First, here's the formula for computing the standard deviation.

$$s = \sqrt{\frac{\Sigma(X - \bar{X})^2}{n - 1}} \tag{3.2}$$

where

s is the standard deviation

Σ is sigma, which tells you to find the sum of what follows

X is each individual score

$\bar{X}$ is the mean of all the scores

n is the sample size

This formula finds the difference between each individual score and the mean $(X - \overline{X})$, *squares each difference, and sums them all together. Then it divides the sum by the size of the sample (minus 1) and takes the square root of the result. As you can see, and as we mentioned earlier, the standard deviation is an average deviation from the mean.*

Here are the data we'll use in the following step-by-step explanation of how to compute the standard deviation.

$$5, 8, 5, 4, 6, 7, 8, 8, 3, 6$$

1 List each score. It doesn't matter whether the scores are in any particular order.

2 Compute the mean of the group.

3 Subtract the mean from each score.

Here's what we've done so far, where $X - \overline{X}$ represents the difference between the actual score and the mean of all the scores, which is 6.

X	$\overline{X}$	$X - \overline{X}$
8	6	8 − 6 = +2
8	6	8 − 6 = +2
8	6	8 − 6 = +2
7	6	8 − 7 = +1
6	6	6 − 6 = 0
6	6	6 − 6 = 0
5	6	6 − 7 = −1
5	6	6 − 7 = −1
4	6	6 − 8 = −2
3	6	6 − 9 = −3

4 Square each individual difference. The result is the column marked $(X - \overline{X}^2)$.

X	$(X - \bar{X})$	$(X - \bar{X})^2$
8	+2	4
8	+2	4
8	+2	4
7	+1	1
6	0	0
6	0	0
5	−1	1
5	−1	1
4	−2	4
3	−3	9
Total	0	28

5 Sum all the squared deviations about the mean. As you can see above, the total is 28.

6 Divide the sum by $n - 1$, or 10 − 1 = 9, so then 28/9 = 3.11.

7 Compute the square root of 3.11, which is 1.76. That is the standard deviation for this set of 10 scores.

What we now know from these results is that each score in this distribution differs from the mean by an average of 1.76 points.

Let's take a short step back and examine some of the operations in the standard deviation formula. They're important to review and will increase your understanding of what the standard deviation is.

First, why didn't we just add up the deviations from the mean? Because the sum of the deviations from the mean is always equal to 0. Try it by summing the deviations (2 + 2 + 1 + 0 + 0 − 1 − 1 − 2 − 3). In fact, that's the best way to check if you computed the mean correctly.

TECH TALK

There's another type of deviation that you may read about. You should know what it means. The **mean deviation** (also called the mean absolute deviation) is the sum of the absolute value of the deviations from the mean. You already know that the sum of the deviations from the mean must equal 0 (otherwise the mean is probably computed incorrectly). Instead, let's take the absolute value of each deviation (which is the value regardless of the sign). Sum them together and divide by the number of data points, and you have the mean deviation. (Note: The absolute value of a number is usually represented as that number with a horizontal line on each side of it such as $|5|$. For example, the absolute value of −6, or $|-6|$, is 6.)

Second, why do we square the deviations? So we get rid of the negative sign so that when we do eventually sum them, they don't add up to 0.

And finally, why do we eventually end up taking the square root of the entire value in Step 7? Because we want to return to the same units that we originally started with. We squared the deviations from the mean in Step 4 (to get rid of negative values) and then took the square root of their total in Step 7. Pretty tidy.

Why n − 1? What's Wrong With Just n?

You might have guessed why we square the deviations about the mean and why we go back and take the square root of their sum. But how about subtracting the value of 1 from the denominator of the formula? Why do we divide by $n - 1$ rather than just plain ol' n? Good question.

The answer is that s (the standard deviation) is an estimate of the population standard deviation and is an **unbiased estimate** at that but only when we subtract 1 from n. By subtracting 1 from the denominator, we artificially force the standard deviation to be larger than it would be otherwise. Why would we want to do that? Because as good scientists, we are conservative. Being conservative means that if we have to err, we will do so on the side of overestimating what the standard deviation of the population is. Dividing by a smaller denominator lets us do so. Thus, instead of dividing by 10, we divide by 9. Or instead of dividing by 100, we divide by 99.

**TECH
TALK**
Biased estimates are appropriate if your intent is only to describe the characteristics of the sample. But if you intend to use the sample as an estimate of a population parameter, then the unbiased statistic is best to calculate.

Take a look in the following table and see what happens as the size of the sample gets larger (and moves closer to the population in size). The $n-1$ adjustment has far less of an impact on the difference between the biased and the unbiased estimates of the standard deviation (the bold column in the table). All other things being equal, then, the larger the size of the sample, the less the difference there is between the biased and the unbiased estimates of the standard deviation. Check out the following table, and you'll see what we mean.

Sample Size	Value of Numerator in Standard Deviation Formula	Biased Estimate of the Population Standard Deviation (dividing by n)	Unbiased Estimate of the Population Standard Deviation (dividing by n − 1)	Difference Between Biased and Unbiased Estimates
10	500	7.07	7.45	**.38**
100	500	2.24	2.25	**.01**
1,000	500	0.7071	0.7075	**.0004**

The moral of the story? When you compute the standard deviation for a sample, which is an estimate of the population, the closer to the size of the population the sample is, the more accurate the estimate will be.

What's the Big Deal?

The computation of the standard deviation is very straightforward. But what does it mean? As a measure of variability, all it tells us is how much each score in a set of scores, on the average, varies from the mean. But it has some very practical applications as you will find out in Chapter 4. Just to whet your appetite, consider this: The standard deviation can be used to help us compare scores from different distributions, *even when the means and standard deviations are different*. Amazing! This, as you will see, can be very cool.

THINGS TO REMEMBER

- The standard deviation is computed as the average distance from the mean. So you will need to first compute the mean as a measure of central tendency. Don't fool around with the median or the mode in trying to compute the standard deviation.
- The larger the standard deviation, the more spread out the values are, and the more different they are from one another.
- Just like the mean, the standard deviation is sensitive to extreme scores. When you are computing the standard deviation of a sample and you have extreme scores, note that somewhere in your written report.
- If $s = 0$, there is absolutely no variability in the set of scores, and they are essentially identical in value. This will rarely happen.

COMPUTING THE VARIANCE

Here comes another measure of variability and a nice surprise. If you know the standard deviation of a set of scores and you can square a number, you can easily compute the variance of that same set of scores. This third measure of variability, the **variance,** is simply the standard deviation squared.

In other words, it's the same formula you saw earlier, without the square root bracket, like the one shown in Formula 3.3.

$$s^2 = \frac{\Sigma(X - \overline{X})^2}{n - 1} \qquad (3.3)$$

If you take the standard deviation and never complete the last step (taking the square root), you have the variance. In other words, $s^2 = s \bullet s$, or the variance equals the standard deviation squared. In our earlier example, where the standard deviation was equal to 1.76, the variance is equal to 1.76^2, or 3.11.

You are not likely to see the variance mentioned by itself in a journal article or see it used as a descriptive statistic. This is because the variance is a difficult number to interpret and apply to a set of data. After all, it is based on squared deviation scores.

But the variance is important since it is used both as a concept and as a practical measure of variability in many statistical formulas and techniques. You will learn about these later in *Statistics for People Who (Think They) Hate Statistics.*

The Standard Deviation Versus the Variance

How are standard deviation and the variance the same, and how are they different?

Well, they are both measures of variability, dispersion, or spread. The formulas used to compute them are very similar. You see them all over the place in the "Results" sections of journals.

They are also quite different.

First, and most important, the standard deviation (because we take the square root of the average summed squared deviation) is stated in the original units from which it was derived. The variance is stated in units that are squared (the square root is never taken).

What does this mean? Let's say that we need to know the variability of a group of production workers assembling circuit boards. Let's say that they average 8.6 boards per hour, and the standard deviation is 1.59. The value 1.59 means that the difference in the average number of boards assembled per hour is about 1.59 circuit boards from the mean.

Let's look at an interpretation of the variance, which is 1.59^2, or 2.53. This would be interpreted as meaning that the average difference between the workers is about 2.53 circuit boards *squared* from the mean. Which of these two makes more sense?

USING THE COMPUTER TO COMPUTE MEASURES OF VARIABILITY

Let's use SPSS to compute some measures of variability. We are using the file named Chapter 3 Data Set 1.

There is one variable in this data set:

Variable	Definition
reac_tm	Reaction time on a tapping task

Here are the steps to compute the measures of variability that we discussed in this chapter.

1. Open the file named Chapter 3 Data Set 1
2. Click Analyze → Descriptive Statistics → Frequencies.
3. Double-click on the reac_tm variable to move it to the Variable(s) box.
4. Click Statistics, and you will see the Frequencies: Statistics dialog box. Use this dialog box to select the variables and procedures you want to perform.

5. Under Dispersion, click Std. Deviation.

6. Under Dispersion, click Variance.

7. Under Dispersion, click Range.

8. Click Continue.

9. Click OK.

The SPSS Output

Figure 3.1 shows selected output from the SPSS procedure for reac_tm. There are 30 valid cases with no missing cases, and the standard deviation is .7025. The variance equals .4936 (or s^2), and the range is 2.60.

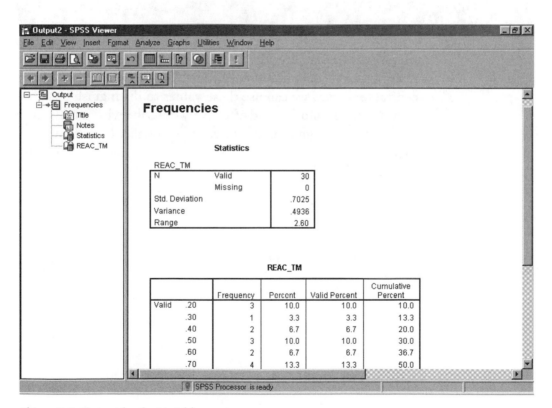

Figure 3.1. Output for the Variable react_tm

You've probably noticed that Version 10 of SPSS allows only for labels that are no more than eight characters long and have no capitals and no spaces. That's because this version is still stuck in the eight-character limit of the old MS-DOS (disk operating system) days. These limits make for some inconvenience, so you need to be creative. For example, the variable named Reaction time becomes reac_tm. Just be sure to define what a label means if it is not obvious.

SUMMARY

Measures of variability help us even more fully understand what a distribution of data points looks like. Along with a measure of central tendency, we can use these values to distinguish distributions from one another and effectively describe what a collection of test scores, heights, or measures of personality looks like. Now that we can think and talk about distributions, let's look at ways we can look at them.

TIME TO PRACTICE

1. Why is the range the most convenient measure of dispersion, yet the most imprecise measure of variability? When would you use the range?

2. For the following set of scores, compute the range and the unbiased and the biased standard deviation, and variance. Do the exercise by hand.

   31, 42, 35, 55, 54, 34, 25, 44, 35

3. Why is the unbiased estimate greater than the biased estimate?

ANSWERS TO PRACTICE QUESTIONS

1. The range is the most convenient measure of dispersion since it requires you only to subtract one number (the lowest value) from another number (the highest value). It's imprecise because it does not take into account the values that fall between the highest and the lowest values in a distribution. Use the range when you want a very gross (and not very precise) estimate of the variability in a distribution.

2. The range is 30.

	Unbiased	Biased
s	10.19	9.60

The unbiased sample standard deviation equals 10.19. The biased estimate equals 9.60. The difference is due to dividing by a sample size of 8 (for the unbiased estimate) as compared to a sample size of 9 (for the biased estimate). The unbiased estimate of the variance is 92.25, and the biased estimate is 103.78.

3. The unbiased estimate should be larger than the biased one since we are intentionally being conservative and overestimating the size of the sample standard deviation.

4 A Picture Really Is Worth a Thousand Words

Difficulty Scale ☺☺☺☺ (pretty easy, but not a cinch)

What you'll learn about in this chapter

- Why a picture is really worth a thousand words
- How to create a histogram and polygon
- Different types of charts and their uses
- Using Excel and SPSS to create charts

WHY ILLUSTRATE DATA?

In the last two chapters, you learned about two important types of descriptive statistics, measures of central tendency and measures of variability. Both of these provide you with the one best score for describing a group of data (central tendency) and a measure of how diverse or different scores are from one another (variability).

What we did not do, and what we will do here, is examine how differences in these two measures result in different looking distributions. Numbers alone (such as $\overline{X} = 10$ and $s = 3$) may be important, but a visual representation is a much more effective way of examining the characteristics of a distribution as well as the characteristics of any set of data.

So, in this chapter, we'll learn how to visually represent a distribution of scores as well as how to use different types of graphs to represent different types of data.

Ten Ways to a Great Figure (Eat Less and Exercise More?)

Whether you create illustrations by hand or use a computer program, the principles of decent design still apply. Here are 10 to copy and put above your desk.

1. **Minimize chart or graph junk.** "Chart junk" (a close cousin to "word junk") is where you use every function, every graph, and every feature a computer program has to make your charts busy, full, and uninformative. Less is definitely more.

2. **Plan out your chart before you start creating the final copy.** Use graph paper even if you will be using a computer program to generate the graph.

3. **Say what you mean and mean what you say—no more and no less.** There's nothing worse than a cluttered graph to confuse the reader.

4. **Label everything so nothing is left to the misunderstanding of the audience.**

5. **A graph should communicate only one idea.**

6. **Keep things balanced.** When you construct a graph, center titles and axes labels.

7. **Maintain the scale in a graph.** The scale refers to the relationship between the horizontal and vertical axes. This ratio should be about three to four, so a graph that is three inches wide will be about four inches tall.

8. **Simple is best.** Keep the chart simple, but not simplistic. Convey the one idea in as straightforward a way as possible with distracting information saved for the accompanying text. Remember, a chart or graph should be able to stand alone.

9. **Limit the number of words you use.** Too many words or words that are too large can detract from the visual message your chart should convey.

10. **A chart alone should convey what you want to say.** If it doesn't, go back to your plan and try it again.

FIRST THINGS FIRST: CREATING A FREQUENCY DISTRIBUTION

The most basic way to illustrate data is through the creation of a frequency distribution. A **frequency distribution** is a method of tallying, and representing, how often certain scores occur. In the creation of a frequency distribution, scores are usually grouped into class intervals, or ranges of numbers.

Here are 50 scores on a test of reading comprehension and what the frequency distribution for these scores looks like.

Here's the raw data on which it is based.

```
47  10  31  25  20
 2  11  31  25  21
44  14  15  26  21
41  14  16  26  21
 7  30  17  27  24
 6  30  16  29  24
35  32  15  29  23
38  33  19  28  10
35  34  18  29  21
36  32  16  27  20
```

And here's the frequency distribution.

Class Interval	Frequency
45-49	1
40-44	2
35-39	4
30-34	8
25-29	10
20-24	10
15-19	8
10-14	4
5-9	2
0-4	1

The Classiest of Intervals

As you can see from the above table, a **class interval** is a range of numbers, and the first step in the creation of a frequency distribution is to define how large each interval will be. You can see in the frequency distribution that we created that each interval spans five possible scores such as 5-9 (which includes scores 5, 6, 7, 8, and 9) and 40-44 (which includes scores 40, 41, 42, 43, and 44). How did we decide to have an interval that includes only five scores? Why not five intervals each consisting of 10 scores? Or two each consisting of 25 scores?

Here are some general rules to follow in the creation of a class interval, regardless of the size of values in the data set you are dealing with.

1. Select a class interval that has a range of 2, 5, 10, or 20 data points. In our example, we chose 5.

2. Select a class interval so that 10 to 20 such intervals cover the entire range of data. A convenient way to do this is to compute the range, then divide by a number that represents the number of intervals you want to use (between 10 and 20). In our example, there are 50 scores and we wanted 10 intervals: $50/10 = 5$, which is the size of each class interval. If you had a set of scores ranging from 100 to 400, you can start with the following estimate and work from there: $300/20 = 15$, so 15 would be the class interval.

3. Begin listing the class interval with a multiple of that interval. In our frequency distribution shown earlier, the class interval is 5 and we started the lowest class interval of 0.

4. Finally, the largest interval goes at the top of the frequency distribution.

Once class intervals are created, it's time to complete the frequency part of the frequency distribution. That's simply counting the number of times a score occurs in the raw data and entering that number in each of the class intervals represented by the count.

In the frequency distribution that we created earlier, the number of scores that occur between 30 and 34 and are in the 30-34 class interval is 8. So, an 8 goes in the column marked Frequency. There's your frequency distribution.

THE PLOT THICKENS: CREATING A HISTOGRAM

Now that we've got a tally of how many scores fall in what class intervals, we'll go to the next step and create what is called a **histogram**, a visual representation of the frequency distribution where the frequencies are represented by bars. This is also sometimes called a bar graph or a column graph.

Depending on the book you read and the software you use, visual representations of data are called graphs (such as in SPSS) or charts (such as in the Microsoft spreadsheet Excel). It really makes no difference. All you need to know is that a graph or a chart is the visual representation of data.

To create a histogram, do the following.

1 Using a piece of graph paper, place values at equal distances along the x-axis as shown in Figure 4.1. Now, identify the midpoint of the class intervals, which is the middle point in the class interval. It's pretty easy to just eyeball, but you can also just add the top and bottom values of the class interval and divide by 2. For example, the midpoint of the class interval 0-4 is the average of 0 and 4, or 4/2 = 2.

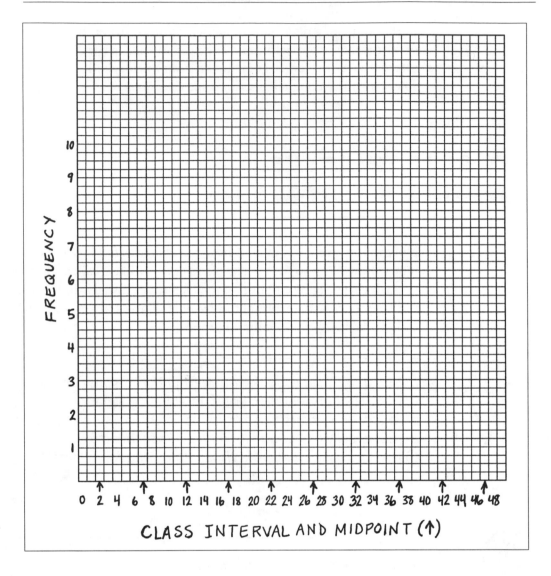

Figure 4.1. Class Intervals Along the x-Axis

2   Draw a bar or column around each **midpoint** that represents the entire class interval to the height representing the frequency of that class interval. For example, in Figure 4.2 you can see our first entry where the class interval of 0-4 is represented by the frequency of 1 (representing the one time a value between 0 and 4 occurs). Continue drawing bars or columns until each of the frequencies for each of the class intervals is represented. Here's a nice hand-drawn (really!) histogram for the frequency distribution of 50 scores we have been working with so far.

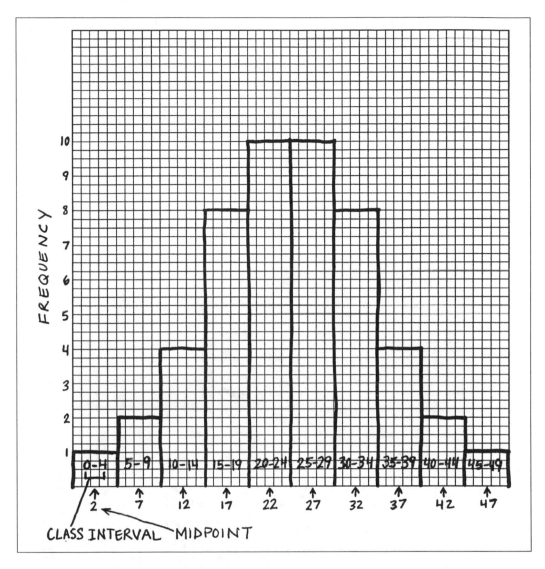

Figure 4.2. Hand-Drawn Histogram

Notice how each class interval is represented by a range of scores along the x-axis.

The Tally-Ho Method

You can see by the simple frequency distribution that you saw at the beginning of the chapter that you already know more about the distribution of scores than just a simple listing of them. You have a good idea of what values occur with what frequency. But another visual representation (besides a histogram) can be done by using tallies for each of the occurrences, as shown in Figure 4.3.

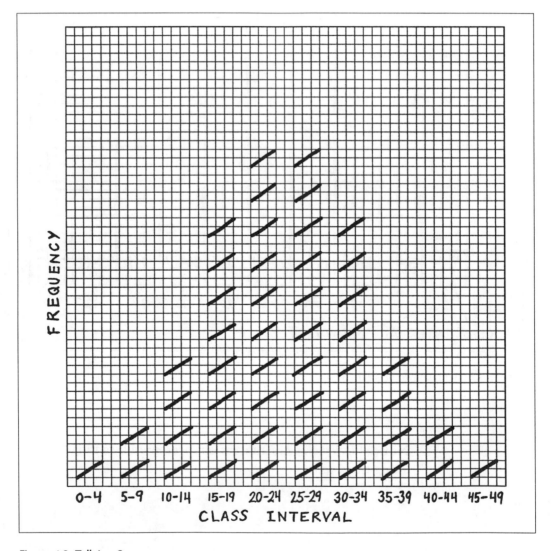

Figure 4.3. Tallying Scores

We used tallies that correspond with the frequency of scores that occur within a certain class. This gives you an even better visual representation of how often certain scores occur relative to other scores.

The Next Step: A Frequency Polygon

Creating a histogram or a tally of scores wasn't so difficult, and the next step (and the next way of illustrating data) is even easier. We're going to use the same data, and in fact the histogram that you just saw created, to create a frequency polygon. A **frequency polygon** is a continuous line that represents the frequencies of scores within a class interval, as shown in Figure 4.4.

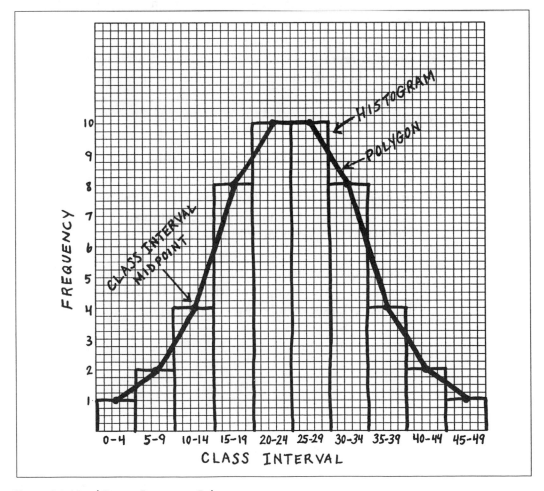

Figure 4.4. Hand-Drawn Frequency Polygon

How did we draw this? Here's how.

 1 Place a midpoint at the top of each bar or column in a histogram (see Figure 4.2).

2 Connect the lines and you've got it—a frequency polygon!

Note that in Figure 4.4, the histogram on which the frequency polygon is based is drawn using vertical and horizontal lines, and the polygon is drawn using curved lines. That's because while we want you to see what a frequency polygon is based on, you usually don't see the underlying histogram.

Why use a frequency polygon rather than a histogram to represent data? It's more a matter of preference than anything else. A frequency polygon appears more dynamic than a histogram (a line that represents change in frequency always looks neat), but you are basically conveying the same information.

Cumulating Frequencies

Once you have created a frequency distribution and have visually represented that data using a histogram or a frequency polygon, another option is to create a visual representation of the cumulative frequency of occurrences by class intervals. This is called a **cumulative frequency distribution.**

A cumulative frequency distribution is based on the same data as a frequency distribution, but with an added column (Cumulative Frequency), as shown below.

Class Interval	Frequency	Cumulative Frequency
45-49	1	50
40-44	2	49
35-39	4	47
30-34	8	43
25-29	10	35
20-24	10	25
15-19	8	15
10-14	4	7
5-9	2	3
0-4	1	1

The cumulative frequency distribution begins by the creation of a new column labeled Cumulative Frequency. Then, we add the frequency in a class interval to all the frequencies below it. For example, for the class interval of 0-4, there is 1 occurrence and none below it, so the cumulative frequency is 1. For the class interval of 5-9, there are 2 occurrences in that class interval and one below it for a total of 3 (2 + 1) occurrences in that class interval or below it. The last class interval (45-49) contains 1 occurrence, but there is a total of 50 occurrences at or below that class interval.

Once we create the cumulative frequency distribution, then the data can be plotted just as they were for a histogram or a frequency polygon. Only this time we'll skip right ahead and plot the midpoint of each class interval as a function of the cumulative frequency of that class interval. You can see the cumulative frequency distribution in Figure 4.5 based on the 50 scores from the beginning of this chapter.

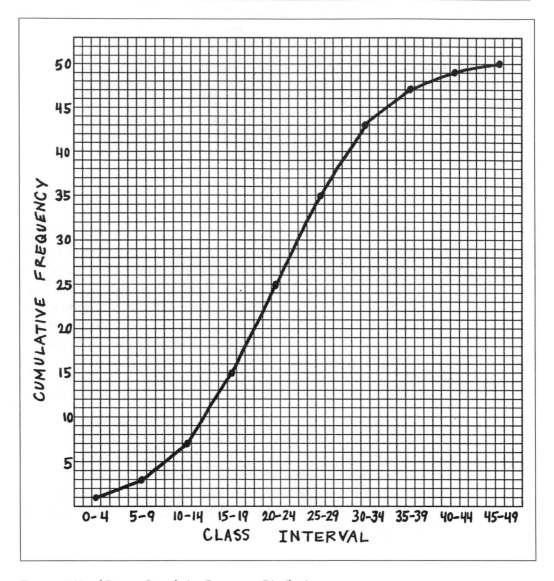

Figure 4.5 Hand-Drawn Cumulative Frequency Distribution

TECH
TALK

Another name for a cumulative frequency polygon is an **ogive.** And, if the distribution of the data is normal (see Chapter 8 for more on this), then the ogive represents what is popularly known as a bell curve or a normal distribution. SPSS creates a really nice ogive—it's called a P-P plot (for probability plot) and is really easy to create. See Appendix A for an introduction to creating graphs using SPSS and also see the material toward the end of this chapter.

FAT AND SKINNY FREQUENCY DISTRIBUTIONS

You could certainly surmise by now that distributions can be very different from one another in a variety of ways. In fact, there are four different ways—in their average value, their variability, their skewness, and their kurtosis. Those last two are new terms, and we'll define them as we show you what they look like. Let's define each of the four characteristics and then illustrate them.

Average Value

We're back once again to measures of central tendency. You can see in Figure 4.6 how three different distributions can differ in their average value. Notice that the average for distribution C is more than the average for distribution B, which, in turn, is more than the average for distribution A.

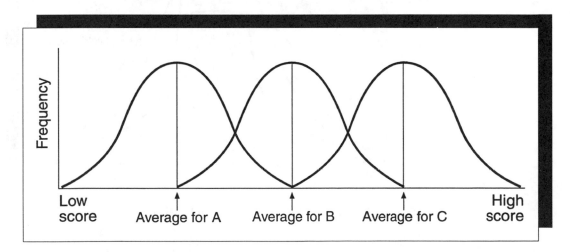

Figure 4.6. How Distributions Can Differ in Their Average Score

Variability

In Figure 4.7, you can see three distributions that all have the same average value, but differ in variability. The variability in distribution A is less than that in distribution B, and, in turn, less than that found in C. Another way to say this is that distribution C has the largest amount of variability of the three distributions, and A has the least.

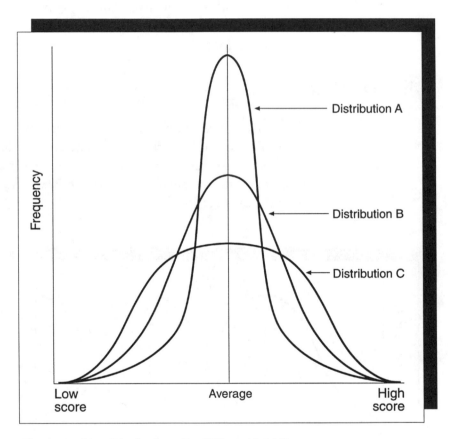

Figure 4.7. How Distributions Can Differ in Variability

Skewness

Skewness is a measure of the lack of symmetry, or the lopsidedness, of a distribution. In other words, one "tail" of the distribution is longer than another. For example, in Figure 4.8, distribution A has a longer right tail than left, corresponding to a smaller number of occurrences at the high end of the distribution. This is a positively skewed distribution. This might be the case when you have a test that is very difficult, and few people get scores that are very high and many more get scores that are relatively low. Distribution C has a shorter right tail than left, corresponding to a larger number of occurrences at the high end of the distribution. This is a negatively skewed distribution and would be the case for an easy test (lots of high scores and relatively few low scores). And distribution B—well, it's just right, equal lengths of tails and no skewness. If the mean is greater than the median, the distribution is positively skewed. If the median is greater than the mean, the distribution is negatively skewed.

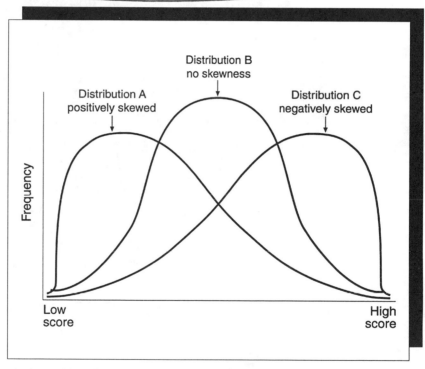

Figure 4.8. Degree of Skewness in Different Distributions

Kurtosis

Even though this sounds like a medical condition, it's the last of the four ways that we can classify how distributions differ from one another. **Kurtosis** has to do with how flat or peaked a distribution appears, and the terms used to describe this characteristic are relative ones. For example, the term **platykurtic** refers to a distribution that is relatively flat compared to a normal, or bell-shaped, distribution. The term **leptokurtic** refers to a distribution that is relatively peaked compared to a normal, or bell-shaped, distribution. In Figure 4.9, distribution A is platykurtic compared to distribution B. Distribution C is leptokurtic compared to distribution B. Figure 4.9 looks similar to Figure 4.7 for a good reason—distributions that are platykurtic, for example, are relatively more disperse than those that are not. Similarly, a distribution that is leptokurtic is less variable or dispersed relative to others.

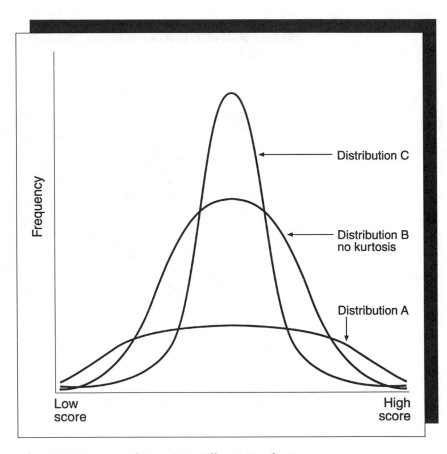

Figure 4.9. Degrees of Kurtosis in Different Distributions

TECH TALK

While skewness and kurtosis are used mostly as descriptive terms (such as "That distribution is negatively skewed"), there are mathematical indicators of how skewed or kurtotic a distribution is. For example, skewness is computed by subtracting the value of the median from the mean. For example, if the mean of a distribution is 100 and the median is 95, the skewness value is 100 – 95 = 5, and the distribution is positively skewed. If the mean of a distribution is 85 and the median is 90, the skewness value is 85 – 90 = –5, and the distribution is negatively skewed. There's an even more sophisticated formula, which is not relative, but takes the standard deviation of the distribution into account so skewness indicators can be compared to one another (see Formula 4.1).

$$Sk = \frac{3(\overline{X} - M)}{s} \qquad (4.1)$$

where

Sk is Pearson's (it's the correlation guy you'll learn about in Chapter 5) measure of skew

$\overline{X}$ is the mean

M is the median

s is the standard deviation

Using this formula, we can compare the skewness of one distribution to another in absolute, and not relative, terms. For example, the mean of distribution A is 100, the median is 105, and the standard deviation is 10. For distribution B, the mean is 120, the median is 116, and the standard deviation is 10. Using Pearson's skew formula, the skewness of distribution A is –.5, and the skewness of distribution B is .4. Distribution A is negatively skewed, and distribution B is positively skewed. However, distribution A is more skewed than distribution B, regardless of the direction.

OTHER COOL WAYS TO CHART DATA

What we did so far in this chapter is take some data and show how such charts as histograms and polygons can be used to communicate visually. But there are several other types of charts that are used in the behavioral and social sciences, and while it's not necessary for you to know exactly how to create them (manually), you should at least be familiar with their names and what they do. So here are some popular charts, what they do, and how they do it.

There are several very good personal computer applications for creating charts, among them the spreadsheet Excel (a Microsoft product) and, of course, SPSS. For your information, the charts that you see in this section of the chapter were created using Excel. The charts in the "Using the Computer to Illustrate Data" section were created using SPSS.

Column Charts

A column chart should be used when you want to show how data change over a period of time or when comparing different categories with one another. Categories are organized horizontally on the x-axis, and values are shown vertically on the y-axis. Here are some examples of when you might want to use a column chart.

- Number of voters by political affiliation
- The sales of three different types of products
- Number of children in each of six different grades

Figure 4.10 shows a graph of number of voters by political affiliation.

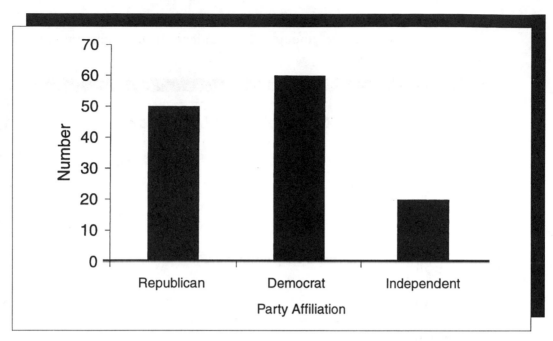

Figure 4.10. A Column Chart That Compares Different Categories With One Another

Bar Charts

A bar chart is identical to a column chart, but in this chart, categories are organized vertically on the x-axis and values are shown horizontally on the y-axis.

Line Charts

A line chart should be used when you want to show a trend in the data at equal intervals. Here are some examples of when you might want to use a line chart.

- Number of cases of mononucleosis (mono) among college students at three state universities per season
- Change in student enrollment over the school year
- Number of travelers on two different airlines for each quarter

In Figure 4.11, you can see a chart of the number of reported cases of mono among college students at three state universities by season.

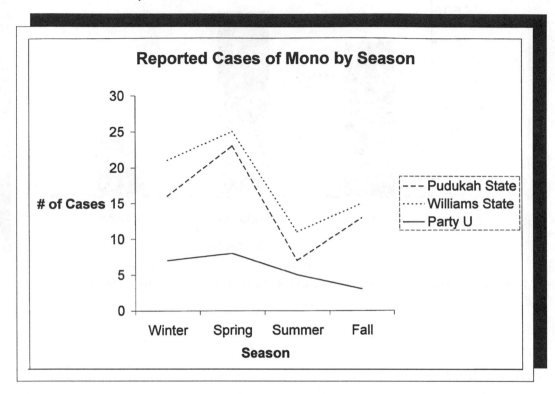

Figure 4.11. Using a Line Chart to Show a Trend Over Time

Pie Charts

A pie chart should be used when you want to show the proportion of an item that makes up a series of data points. Here are some examples of when you might want to use a pie chart.

- Percentage of children living in poverty by ethnicity
- Proportion of night and day students enrolled
- Age of participants by gender

In Figure 4.12, you can see a pie chart of the number of children living in poverty by ethnicity.

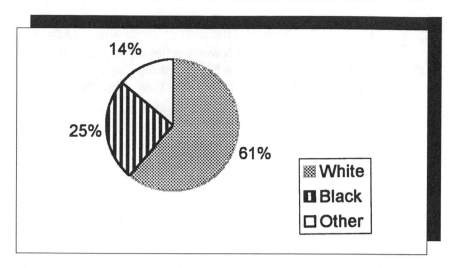

Figure 4.12. A Pie Chart Illustrating the Relative Proportion of One Category to Others

USING THE COMPUTER TO ILLUSTRATE DATA

Now let's use SPSS and go through the steps in creating some of the charts that we explored in this chapter. First, some general SPSS charting rules.

1. To create a chart, you must first enter the data you want to chart and then select the type of chart you want to create from the Graphs menu (see, we told you they were called different things in different settings). SPSS calls these visual impressions graphs.

2. To edit a graph, double-click on the chart itself and the Chart Editor will open up. Make the edits as you see fit.

3. To return to the original graph, close the Chart Editor by clicking on the icon in the upper-left-hand corner of the window.

TECH TALK   New to Version 10.0 of SPSS is the ability to create a chart based on the data in the Viewer window. Just highlight the data you want to chart to enter the Chart Editor, select the data you want to chart, right-click, and select Create Graph and the type of graph you want to create. Then edit to your heart's content.

Creating a Histogram Graph

To create a histogram, follow these steps.

1   Enter the data you want to use to create the graph. In this example, we will be using the same data that were used to create the histogram shown at the beginning of this chapter.

2   Click Graphs → Histogram, and you will see the Histogram dialog box as shown here.

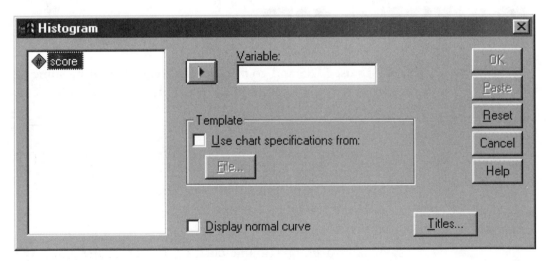

Figure 4.13. Histogram Dialog Box

3 Double-click the variable named score to move it to the Variable box.

4 Click OK, and the histogram will appear as shown here.

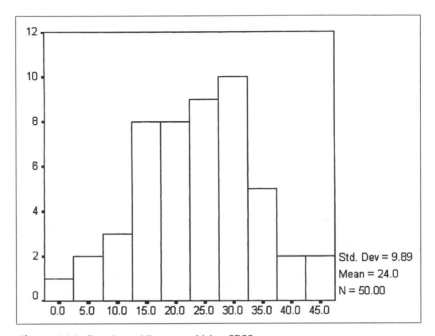

Figure 4.14. Creating a Histogram Using SPSS

The histogram in Figure 4.14 looks a bit different from the one for 50 cases that was hand drawn earlier. The difference is because SPSS defines class intervals using its own idiosyncratic method. SPSS took as the middle of a class interval the bottom number of the interval (such as 10), rather than the midpoint (such as 12.5). Consequently, scores are allocated to different groups. The lesson here? How you group data makes a big difference in the way they look.

Creating a Bar Graph

To create a bar graph, follow these steps. Enter the data you want to use to create the graph. Here are the data we used:

Republican	Democrat	Independent
54	63	19

1   Click Graphs → Bar, and you will see the Bar Charts dialog box as shown here.

2   Click define.

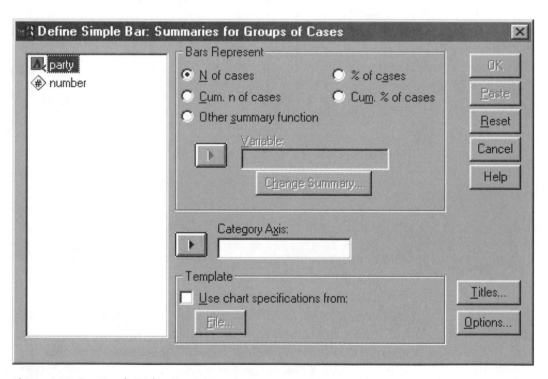

Figure 4.15. Bar Graph Dialog Box

3 Click Summaries for groups of cases and then click Define.

4 Click Other summary function.

5 Click ▶ to move variable number to the Bars Represent box.

6 Click party, and then click ▶ to move the variable to the Category Axis box.

7 Click OK, and the bar graph will appear as shown here.

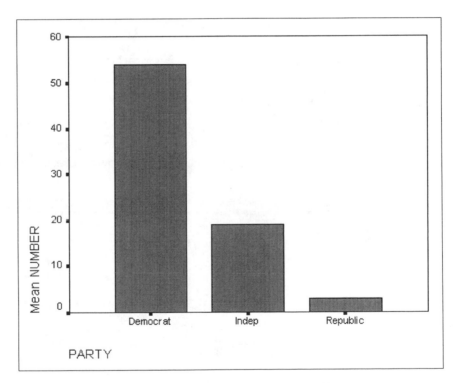

Figure 4.16. Creating a Bar Graph (just like a column graph) Using SPSS

Creating a Line Graph

To create a line graph, follow these steps.

1 Enter the data you want to use to create the graph. In this example, we will be using of the number reported cases of mono among college students at three state universities. Here's the data.

Pudukah State	Williams State	Party U
59	72	23

2 Click Graphs → Line, and you will see the Line Charts dialog box.

Once again, we run into language conflicts. SPSS uses the Graphs menu to create visual picture of data, but uses the word Chart in the dialog box. The lesson is that if it looks like a duck (or a chart), it is chart or a graph—your choice.

3 Click Simple, and click Summaries for groups of cases.

4 Click Define. You will see the Define Simple Line: Summaries for Groups of Cases dialog box as shown here.

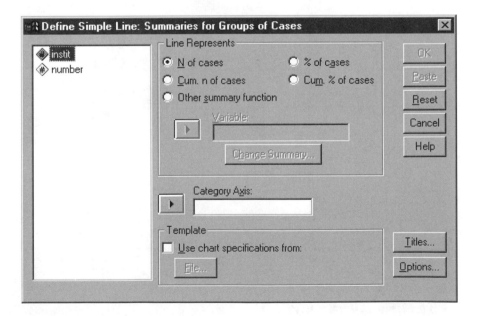

Figure 4.17. Define Simple Line Dialog Box

5   Click number, then click Other summary function, and then click ▶ to move variable to the Lines Represent box.

6   Move the instit variable to the Category Axis box.

7   Click OK, and the line graph will appear as shown here.

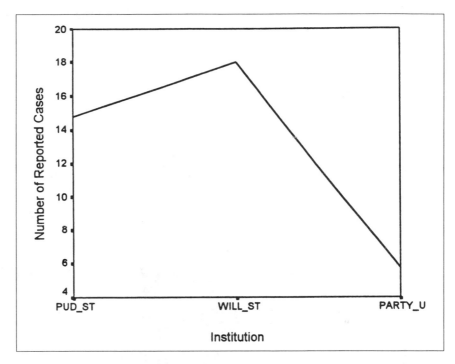

Figure 4.18. A Line Graph That Represents the Number of Cases of Mono at Three Institutions

Creating a Pie Graph

To create a pie graph, follow these steps.

Enter the data you want to use to create the graph. In this example, the pie chart represents the number of children living in poverty by ethnicity. Here's the data.

Ethnicity	Percentage
White	61
Black	25
Other	14

1 Click Graphs → Pie, and you will see the Pie Charts dialog box.

2 Click Values of Individual cases.

3 Click Define. You will see the Define Pie: Values of individual cases dialog box.

4 Click percentage, and then click ▶ to move the variable to the Slices Represent variable box. Click percentage and then click ▶ to move the variable to the Slices Labels box.

5 Click OK, and the pie graph will appear as shown here.

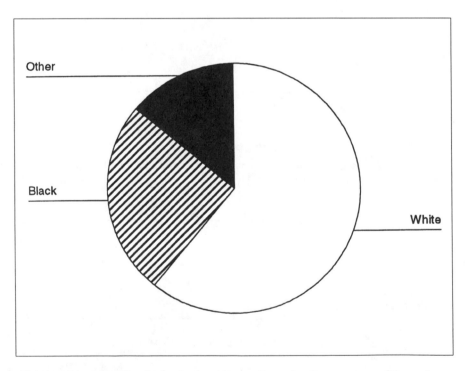

Figure 4.19   A Pie Graph, the Perfect Way to Show the Occurrences of Several Variables Relative to the Total

SUMMARY

There's no question that charts are fun to create and can add enormous understanding to what appears to be disorganized data. Follow our suggestions in this chapter and use charts well, but only when they enhance, not just add to, what's already there.

TIME TO PRACTICE

1. A data set of 50 comprehension scores (named comp_sc) is contained in Appendix C, called Chapter 4 Data Set 1. Answer the following questions and/or complete the following tasks.

    a. Create a frequency distribution and a histogram for the set.

    b. Why did you select the class interval you used?

    c. Is this distribution skewed? How do you know?

2. For each of the following, indicate whether you would use a pie, line, or bar chart and why.

    a. The proportion of freshmen, sophomores, juniors, and seniors in a particular university.

    b. Change in GPA over four semesters.

    c. Number of applicants for four different jobs.

    d. Reaction time to four different stimuli.

    e. Number of scores in each of 10 categories.

3. Go to the library and find a journal article in your area of interest that does contain empirical data, but does not contain any visual representation of that data. Use the data to create a chart. Be sure to specify what type of chart you are creating and why you chose the one you did. You can create the chart manually or using SPSS or Excel.

ANSWERS TO PRACTICE QUESTIONS

1a. Here's the frequency distribution.

Class Interval	Frequency
45-50	1
40-44	2
35-39	3
30-34	8
25-29	10
20-24	10
15-19	8
10-14	4
5-9	2
0-4	2

Here's what the histogram should look like.

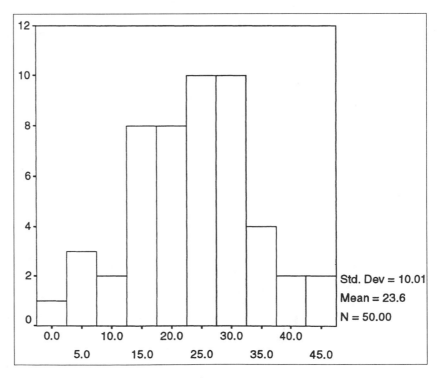

Std. Dev = 10.01
Mean = 23.6
N = 50.00

Figure 4.20. Histogram of Data in Chapter 4 Data Set 1

b. We settled on a class interval of 5 since it allowed us to have close to 10 class intervals and it fit the criteria that we discussed in this chapter for deciding on a class interval.

c. The distribution is positively skewed since the mean is greater than the median.

2. a. Pie.

   b. Line.

   c. Bar or histogram.

   d. Line.

   e. Bar or histogram.

3. On your own!

Ice Cream and Crime
Computing Correlation Coefficients

Difficulty Scale ☺☺ (moderately hard)

What you'll learn about in this chapter

- What correlations are and how they work
- How to compute a simple correlation coefficient
- How to interpret the value of the correlation coefficient
- What other types of correlations exist

WHAT ARE CORRELATIONS ALL ABOUT?

Measures of central tendency and measures of variability are not the only descriptive statistics that we are interested in using to get a picture of what a set of scores looks like. You have already learned that knowing the values of the one most representative score (central tendency) and a measure of spread or dispersion (variability) is critical for describing the characteristics of a distribution.

However, sometimes we are as interested in the relationship between variables—or to be more precise, how the value of one variable changes when the value of another variable changes. The way we express this interest is through the computation of a simple correlation coefficient.

A **correlation coefficient** is a numerical index that reflects the relationship between two variables. The value of this descriptive statistic ranges between a value of −1 and a value of +1. A correlation between two variables is sometimes referred to as a bivariate (for two variables) correlation. Even more specifically, the type of correlation that we will talk about in the majority of this chapter is called the **Pearson product-moment correlation,** named for its inventor, Karl Pearson.

TECH TALK

The Pearson correlation coefficient examines the relationship between two variables, but both those variables are continuous in nature. In other words, they are variables that can assume any value along some underlying continuum, such as height, age, test score, or income. But there is a host of other variables that are not continuous. They're called discrete or categorical variables, such as race, social class, and political affiliation.

You need to use other correlational techniques such as the point-biserial correlation in these cases. These topics are for a more advanced course, but you should know they are acceptable and very useful techniques. We mention them briefly later on in this chapter.

There are other types of correlation coefficients, which measure the relationship between more than two variables, and we'll leave those for the next statistics course (which you are looking forward to already, right?).

Types of Correlation Coefficients: Flavor 1 and Flavor 2

A correlation reflects the dynamic quality of the relationship between variables. In doing so, it allows us to understand whether variables tend to move in the same or opposite directions when they change. If variables change in the same direction, the correlation is called a **direct correlation** or a **positive correlation**. If variables change in opposite directions, the correlation is called an **indirect correlation** or a **negative correlation**. Table 5.1 shows a summary of these relationships.

TABLE 5.1 Types of Correlations and the Corresponding Relationship Between Variables

What Happens to Variable X	What Happens to Variable Y	Type of Correlation	Value	Example
X increases in value	Y increases in value	Direct or positive	Positive, ranging from .00 to +1.00	The more time you spend studying, the higher your test score will be.
X decreases in value	Y decreases in value	Direct or positive	Positive, ranging from .00 to +1.00	The less money you put in the bank, the less interest you will earn.
X increases in value	Y decreases in value	Indirect or negative	Negative, ranging from –1.00 to .00	The more you exercise, the less you will weigh.
X decreases in value	Y increases in value	Indirect or negative	Negative, ranging from –1.00 to .00	The less time you take to complete a test, the more you'll get wrong.

Now, keep in mind that the examples in the table reflect generalities. For example, regarding time to completion and the number of items correct on a test: in general, the less time that is taken on a test, the lower the score.

Such a conclusion is not rocket science, since the faster one goes, the more likely one is to make careless mistakes such as not reading instructions correctly. But of course, there are people who can go very fast and do very well. And there are people who go very slow and don't do well at all. The point is that we are talking about the performance of a group of people on two different variables. We are computing the correlation between the two variables for the group, not for any one particular person.

THINGS TO REMEMBER

There are several (easy, but important) things to remember about the correlation coefficient.

- A correlation can range in value from –1 to +1.

- The absolute value of the coefficient reflects the strength of the correlation. So a correlation of −.70 is stronger than a correlation of +.50. One of the frequently made mistakes regarding correlation coefficients is when students assume that a direct or positive correlation is always stronger (i.e., "better") than an indirect or negative correlation because of the sign and nothing else.

- A correlation always reflects the situation where there are at least two data points (scores on two variables) per case.

- Another easy mistake is to assign a value judgment to the sign of the correlation. Many students assume that a negative relationship is not good and a positive one is good. That's why instead of using the terms negative and positive, the terms indirect and direct communicate meaning more clearly.

- The Pearson product-moment correlation coefficient is represented by the small letter r with a subscript representing the variables that are being correlated. For example,

r_{xy} is the correlation between variable X and variable Y

$r_{\text{weight-height}}$ is the correlation between weight and height

$r_{\text{SAT-GPA}}$ is the correlation between SAT score and grade point average (GPA)

TECH TALK
The correlation coefficient reflects the amount of variability that is shared between two variables and what they have in common. For example, you can expect an individual's height to be correlated with an individual's weight because they share many of the same characteristics such as the individual's nutritional and medical history, general health, and genetics. However, if one variable does not change in value and therefore has nothing to share, then the correlation between the two variables is zero. For example, if you computed the correlation between age and number of years of school completed, and everyone was 25 years old, there would be no correlation between the two variables since there's literally nothing (any variability) about age available to share.

Likewise, if you constrain or restrict the range of one variable, the correlation between that variable and another variable is going to be less than if the range is not constrained. For example, if you correlate reading comprehension and grades in school for very high achieving children, you'll find the correlation lower than if you computed the same correlation for children in general. That's because the reading comprehension score of very high achieving students is quite high and much less variable than it would be for all children. The moral? When you are interested in the relationship between two variables, try to collect sufficiently diverse data—that way you'll get the truest representative result.

COMPUTING A SIMPLE CORRELATION COEFFICIENT

The computational formula for finding the simple Pearson product-moment correlation coefficient between a variable labeled X and a variable labeled Y is shown in Formula 5.1.

$$r_{xy} = \frac{n \Sigma XY - \Sigma X \Sigma Y}{\sqrt{[N\Sigma X)^2 - (\Sigma X)^2][N\Sigma Y^2 - (\Sigma Y)^2]}} \tag{5.1}$$

where

r_{xy} is the correlation coefficient between X and Y

N is the size of the sample

X is the individual's score on the X variable

Y is the individual's score on the Y variable

XY is the product of each X score times its corresponding Y score

X^2 is the individual X score, squared

Y^2 is the individual Y score, squared

Here are the data we will use in this example.

X	Y	X^2	Y^2	XY
2	3	4	9	6
4	2	16	4	8
5	6	25	36	30
6	5	36	25	30
4	3	16	9	12
7	6	49	36	42
8	5	64	25	40
5	4	25	16	20
6	4	36	16	24
7	5	49	25	35
Total or Σ　54	43	320	201	247

Before we plug the numbers in, let's make sure you understand what each one represents.

ΣX, or the sum of all the X values, is 54

ΣY, or the sum of all the Y values, is 43

ΣX^2, or the sum of each X value squared, is 320

ΣY^2, or the sum of each Y value squared, is 201

ΣXY, or the sum of the products of X and Y, is 247

It's easy to confuse the sum of a set of values squared and the sum of the squared values. The sum of a set of values squared is taking values such as 2 and 3, summing them (to be 5), and then squaring that (which is 25). The sum of the squared values is taking values such as 2 and 3, squaring them (to get 4 and 9, respectively), and then adding those together (to get 13). Just look for the parentheses as you work.

Here are the steps in computing the correlation coefficient.

1. List the two values for each participant. You should do this in a column format so as not to get confused.

2. Compute the sum of all the X values, and compute the sum of all the Y values.

3. Square each of the X values, and square each of the Y values.

4. Find the sum of all the squared X and Y values.

5. Multiply each X value by its corresponding Y value.

6. Find the sum of the XY products.

These values are plugged into the equation you see in Formula 5.2.

$$r_{xy} = \frac{10 \bullet 247 - 54 \bullet 43}{\sqrt{[10 \bullet 320 - (54)^2][10 \bullet 201 - (43)^2]}} \qquad (5.2)$$

Ta da! And you can see the answer in Formula 5.3.

$$r_{xy} = \frac{148}{213.83} = .692 \qquad (5.3)$$

A Visual Picture of a Correlation: The Scatterplot

There's a very simple way to visually represent a correlation: Create what is called a **scatterplot,** or **scattergram.** This is simply a plot of each set of scores on separate axes.

Here are the steps to complete a scattergram like you see in Figure 5.1 for the 10 sets of scores for which we computed the sample correlation above.

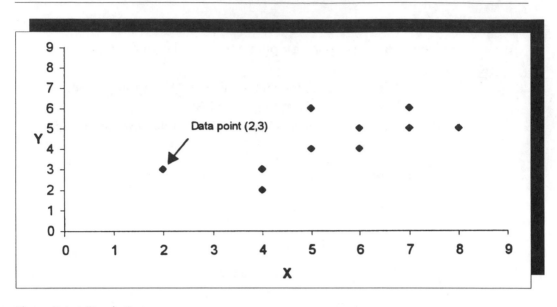

Figure 5.1. A Simple Scattergram

1   Draw the x-axis and the y-axis. Usually, the *X* variable goes on the horizontal axis and the *Y* variable goes on the vertical axis.

2   Mark both axes with the range of values that you know to be the case for the data. For example, the value of the *X* variable in our example ranges from 2 to 8, so we marked the x-axis from 0 to 9. There's no harm in marking them a bit low or high—just as long as you allow room for the values to appear. The value of the *Y* variable ranges from 2 to 6, and we marked that axis from 0 to 9. Having similarly labeled axes can sometimes make the finished scatterplot easier to understand.

3   Finally, for each pair of scores (such as 2 and 3, as shown in Figure 5.1), we entered a dot on the chart by marking the place where 2 falls on the x-axis and 3 falls on the y-axis. The dot represents a **data point,** which is the intersection of the two values, as you can see in Figure 5.1.

When all the data points are plotted, what does such an illustration tell us about the relationship between the variables? To begin with, the general shape of the collection of data points indicates whether the correlation is direct (positive) or indirect (negative).

A positive slope is where the data points group themselves in a cluster from the lower left-hand corner on the x- and y-axes through the upper right-hand corner. A negative slope is where the data points group themselves in a cluster from the upper left-hand corner on the x- and y-axes through the lower right-hand corner.

Here are some scatterplots showing very different correlations where you can see how the grouping of the data points reflects the sign and strength of the correlation coefficient.

Figure 5.2 shows a perfect direct correlation where $r_{xy} = 1.00$ and all the data points are aligned along a straight line with a positive slope.

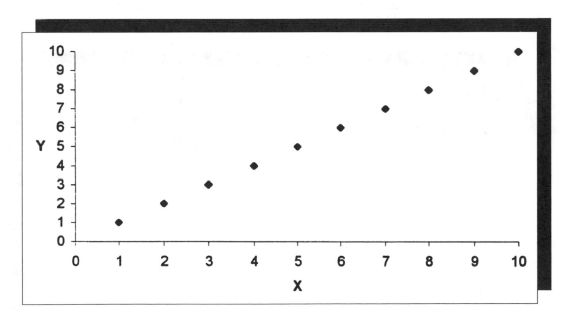

Figure 5.2. A Perfect Direct, or Positive, Correlation

If the correlation were perfectly indirect, the value of the correlation coefficient would be –1.0 and the data points would align themselves in a straight line as well, but from the upper left-hand corner of the chart to the lower right. In other words, the line that connects the data points would have a negative slope.

Don't ever expect to find a perfect correlation between any two variables in the behavioral or social sciences. It would say that two variables are so perfectly correlated, they share everything in common. In other words, knowing one is like knowing the other. Just think about your classmates. Do you think they all share any one thing in common that is perfectly related to another of their characteristics across all these different people? Probably not. In fact, r values approaching .7 and .8 are just about the highest you'll see.

In Figure 5.3, you can see the scatterplot for a strong (but not perfect) direct relationship where $r_{xy} = .70$. Notice that the data points align themselves along a positive slope, although not perfectly.

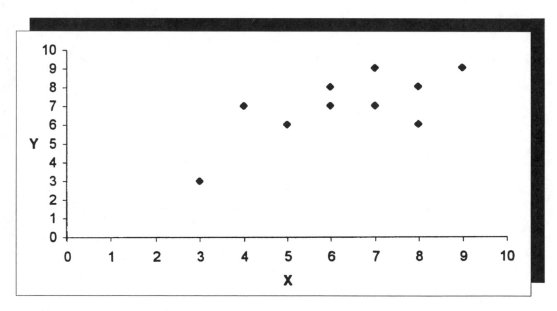

Figure 5.3. A Strong Positive, but Not Perfect, Direct Relationship

Now, we'll show you a strong indirect, or negative, relationship in Figure 5.4 where $r_{xy} = -.82$. Notice how the data points align themselves on a negative slope from the upper left-hand corner of the chart to the lower right-hand corner.

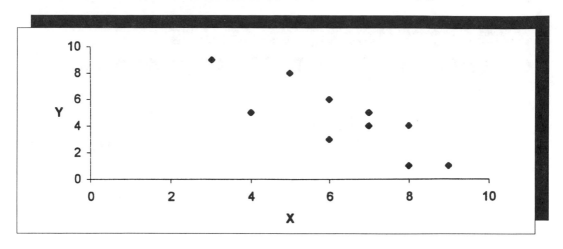

Figure 5.4. A Strong Indirect Relationship

That's what different types of correlations look like, and you can really tell the general strength and direction by examining the way the points are grouped.

TECH TALK

Not all correlations are reflected by a straight line showing the X and the Y values in a relationship called a **linear correlation.** The relationship may not be linear and be reflected by a straight line. Let's take the correlation between age and memory. For the early years, the correlation is probably highly positive—the older children get, the better their memories. Then into young and middle adulthood, there isn't much of a change or much of a correlation since most young and middle adults maintain a good memory. But with old age, memory begins to suffer, and there is an indirect relationship between memory and aging in the later years. If you take these together, you find the correlation between memory and age tends to look something like a curve where memory increases, levels off, and then decreases. It's a curvilinear relationship, and sometimes the best description of the relationship is a curvilinear one.

UNDERSTANDING WHAT THE CORRELATION COEFFICIENT MEANS

Well, we have this numerical index of the relationship between two variables and we know that the higher the value of the correlation (regardless of its sign), the stronger the relationship is. But since the correlation coefficient is a value that is not directly tied to the value of an outcome, just how can we interpret it and make it a more meaningful indicator of a relationship?

Here are different ways to look at the interpretation of that simple r_{xy}.

Using-Your-Thumb Rule

Perhaps the easiest (but not the most informative) way to interpret the value of a correlation coefficient is by eyeballing it and using the information in Table 5.2.

TABLE 5.2   Interpreting a Correlation Coefficient

Size of the Correlation Coefficient	General Interpretation
.8 to 1.0	Very strong relationship
.6 to .8	Strong relationship
.4 to .6	Moderate relationship
.2 to .4	Weak relationship
.0 to .2	Weak or no relationship

So if the correlation between two variables is .5, you could safely conclude that the relationship is a moderate one—not strong, but certainly not weak enough to say that the variables in question don't share anything in common.

This eyeball method is perfectly acceptable for a quick assessment of the strength of the relationship between variables, such as a description in a research report. But since this "rule of thumb" does depend on a subjective judgment (of what's "strong" or "weak"), we would like a more precise method. That's what we'll look at now.

A DETERMINED EFFORT: SQUARING THE CORRELATION COEFFICIENT

Here's the much more precise way to interpret the correlation coefficient: computing the coefficient of determination. The **coefficient of determination** is the percentage of variance in one variable that is accounted for by the variance in the other variable. Quite a mouthful, huh?

Earlier in this chapter, we pointed out how variables that share something in common tend to be correlated with one another. If we correlated math and English grades for 100 fifth-grade students, we would find the correlation to be moderately strong because many of the reasons why children do well (or not well) in math tend to be the same reasons why they do well (or not well) in English. The number of hours they study, how bright they are, how interested their parents are in their schoolwork, the number of books they have at home, and more are all related to both math and English performance and account for differences between children (and that's where the variability comes in).

The more these two variables share in common, the more they will be related. These two variables share variability—or the reason why children differ from one another. And on the whole, the brighter child who studies more will do better.

To determine exactly how much of the variance in one variable can be accounted for by the variance in another variable, the coefficient of determination is computed by squaring the correlation coefficient.

For example, if the correlation between GPA and number of hours of study time is .70 (or $r_{\text{GPA·time}} = .70$), then the coefficient of determination, represented by $r^2_{\text{GPA·time}}$, is $.7^2$, or .49. This means that 49% of the variance in GPA can be explained by the variance in studying time. And the stronger the correlation, the more variance can be explained (which only makes good sense). The more two variables share in common (such as good study habits, knowledge of what's expected in class, and lack of fatigue), the more information about performance on one score can be explained by the other score.

However, if 49% of the variance can be explained, this means that 51% cannot—so even for a strong correlation of .70, a good deal of the reasons why scores on these variables tend to be different from one another goes unexplained. This amount of unexplained variance is called the **coefficient of alienation** (also called the **coefficient of nondetermination**). Don't worry. No aliens here. This isn't *X-Files* stuff, it's just the amount of variance in Y not explained by X.

How about a visual presentation of this sharing variance idea? OK. In Figure 5.5, you'll find a correlation coefficient, the corresponding coefficient of determination, and a diagram that represents how much variance is shared between the two variables. The larger the striped area in each diagram (and the more variance the two variables share), the more highly the variables are correlated.

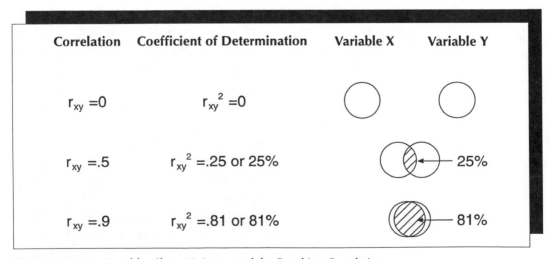

Figure 5.5. How Variables Share Variance and the Resulting Correlation

- The first diagram shows two circles that do not touch. They don't touch because they do not share anything in common. The correlation is 0.
- The second diagram shows two circles that overlap. With a correlation of .5 (and $r^2_{xy} = .25$), they share about 25% of the variance between themselves.
- Finally, the third diagram shows that the two circles are almost placed one on top of the other. With an almost perfect correlation of $r_{xy} = .90$ ($r^2_{xy} = .81$), they share about 81% of the variance between themselves.

As More Ice Cream Is Eaten . . . the Crime Rate Goes Up (or Association vs. Causality)

Now here's the really important thing to be careful about when computing, reading about, or interpreting correlation coefficients. Imagine this. In a small Midwestern town, a phenomenon was discovered that defied any logic. The local police chief observes that as ice cream consumption increases, crime rates tend to increase as well. Quite simply, if you measured both, you would find the relationship was direct, meaning that as people eat more ice cream, the crime rate increases. And as you might expect, as they ate less ice cream, the crime rate went down. The police chief was baffled until he recalled the Stat 1 class he took in college and still fondly remembers.

His wondering how this could be turned into an aha! "Very easily," he thought. The two variables must share something or have something in common with one another. Remember that it must be something that relates to both level of ice cream consumption and level of crime rate. Can you guess what that is?

The *outside temperature* is what they both have in common. When it gets warm outside such as in the summertime, more crimes are committed (it stays light longer, people leave the windows open, etc.). And since it is warmer, people enjoy the ancient treat and art of eating ice cream. And conversely, during the long and dark winter months, less ice cream is consumed and fewer crimes are committed as well.

Joe Bob, recently elected as a city commissioner, learns about these findings and has a great idea, or at least one that he thinks his constituents will love. (Keep in mind, he skipped the statistics offering in college.) Why not just limit the consumption of ice cream in the summer months and there will surely be a decrease in the crime rate? Sounds good, right? Well, on closer inspection, it really makes no sense at all.

That's because of the simple principle that correlations express the association that exists between two or more variables and has nothing to do with causality. In other words, just because level of ice cream consumption and crime rate increase together (and decrease together as well) does not mean that a change in one results in a change in another.

For example, if we took all the ice cream out of all the stores in town and no more was available, do you think the crime rate would decrease? Of course not, and it's preposterous to even think such. But strangely enough, that's often how associations are interpreted—as being causal in nature, and complex issues in the social and behavioral sciences are reduced to trivialities because of this misunderstanding. Did long hair and hippiedom have anything to do with the Vietnam conflict? Of course not. Does the rise in the number of crimes committed have anything to do with more efficient and safer cars? Of course not. But they all happen at the same time, creating the illusion of being associated.

OTHER COOL CORRELATIONS

There are different ways variables can be assessed. For example, nominal-level variables are categorical in nature such as race (black or white) or political affiliation (Independent or Republican). Or, if you are measuring income and age, these are both interval-level variables since the underlying continuum on which they are based has equally appearing intervals. As you continue your studies, you're likely to come across correlations between data that occur at different levels of measurement. And to compute these correlations, you need some specialized techniques. Table 5.3 summarizes what these different techniques are and how they differ from one another.

TABLE 5.3   Correlation Coefficient Shopping, Anyone?

Level of Measurement and Examples			
Variable X	*Variable Y*	*Type of Correlation*	*Correlation Being Computed*
Nominal (voting preference such as Republican or Democrat)	Nominal (sex such as male or female)	Phi coefficient	The correlation between voting preference and sex
Nominal (social class such as high, medium, or low)	Ordinal (rank in high school graduating class)	Rank biserial coefficient	The correlation between social class and rank in high school
Nominal (family configuration such as intact or single parent)	Interval (grade point average)	Point biserial	The correlation between family configuration and grade point average
Ordinal (height converted to rank)	Ordinal (weight converted to rank)	Spearman rank coefficient	The correlation between height and weight
Interval (number of problems solved)	Interval (age in years)	Pearson correlation coefficient	The correlation between number of problems solved and age in years

Bunches of Correlations: The Correlation Matrix

What happens if you have more than two variables? How are the correlations illustrated? Use a **correlation matrix** like the one shown below—a simple and elegant solution.

	Income	*Educ*	*Attitude*	*Vote*
Income	—	.574	−.08	−.291
Educ	.574	—	−.149	−.199
Attitude	−.08	−.149	—	−.169
Vote	−.291	−.199	−.169	—

As you can see, there are four variables in the matrix: level of income (Income), level of education (Educ), attitude toward voting (Attitude), and whether the individual voted in the last election (Vote).

For each pair of variables, there is a correlation coefficient. For example, the correlation between income level and education is .574. Similarly, the correlation between income level and whether the person participated in the last election is –.291 (meaning that the higher the level of income, the less likely people are to vote).

In such a matrix, there are always 4!/(4–2)!2!, or four things taken two at a time for a total of six correlation coefficients. Since variables correlate perfectly with themselves (those are the dashes down the diagonal), and since the correlation between Income and Vote is the same as the correlation between Vote and Income, the matrix crates a mirror image of itself.

You will see such matrices (the plural of matrix) when you read journal articles that use correlations to describe the relationship between several variables.

USING THE COMPUTER TO COMPUTE A CORRELATION COEFFICIENT

Let's use SPSS to compute a correlation coefficient. The data set we are using is an SPSS data file named Chapter 5 Data Set 1.

There are two variables in this data set:

Variable	Definition
Income	Annual income in thousands of dollars
Education	Level of education measured in years

To compute the Pearson correlation coefficient, follow these steps.

1. Open the file named Chapter 5 Data Set 1.
2. Click Analyze → Correlate → Bivariate, and you will see the Bivariate Correlations dialog box as shown in Figure 5.6.

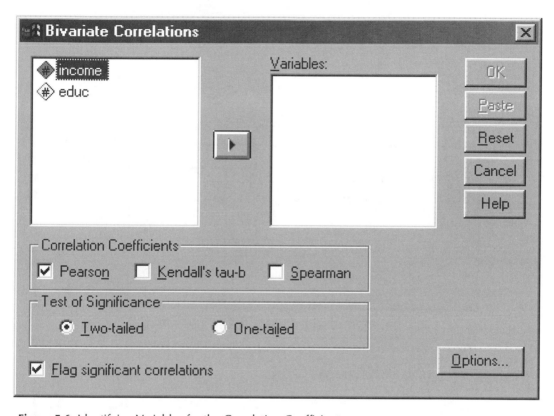

Figure 5.6. Identifying Variables for the Correlation Coefficient

3. Double-click on the variable named income to move it to the Variable(s) box.
4. Double-click on the variable named educ to move it to the Variable(s) box.
5. Click OK.

The SPSS Output

The output in Figure 5.7 shows the correlation coefficient to be equal to .574. Also shown are the sample size 20 and a measure of the statistical significance of the correlation coefficient (which we'll cover in Chapter 13).

➡ **Correlations**

Correlations

		INCOME	EDUC
INCOME	Pearson Correlation	1.000	.574**
	Sig. (2-tailed)	.	.008
	N	20	20
EDUC	Pearson Correlation	.574**	1.000
	Sig. (2-tailed)	.008	.
	N	20	20

**. Correlation is significant at the 0.01 level

Figure 5.7 SPSS Output for the Computation of the Correlation Coefficient
**Correlation is significant at the .01 level.

SUMMARY

The idea of showing how things are related to one another and what they have in common is a very powerful idea and a very useful descriptive statistic (used in inference as well). Keep in mind that correlations express a relationship that is only associative and not causal, and you'll be able to understand how this statistic gives us valuable information about the relationships and how variables change or remain the same in concert with others.

TIME TO PRACTICE

1. Use these data to answer Questions 1a and 1b. These data are saved as Chapter 5 Data Set 2.

Total No. of Problems Correct (out of a possible 20)	Attitude Toward Test Taking (out of a possible 100)
17	94
13	73
12	59
15	80
16	93
14	85
16	66
16	79
18	77
19	91

a. Compute the Pearson product-moment correlation coefficient.

b. Construct a scatterplot for these 10 values. Based on the scatterplot, would you predict the correlation to be direct or indirect? Why?

2. Use these data to answer Questions 2a and 2b.

Speed (to complete a 50-yard swim)	Strength (no. of pounds bench-pressed)
21.6	135
23.4	213
26.5	243
25.5	167
20.8	120
19.5	134
20.9	209
18.7	176
29.8	156
28.7	177

a. Using either a calculator or a computer, compute the Pearson correlation coefficient.

b. Interpret these data using both the general range of very weak to very strong and also compute the coefficient of determination. How does the subjective analysis compare to the value of r^2?

3. The coefficient of determination between two variables is .64. Answer the following questions.

   a. What is the Pearson correlation coefficient?

   b. How strong is the relationship?

   c. How much of the variance in the relationship between these two variables is unaccounted for?

4. Look at Table 5.3. What type of correlation coefficient would you use to examine the relationship between ethnicity (defined as different categories) and political affiliation? How about club membership (yes or no) and high school GPA? Explain why you selected the answers you did.

ANSWERS TO PRACTICE QUESTIONS

1. a. $r = .596$.

    b. From the answer to 1a, you already now that the correlation is direct. But from the scatterplot shown in Figure 5.8, you can predict it to be such (without actually knowing the sign of the coefficient), since the data points group themselves from the lower left corner of the graph to the upper right corner and assume a positive slope.

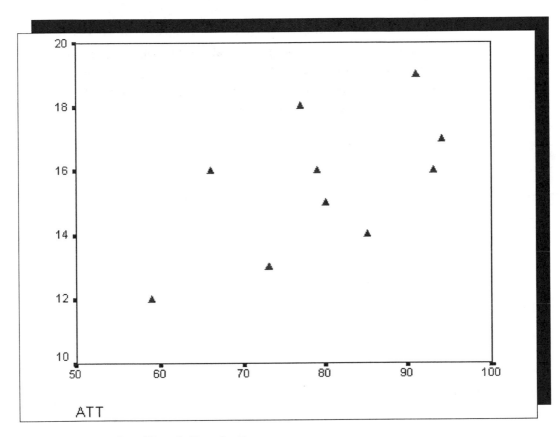

Figure 5.8. Scatterplot of Data in Data Set 2

2. a. $r = .269$.

   b. According to the table presented earlier in the chapter, the general strength of the correlation of this magnitude is weak. The coefficient of determination is $.269^2$, or 7.2% (.072) of the variance is accounted for. The subjective analysis (weak) and the objective one (7.2% of the variance accounted for) are consistent with one another.

3. a. .8.

   b. Very strong.

   c. $1 - .64$, or 36% (.36).

4. To the examine the relationship between ethnicity and political affiliation, you would use the phi coefficient since both variables are nominal in nature. To examine the relationship between club membership and high school GPA, you would use the point biserial correlation since one variable is nominal (club membership) and the other is interval (GPA).

Predicting Who'll Win the Super Bowl

Using Linear Regression

Difficulty Scale ☺ (as hard as they get!)

What you'll learn about in this chapter

- How prediction works and how it can be used in the social and behavioral sciences
- Why linear regression works when predicting one variable from another
- How to judge the accuracy of predictions
- The usefulness of multiple regression

WHAT IS PREDICTION ALL ABOUT?

Here's the scoop. Not only can you compute the degree to which two variables are related to one another (by computing a correlation coefficient as we did in Chapter 5), but you can also use these correlations as the basis for the prediction of the value of one variable from the value of another. This is a very special case of how correlations can be used, and it is a very powerful tool for social and behavioral sciences researchers.

The basic idea is to use a set of previously collected data (such as data on variables X and Y), calculate how correlated these variables are with one another, and then use that correlation and the knowledge of X to predict Y. Sound difficult? It's not really, especially once you see it illustrated.

For example, a researcher collects data on total high school grade point average (GPA) and first-year college GPA for 400 students in their freshman year at the state university. He computes the correlation between the two variables. Then he uses the techniques you'll learn about later in this chapter to take a *new* set of high school GPAs and (knowing the relationship between high school GPA and first-year college GPA from the previous set of students) predict what first-year GPA should be for the 400 new students. Pretty nifty, huh?

Here's another example. A group of teachers is interested in finding out how well retention works. That is, do children who are retained in kindergarten (and not passed on to first grade) do better in first grade? Once again, these teachers know the correlation between being retained and first-grade performance and can apply it to a new set of students and predict first-grade performance based on kindergarten performance. How does this work? Easy. Data are collected on past events (such as the existing relationship between two variables), and then applied to a future event given knowledge of only one variable. It's easier than you think.

The higher the absolute value of the correlation coefficient, the more accurate the prediction is of one variable from the other based on that correlation because the more two variables share in common, the more you know about the second variable from your knowledge of the first variable. And you may already surmise that when the correlation is perfect (+1.0 or –1.0), then the prediction is perfect as well. If $r_{xy} = -1.0$ or +1.0, and if you know the value of X, then you also know the exact value of Y. Likewise, if $r_{xy} = -1.0$ or +1.0, and you know the value of Y, then you also know the exact value of X. Either way works just fine.

What we'll do in this chapter is to go through the process of using linear regression to predict a *Y* score from an *X* score. We'll begin by discussing the general logic that underlies prediction, then go to a review of some simple line-drawing skills, and finally discuss the prediction process using specific examples.

THE LOGIC OF PREDICTION

Before we begin with the actual calculations and show you how correlations are used for prediction, let's create the argument why and how prediction works. Then we will continue with the example of predicting college GPA from high school GPA.

Prediction is an activity that computes future outcomes from present ones. When we want to predict one variable from another, we need to first compute the correlation between the two variables. Table 6.1 shows the data we will be using in this example. Figure 6.1 shows the scatterplot (see Chapter 5) of the two variables that are being computed.

TABLE 6.1	Total High School GPA and First-Year College GPA Are Correlated
High School GPA	*First-Year College GPA*
3.50	3.30
2.50	2.20
4.00	3.50
3.80	2.70
2.80	3.50
1.90	2.00
3.20	3.10
3.70	3.40
2.70	1.90
3.30	3.70

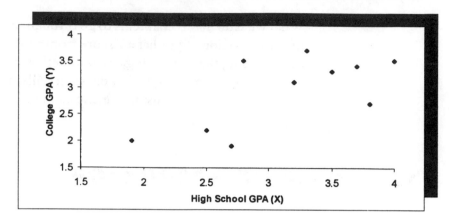

Figure 6.1. Scatterplot of High School GPA and College GPA

To predict college GPA from high school GPA, we have to create a **regression equation** and use that to plot what is called a **regression line**. A regression line reflects our best guess as to what score on the Y variable (college GPA) would be predicted by a score on the X variable (high school GPA). For all the data you see in Table 6.1, it's the line that minimizes the distance between the line and each of the points on the predicted (Y) variable. You'll shortly learn how to draw that line shown in Figure 6.2. What does this regression line represent?

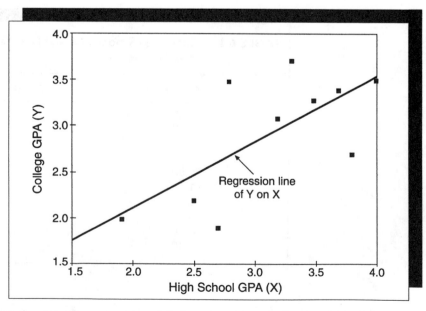

Figure 6.2. Regression Line of College GPA (Y) on High School GPA (X)

First, it's the regression of the Y variable on the X variable. In other words, Y (college GPA) is being predicted from X (high school GPA). This regression line is also called the **line of best fit.** It best fits these data since it minimizes the distance between each individual point and the regression line. For example, if you take all these points and try to find the line that best fits them all at once, the line you see in Figure 6.2 is the one you would use.

Second, it's the line that allows us our best guess (at estimating what college GPA would be, given each high school GPA). For example, if high school GPA is 3.0, then college GPA should be around (remember, this is only an eyeball prediction) 2.8. Take a look at Figure 6.3 to see how we did this. We located the predictor value (3.0) on the X-axis, then drew a perpendicular line from the X-axis to the regression line, then drew a horizontal line to the Y-axis and *estimated* what the value would be.

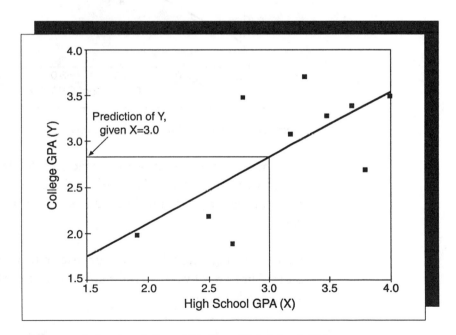

Figure 6.3. Estimating College GPA Given High School GPA

Third, the distance between each individual data point and the regression line is the **error in prediction**—a direct reflection of the correlation between the two variables. For example, if you look at data point 3.3, 3.7 (marked in Figure 6.4), you can see that this X,

Y data point is above the regression line. The distance between
that point and the line is the error in prediction, as marked in Figure 6.4, because if the prediction were perfect, then all the predicted points would fall where? Right on the regression or prediction line.

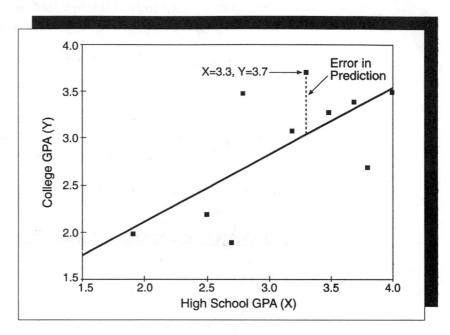

Figure 6.4. Prediction Is Rarely Perfect: Estimating the Error in Prediction

Fourth, if the correlation were perfect, all the data points would
align themselves along a 45° angle and the regression line would
pass through each point (just like we said in the third point
above).

Given the regression line, we can use it to predict any future
score. That's what we'll do right now—create the line and then do
some prediction work.

DRAWING THE WORLD'S BEST LINE (FOR YOUR DATA)

The simplest way to think of prediction is determining the score on one variable (which we'll call Y—the **criterion** or **dependent variable**) from the value of another score (which we'll call X—the **predictor** or **independent variable**).

The way that we find out how well X can predict Y is through the creation of the regression line we mentioned earlier in this chapter. This line is created from data that have already been collected and drawn based on an equation. The equations are then used to predict scores using a new value for X, the predictor variable.

Formula 6.1 shows the general formula for the regression line, which may look familiar since you probably used it in your high school and college math courses. It's the same as the formula for any straight line.

$$Y' = bX + a \qquad\qquad (6.1)$$

where

- Y' is the predicted score of Y based on a known value of X

- b is the slope, or direction, of the line

- a is the point at which the line crosses the y-axis

- X is the score being used as the predictor

Let's use the same data shown earlier in Table 6.1 with a few more calculations that we will need thrown in.

	X	Y	X^2	Y^2	XY
	3.5	3.3	12.25	10.89	11.55
	2.5	2.2	6.25	4.84	5.50
	4.0	3.5	16.00	12.25	14.00
	3.8	2.7	14.44	7.29	10.26
	2.8	3.5	7.84	12.25	9.80
	1.9	2.0	3.61	4.00	3.80
	3.2	3.1	10.24	9.61	9.92
	3.7	3.4	13.69	11.56	12.58
	2.7	1.9	7.29	3.61	5.13
	3.3	3.7	10.89	13.69	12.21
Total	31.4	29.3	102.50	89.99	94.75

ΣX or the sum of all the X values is 31.4

ΣY or the sum of all the Y values is 29.3

ΣX^2 or the sum of each X value squared is 102.5

ΣY^2 or the sum of each Y value squared is 89.99

ΣXY or the sum of the products of X and Y is 94.75

Formula 6.2 is used to compute the slope of the regression line (*b* in the equation for a straight line):

$$b = \frac{\Sigma XY - (\Sigma X \Sigma Y / n)}{\Sigma X^2 - [(\Sigma X)^2 / n]} \tag{6.2}$$

In Formula 6.3, you can see the computed value for *b*, the slope of the line.

$$b = \frac{94.75 - (31.4 \bullet 29.3) / 10}{102.5 - [(31.4)^2 / 10]} \tag{6.3}$$

$$b = \frac{2.748}{3.904} = .704$$

Formula 6.4 is used to compute the point at which the line crosses the y-axis (*a* in the equation for a straight line):

$$a = \frac{\Sigma Y - b\Sigma X}{n} \tag{6.4}$$

In Formula 6.5, you can see the computed value for a, the intercept of the line.

$$a = \frac{29.3 - (.704 \bullet 31.4)}{10}$$

$$a = \frac{7.19}{10} = .719 \qquad (6.5)$$

Now, if we go back and substitute b and a into the equation for a straight line $(Y = bX + a)$, we come up with the final regression line:

$$Y' = .704X + .719$$

Why the Y' and not just a plain Y? Remember, we are using X to predict Y and Y' (read: Y *prime*) is the predicted and not the actual value of Y. So, now that we have this equation, what can we do with it? Predict Y, what else?

For example, let's say that high school GPA equals 2.8 (or $X = 2.8$). If we substitute the value of 2.8 into the equation, we get the following formula:

$$Y' = .704(2.8) + .719 = 2.69$$

So, 2.69 is the predicted value of Y (or Y') given X is equal to 2.8. Now for any X score, we can easily and quickly compute a predicted Y score.

TECH TALK

Not all lines that fit best between a bunch of data points are straight. Rather, they could be curvilinear just like you can have a curvilinear relationship as we discussed in the last chapter. For example, the relationship between anxiety and performance on an achievement test is such that when people are not at all anxious or very anxious, they don't perform very well. But if they're moderately anxious, then performance can be maximized. The relationship between these two variables is curvilinear, and the prediction of Y from X takes that into account.

How Good Is Our Prediction?

How can we measure how good a job we have done predicting one outcome from another? We know that the higher the absolute magnitude of the correlation between two variables, the better the prediction. In theory, that's great. But being practical, we can also look at the difference between the predicted value (Y') and the actual value (Y) when we first compute the formula of the regression line.

For example, if the formula for the regression line is $Y' = .704X + .719$, the predicted Y (or Y') for an X value of 2.8 is $.704(2.8) + .719$, or 2.72. We know that the actual Y value that corresponds to an X value is 3.5 (from the data set shown in Table 6.1). The difference between 3.5 and 2.69 is .81 and is known as an **error of estimate.**

If we take all of these differences, we can compute the average amount that each data point differs from the predicted data point, or the **standard error of estimate.** This value tells us how much imprecision there is in our estimate. As you might expect, the higher the correlation between the two values (and the better the prediction), the lower this error will be. In fact, if the correlation between the two variables is perfect (either +1 or −1), then the standard error of estimate is 0. Why? Because prediction is perfect, all the actual data points fall on the regression line and there's no error in estimating Y from X.

The predicted, Y', or dependent variable, need not always be a continuous one like height, test score, or problem-solving skills. It can be a categorical variable such as admit/don't admit, or level A/level B, or social class 1/social class 2. The score that's used in the prediction is "dummy coded" to be a 1 or a 2 and then used in the same equation.

USING THE COMPUTER TO COMPUTE THE REGRESSION LINE

Let's use SPSS to compute the regression line in predicting Y from X. The data set we are using is Chapter 6 Data Set 1. We will be using the number of hours of training to predict how severe injuries are when someone is injured playing football.

There are two variables in this data set:

Variable	Definition
Training (X)	Number of hours per week of strength training
Injuries (Y)	Severity of injuries on a scale from 1 to 10

Here are the steps to compute the regression line that we discussed in this chapter. Follow along and do it yourself.

1. Open the file named Chapter 6 Data Set 1.
2. Click Analyze → Regression → Linear. You'll see the Linear Regression dialog box shown in Figure 6.5.

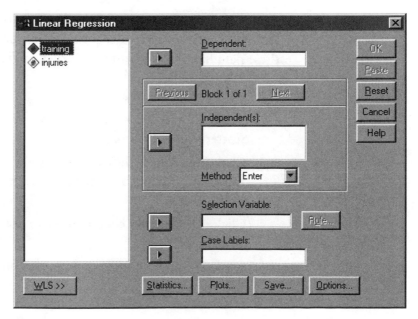

Figure 6.5. Linear Regression Dialog Box

3. Click on the variable named injuries, and click ▶ to move it to the Dependent variable box. It's the dependent variable since its value *depends* on the value of number of hours of training. It's the variable being predicted.

4. Click on the variable named training, and click ▶ to move it to the Independent(s) variable box.

5. Click OK, and you will see the partial results of the analysis as shown in Figure 6.6.

		Unstandardized Coefficients		Standardized Coefficients		
Model		B	Std. Error	Beta	t	Sig.
1	(Constant)	6.847	1.004		6.818	.000
	TRAINING	-.125	.046	-.458	-2.727	.011

Coefficients[a]

a. Dependent Variable: INJURIES

Figure 6.6. Results of the SPSS Analysis

We'll get to the interpretation of this output in a moment. First, let's have SPSS overlay a regression line on the scatterplot for these data like the one you saw earlier in Figure 6.2.

1. Click Graphs → Scatter.

2. Click Simple, then click Define. You'll see the simple Scatterplot dialog box.

3. Click injury, and click ▶ to move the variable label to the Y-axis box. Remember, the predicted variable is represented by the Y-axis.

4. Click training, and click ▶ to move the variable label to the X-axis box.

5. Click OK, and you will see the scatterplot as shown in Figure 6.7.

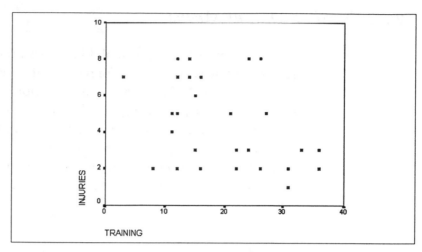

Figure 6.7. A Scatterplot Generated Using SPSS

Now let's draw the regression line.

6. Double-click on the chart to select it for editing.

7. Click Chart → Options. You'll see the Scatterplot Options dialog box.

8. Click Total in the Fit Line area.

9. Click OK. The completed scatterplot, with the regression line, is shown in Figure 6.8.

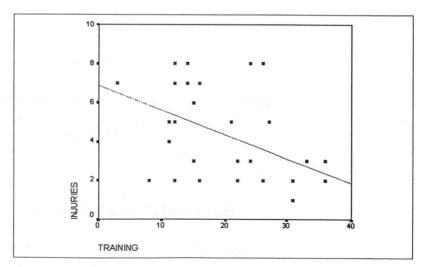

Figure 6.8. SPSS Scatterplot With Regression Line

What the SPSS Output Means

The SPSS output tells us several things. First, the formula for the regression line is taken from the first set of output shown in Figure 6.6 as $Y' = -.125X + 6.847$. This equation can be used to predict level of injury given any number of hours spent in strength training. In fact, as you can see in Figure 6.8, the regression line has a negative slope, reflecting a negative correlation (of $-.458$) between hours of training and severity of injuries. So it appears, given the data, that the more one trains, the fewer severe injuries occur.

THE MORE PREDICTORS THE BETTER? MAYBE

All the examples that we have used so far in the chapter have been for one criterion or outcome measure and one predictor variable. There is also the case of regression, where more than one predictor or independent variable is used to predict a particular outcome. If one variable can predict an outcome with some degree of accuracy, then why couldn't two do a better job?

For example, if high school GPA is a pretty good indicator of college GPA, then how about high school GPA plus number of hours of extracurricular activities? So instead of

$$Y' = bX + a$$

the model for the regression equation becomes

$$Y' = bX_1 + bX_2 + a$$

where

X_1 is the value of the first independent variable

X_2 is the value of the second independent variable

b is the regression weight for the particular variable

As you may have guessed, this model is called **multiple regression.** So, in theory anyway, you are predicting an outcome from two independent variables, rather than one. But you only want to add additional independent variables under certain conditions.

First, any variable you add has to make a unique contribution to understanding the dependent variable. Otherwise, why use it? What do we mean by unique? The additional variable needs to explain differences in the predicted variable that the first predictor does not. That is, the two variables in combination would have to predict Y better than any one of the variables would do alone.

In our example, level of participation in extracurricular activities could make a unique contribution. But should we add a variable such as the number of hours each student studied in high school as a third independent variable or predictor? Since number of hours of study is probably highly related to high school GPA (another of our predictor variables, remember?), study time would probably not add very much to the overall prediction of college GPA. We might be better off looking for another variable (such as ratings on letters of recommendation) rather than spending our time collecting the data on study time.

The Big Rule When It Comes to Multiple Prediction

If you are going to use more than one predictor variable, try to keep the following two important guidelines in mind.

1. When selecting a dependent variable to predict an outcome, select a predictor variable (X) that is related to the predicted variable (Y). That way, the two share something in common (remember, they should be correlated).

2. When selecting more than one independent variable (such as X_1 and X_2), try to select variables that are independent or uncorrelated with one another, but are both related to the outcome or predicted (Y) variable.

In effect, you want only independent or predictor variables that are related to the dependent variable and are unrelated to each other. That way, each one makes as unique as possible a contribution in predicting the dependent or predicted variable.

TECH TALK

How many predictor variables are too many? Well, if one variable predicts some outcome, and two is even more accurate, then why not three, four, or five predictor variables? In practical terms, every time you add a variable, an expense is incurred. Someone has to go collect the data, it takes time (which is $$$ when it comes to research budgets), and so on. From a theoretical sense, there is a fixed limit on how many variables can contribute to an understanding of what we are trying to predict. Remember that it is best when the predictor or independent variables are independent or unrelated to each other. The problem is that once you get to three or four variables, few things remain unrelated. Better to be accurate and conservative than include too many variables and waste money and the power of prediction.

SUMMARY

Prediction is a special case of simple correlations, and it is a very powerful tool for examining complex relationships. This might have been a little more difficult of a chapter than others, but you'll be well served by what you have learned, especially if you can apply it to the research reports and journal articles that you have to read. With the end of Part II, it's time to move on to the conceptual basis for inferential statistics, including probability and hypothesis testing.

TIME TO PRACTICE

1. Chapter 6 Data Set 2 contains the data for a group of participants who took a timed test. The data are the average amount of time the participants took on each item (response time) and the number of guesses it took to get each item correct (number correct).

   a. What is the regression equation for predicting response time from number correct?

   b. What is the predicted response time if the number correct is 8?

   c. What is the difference between the predicted and the actual number correct for each of the predicted response times?

2. Betsy is interested in predicting how many 75-year-olds will develop Alzheimer's disease and is using as predictors level of education and general physical health graded on a scale from 1 to 10. But she is interested in using other predictor variables as well. Answer the following questions.

   a. What criteria should she use in the selection of other predictors? Why?

   b. Name two other predictors that you think might be related to the development of Alzheimer's disease.

   c. With the four predictor variables (level of education and general physical health, and the two new ones that you name), draw out what the model of the regression equation would look like.

3. Go to the library and locate three different examples of where linear regression was used in a research study in your area of interest. It's OK if the study contains more than one predictor variable. Answer the following questions for each study.

   a. What is one independent variable? What is the dependent variable?

   b. If there is more than one independent variable, what argument does the researcher make that these variables are independent from one another?

   c. Which of the three studies seems to present the least convincing evidence that the dependent variable is predicted by the independent variable and why?

4. Here's where you can apply the information in one of this chapter's tips and get a chance to predict a Super Bowl winner! Joe Coach was curious to know if the average number of games won in a year predicts Super Bowl performance (win or lose). The X variable was the average number of games won during the past 10 seasons. The Y variable was whether the team ever won the Super Bowl during the past 10 seasons. Here are the data:

Team	Average Number of Wins Over 10 Years	Ever Win a Super Bowl? (1= yes/0 = no)
Savannah Sharks	12	1
Pittsburgh Pelicans	11	0
Williamstown Warriors	15	0
Bennington Bruisers	12	1
Atlanta Angels	13	1
Trenton Terrors	16	0
Virginia Vipers	15	1
Charleston Crooners	9	0
Harrisburg Heathens	8	0
Eaton Energizers	12	1

a. How would you assess the usefulness of the average number of wins as a predictor of whether a team ever won a Super Bowl?

b. What's the advantage of being able to use a categorical variable (such as 1 or 0) as a dependent variable?

c. What other variables might you use to predict the dependent variable, and why would you choose them?

ANSWERS TO PRACTICE QUESTIONS

1.   a. The regression equation is $Y' = -.214$ (number correct) $+ 17.202$.

     b. $Y' = -.214(8) + 17.202 = 15.49$.

     c.

Time	# Correct	Y'	Y - Y'
14.5	5	16.13	−1.6
13.4	7	15.70	−2.3
12.7	6	15.92	−3.2
16.4	2	16.77	−0.4
21.0	4	16.35	4.7
13.9	3	16.56	−2.7
17.3	12	14.63	2.7
12.5	5	16.13	−3.6
16.7	4	16.35	0.4
22.7	3	16.56	6.1

2.   a. The other predictor variables should not be related to any other predictor variable. If they are independent of one another, they could each contribute unique information.

     b. For example, living arrangements (single or in a group) and access to health care (high, medium, or low).

     c. Presence of Alzheimer's = (level of education)X_1 + (general physical health)X_2 + (living arrangements)X_3 + (access to health care)X_4 + a.

3.   This one you do on your own.

4.   a. You could compute the correlation between the two variables, which is .204. According to the information in Chapter 5, the magnitude of such a correlation is quite low. You could reach the conclusion that the number of wins is not a very good predictor of whether a team ever won a Super Bowl.

     b. Many variables are categorical by nature (gender, race, social class, and political party) and cannot be easily measured on a scale from 1 to 100, for example. Using categorical variables allows us more flexibility.

     c. Some other variables might be number of All-American players, win-loss record of coaches, and home attendance.

PART III

Taking Chances for Fun and Profit

SNAPSHOTS

A scatterplot of student test scores.

What do you know so far, and what's next? To begin with, you've got a really solid basis for understanding how to describe the characteristics of a set of scores and how distributions can differ from one another. That's what you learned in Chapters 2, 3, and 4 of *Statistics for People Who (Think They) Hate Statistics.* You've also learned how to describe the relationship between variables in Chapter 5 and predict one from the other in Chapter 6.

Now it's time to bump up the ante a bit and start playing for real. In Part III of *Statistics for People,* you will be introduced in Chapter 7 to the importance, and nature, of hypothesis testing including an in-depth discussion of what a hypothesis is, what different types there are, the function of the hypothesis, and why and how they are tested.

Then we'll get to the all-important topic of probability, represented by a discussion of the normal curve and the basic principles underlying probability—the part of statistics that helps us define how likely it is that some event (such as a specific score on a test) will occur. We'll use the normal curve as a basis for these arguments, and you'll see how any score or occurrence within any distribution has likelihood associated with it.

After some fun with probability and the normal curve, we'll be ready to start our extended discussion in Part IV regarding the application of hypothesis testing and probability theory to the testing of specific questions regarding relationships between variables. It only gets better from here!

Hypotheticals and You

Testing Your Questions

Difficulty Scale ☺☺☺☺ (you can go out tonight, but don't stay out too late)

What you'll learn about in this chapter

- More about the difference between a sample and a population
- The importance of the null and research hypotheses
- The criteria for judging a good hypothesis

SO YOU WANT TO BE A SCIENTIST

You might have heard the term *hypothesis* used in other classes. You may even have had to formulate one for a research project you did for another class or you may have read one or two in a journal article. If so, then you probably have a good idea what a hypothesis is. For those of you who are unfamiliar with this often used term, a **hypothesis** is basically "an educated guess." Its most important role is to reflect the general problem statement or question that was the motivation for asking the research question in the first place.

That's why taking the care and time to formulate a really precise and clear research question is so important. This research question will be your guide in the creation of a hypothesis, and in turn, the hypothesis will determine the techniques you will use to test the hypothesis and answer the question that was originally asked.

So, a good hypothesis translates a problem statement or a research question into a form that is more amenable to testing. This form is called a hypothesis. We will talk about what makes a good hypothesis later in this chapter. Before that, let's talk in more detail about the difference between a sample and a population. This is an important distinction since hypothesis testing deals with a sample and then the results are generalized to the larger population. Let's turn our attention to the two main categories of hypotheses (the null hypothesis and research hypothesis). But first, let's formally define some simple terms that we have used earlier in *Statistics for People Who (Think They) Hate Statistics*.

Samples and Populations

As a good scientist, you would like to be able to say that if Method A is better than Method B this is true forever and always and for all people in the universe, right? Or at least to the people to whom the results are important. Indeed. And if you do enough research on the relative merits of Methods A and B and test enough people, you may someday be able to say that.

But don't get too excited since it's unlikely you will able to speak with such a high degree of confidence. It takes too much money ($$$) and too much time (all those people!) to do all that research and besides, it's not even necessary. Instead, you can just select a representative sample from the population and test your hypothesis about Methods A and B.

Given the constraints of never enough time and never enough research funds with which almost all scientists live, the next best strategy is to take a portion of a larger group of participants and do the research with that smaller group. In this context, the larger group is referred to as a **population,** and the smaller group selected from that population is referred to as a **sample.**

Samples should be selected from populations in such a way that the sample as closely as possible matches the characteristics of the population. The goal is to have the sample as much like the population as possible. The most important implication of ensuring

TECH TALK

A measure of how well a sample approximates the characteristics of a population is called **sampling error.** Sampling error is basically the difference between the values of the sample statistic (a measure that describes a sample value but *estimates* a value in the population) and the population parameter (the value of a certain measure in the population). The higher the sampling error, the less precise the sample and the more difficult it will be to make the case that what you find in the sample indeed reflects what you expect to find in the population.

similarity between the two is that the research results based on the sample can be generalized to the population. When the sample accurately represents the population, the results of the study are said to have a high degree of generalizability.

A high degree of generalizability is an important quality of good research since it means that the time and effort (and $$$) that went into the research may have implications for groups of people other than the original participants.

THE NULL HYPOTHESIS

OK. So we have a sample of participants selected from a population, and to begin the test of our research hypothesis we first formulate the **null hypothesis.**

The null hypothesis is an interesting little creature. If it could talk, it would say something like, "I represent no relationship between the variables that you are studying." In other words, null hypotheses are statements of equality demonstrated by the following real-life (brief) null hypotheses taken from a variety of popular social and behavioral sciences journals. Names have been changed to protect the innocent.

- There will be no difference in the average score of 9th graders and the average score of 12th graders on the ABC memory test.
- There is no difference between the reading levels of learning disabled children in resource rooms when compared with learning disabled children in regular classrooms.
- There is no relationship between reaction time and problem-solving ability.
- There is no difference between the amount of assistance offered by white and black families to their children in school-related activities.

What these four null hypotheses have in common is that they all contain a statement that two or more things are equal to, or unrelated to, each other.

The Purposes of the Null Hypothesis

What are the basic purposes of the null hypothesis? The null hypothesis acts as both a starting point and a benchmark against which the actual outcomes of a study can be measured.

Let's examine each of these purposes in more detail.

First, the null hypothesis acts as a starting point since it is the state of affairs that is accepted as true in the absence of any other information. For example, let's look at the first null hypothesis we stated above:

> There will be no difference in the average score of 9th graders and the average score of 12th graders on the ABC memory test.

Given no *a priori* (before the fact) knowledge of 9th- and 12th-graders' memory skills, you have no reason to believe there will be differences between the two groups, right? If you know nothing about the relationship between these variables, the best you could do is guess. And that's taking a chance. You might speculate as to why one group might outperform another, but if you have no evidence a priori (before the fact), then what choice do you have but to assume that they are equal?

This lack of a relationship as a starting point is a hallmark of this whole topic. In other words, until you show that there is a systematic difference, you have to assume that any difference you observe is due to chance.

Furthermore, if there are any differences between these two groups, you have to assume that these differences are due to the most attractive explanation for differences between any groups on any variable—chance! Sound familiar? That's right—given no other information, chance is always the most likely and attractive explanation for the observed differences between two groups or the relationship between variables. Chance explains what we cannot.

For example, you could take a group of soccer players and a group of football players and compare their running speeds. But look at all the factors we don't know about that could contribute to differences. Who is to know whether some soccer players practice more, if some football players are stronger, or if both groups are receiving additional training? What's more, perhaps the way their speed is being measured leaves room for chance; a faulty stopwatch or a windy day can contribute to differences unrelated to true running speed. As good researchers, our job is to eliminate chance factors from explaining observed differences and to evaluate other factors that might contribute to group differences such as intentional training or nutrition programs and see how they affect speed. The point is, if we find differences between groups and the differences are not due to training, we are at a loss as to what to attribute the difference to other than chance.

The second purpose of the null hypothesis is to provide a benchmark against which observed outcomes can be compared to see how likely it is that these outcomes are due to some other factor. The null hypothesis helps to define a range within which any observed differences between groups can be attributed to chance (which is the null hypothesis' contention) or due to something other than chance (which perhaps would be the result of the manipulation of some variable such as training in the above example).

Most research studies have an implied null hypothesis, and you may not find it clearly stated in a research report or journal article. Instead, you'll find the research hypothesis clearly stated, which is now where we turn our attention.

THE RESEARCH HYPOTHESIS

While a null hypothesis is a statement of no relationship between variables, a **research hypothesis** is a definite statement of the relationship between variables. For example, for each of the null hypotheses stated earlier, here is a corresponding research hypothesis. Notice that we said "a" and not "the" corresponding research hypothesis since there could certainly be more than one research hypotheses for any one null hypothesis.

- The average score of 9th graders *is different* from the average score of 12th graders on the ABC memory test.
- The reading level of learning disabled children in resource rooms *is higher* than the reading level of learning disabled children in regular classrooms.
- Slower reaction time and problem-solving ability *are positively related.*
- There *is a difference* between the amount of assistance offered by white and black families to their children in school-related activities.

Each of these four research hypotheses has one thing in common. They are all statements of *inequality.* They posit a relationship between variables and not an equality, as does the null hypothesis.

The nature of this inequality can take two different forms—a directional or a nondirectional research hypothesis. If the research hypothesis posits no direction to the inequality (such as different from), the hypothesis is a nondirectional research hypothesis. If the research hypothesis posits a direction to the inequality (such as more than or less than), the research hypothesis is a directional research hypothesis.

The Nondirectional Research Hypothesis

A **nondirectional research hypothesis** reflects a difference between groups, but the direction of the difference is not specified.

For example, the research hypothesis

> The average score of 9th graders is different from the average score of 12th graders on the ABC memory test

is nondirectional in that the direction of the difference between the two groups is not specified. The hypothesis states only that there is a difference and says nothing about the direction of that difference. It is a research hypothesis because a difference is hypothesized, but the nature of the difference is not specified.

A nondirectional research hypothesis such as the one described here would be represented by the following equation.

$$H_1: \overline{X}_9 \neq \overline{X}_{12} \tag{7.1}$$

where

H_1:   is the symbol for the first (of possibly several) research hypothesis

$\overline{X}_9$ is the average memory score for the sample of 9th graders

$\overline{X}_{12}$ is the average memory score for the sample of 12th graders

$\neq$ is not equal

The Directional Research Hypothesis

A **directional research hypothesis** reflects a difference between groups, and the direction of the difference is specified.

For example, the research hypothesis

The average score of 12th graders is greater than the average score of 9th graders on the ABC memory test

is directional, since the direction of the difference between the two groups is specified. One is hypothesized to be greater than (not just different from) the other.

An example of two other directional hypotheses is

A　is greater than B (or A > B), or

B　is greater than A (or A < B).

These both represent inequalities, but of a specific nature (greater than or less than). A directional research hypothesis such as the one described above, where 12th graders are hypothesized to score better than 9th graders, would be represented by the equation in Formula 7.2.

$$H_1: \overline{X}_{12} > \overline{X}_9 \tag{7.2}$$

where

H_1:　is the symbol for the first (of possibly several) research hypothesis

$\overline{X}_9$　is the average memory score for the sample of 9th graders

$\overline{X}_{12}$　is the average memory score for the sample of 12th graders

>　is greater than

What is the purpose of the research hypothesis? It is this hypothesis that is tested directly as an important step in the research process. The results of this test are compared with what you expect by chance alone (reflecting the null hypothesis) to see which of the two is the more attractive explanation for any differences between groups you might observe.

Table 7.1 shows the four null hypotheses stated as both directional and nondirectional research hypotheses.

TABLE 7.1   Null Hypothesis and Corresponding Research Hypotheses

Null Hypothesis	Nondirectional Research Hypothesis	Directional Research Hypothesis
There will be no difference in the average score of 9th graders and the average score of 12th graders on the ABC memory test.	12th graders and 9th graders will differ on the ABC memory test.	12th graders will have a higher average score on the ABC memory test than will 9th graders.
There is no difference between the reading levels of learning disabled children in resource rooms when compared with learning disabled children in regular classrooms.	The reading scores of learning disabled children who are taught in resource rooms will differ from those of learning disabled children taught in regular classrooms.	Learning disabled children who are taught in resource rooms will have higher reading scores when compared with learning disabled children taught in regular classrooms.
There is no relationship between reaction time and problem-solving ability.	There is a relationship between reaction time and problem-solving ability.	There is a positive relationship between reaction time and problem-solving ability.
There is no difference between the amount of assistance offered by white and black families to their children in school-related activities.	The amount of assistance offered by white families to their children is different from the amount of support offered by black families to their children in school-related activities.	The amount of assistance offered by white families to their children is more than the amount of support offered by black families to their children in school-related activities.

TECH TALK   **What About Those Tails?**

Another way to talk about directional and nondirectional hypotheses is to talk about one- and two-tailed tests. A **one-tailed test** (reflecting a directional hypothesis) posits a difference in a particular direction such as when we hypothesize that Group 1 will score higher than Group 2. A **two-tailed test** (reflecting a nondirectional hypothesis) posits a difference but in no particular direction. The importance of this distinction begins when you test different types of hypotheses (one and two tailed) and establish probability levels for rejecting or not rejecting the null hypothesis. More about this in Chapter 9. Promise.

Some Differences Between the Null Hypothesis and the Research Hypothesis

First, a bit of review. The two differ in that one (the null hypothesis) states there is no relationship between variables (an equality) while the research hypothesis states there is a relationship between the variables (an inequality). This is the primary difference.

Second, null hypotheses always refer to the population whereas research hypotheses always refer to the sample. We select a sample of participants from a much larger population. We then try to generalize the results from the sample back to the population. If you remember your basic philosophy and logic (you did take these courses, right?), you'll remember that going from small (as in sample) to large (as in population) is a process of inference. So the tool we are learning about is called inferential statistics.

Third, since the entire population cannot be directly tested (again, it is impractical, uneconomical, and often impossible), you can't say with 100% certainty that there is no real difference between samples on some variable. Rather, you have to infer it (indirectly) from the results of the test of the research hypothesis, which is based on the sample. Hence, the null hypothesis must be indirectly tested while the research hypothesis can be directly tested.

Fourth, null hypotheses are always written using Greek letters, and research hypotheses are always written using Roman letters. For example, the null hypothesis that the average score for 9th graders is equal to that of 12th graders is represented in Formula 7.3.

$$H_0: \mu_9 = \mu_{12} \qquad (7.3)$$

where

H_0:   is the null hypothesis

μ_9 is the theoretical average for the population of 9th graders

μ_{12} is the theoretical average for the population of 12th graders

And the research hypothesis that the average score for a sample of 12th graders is greater than the average score for a sample of 9th graders was represented by the equation shown in Formula 7.2.

Finally, because you cannot directly test the null hypothesis, it is an *implied* hypothesis. Yet the research hypothesis is explicit and is stated as such. This is another reason why you rarely see null hypotheses stated in research reports yet almost always see a statement of the research hypothesis.

WHAT MAKES A GOOD HYPOTHESIS?

You now know that hypotheses are educated guesses, a starting point for a lot more to come. As with any guess, some are better than others right from the start. We can't stress enough how important it is to accurately ask the question you want answered and to keep in mind that any hypothesis you present is a direct extension of the original research question you asked. This question will reflect your own personal interests and motivation and what research has been previously been done. With that in mind, here are criteria you might use to decide whether a hypothesis you read in a research report or the ones you formulate are good ones.

To illustrate, let's use an example of a study that examines the effects of after-school child care for employees who work late on the parents' adjustment to work. Here is a well-written hypothesis:

Parents who enroll their children in after-school programs will miss fewer days of work in one year and will have a more positive attitude toward work as measured by the Attitude Toward Work survey than will parents who do not enroll their children in such programs.

Here are the criteria.

First, a good hypothesis is stated in declarative form and not as a question. In the above example, the question, "Do you think parents and the companies they work for will be better . . . ?" was not posed, since hypotheses are most effective when they make a clear and forceful statement.

Second, a good hypothesis posits an expected relationship between variables. The hypothesis that is being used as an example clearly describes the relationship between after-school child care, parents' attitude, and absentee rate. These variables are being tested to see if one (enrollment in the after-school program) has an effect on the others (absentee rate and attitude).

Notice the word *expected* in the above criterion? Defining an expected relationship is intended to prevent the fishing expedition (sometimes called the "shotgun" approach) that may be tempting to take but is not very productive.

TECH TALK

The fishing expedition approach is where you throw out your line and take anything that bites. You collect data on as many things as you can, regardless of your interest or even whether collecting the data is a reasonable part of a scientific investigation. Or you load up them guns and blast away at anything that moves and you're bound to hit something. The problem is that you may not want what you hit, and worse, you may miss what you want to hit, and even worst of all (if possible), you may not know what you hit! Good researchers do not want just anything they can catch or shoot. They want specific results. To get them, researchers need their opening questions and hypotheses to be clear, forceful, and easily understood.

Third, hypotheses reflect the theory or literature on which they are based. The accomplishments of scientists can rarely be attributed to just their own hard work. Their accomplishments are always due, in part, to many other researchers who came before them and laid the framework for later explorations. A good hypothesis reflects this, in that it has a substantive link to existing literature and theory. In the above example, let's assume there is literature indicating that parents are more comfortable knowing their children are being cared for in a structured environment, and parents can then be more productive at work. Knowing this would allow one to hypothesize that an after-school program would provide the security parents are looking for. In turn, this allows them to concentrate on working rather than calling on the telephone to find out whether Rachel or Gregory got home safely.

Fourth, a hypothesis should be brief and to the point. You want your hypothesis to describe the relationship between variables in a declarative form and to be as direct and explicit as possible. The more to the point, the easier it will be for others (such as your master's thesis or doctoral dissertation committee members!) to read your research and understand exactly what you are hypothesizing and what the important variables are. In fact, when people read and evaluate research, the first thing many of them do is find the hypotheses to get a good idea as to the general purpose of the research and how things will be done. A good hypothesis tells you both these things.

Fifth, good hypotheses are testable hypotheses. This means that you can actually carry out the intent of the question reflected by the hypothesis. You can see from the sample hypothesis that the important comparison is between parents who have enrolled their child in an after-school program with those who have not. Then, such things as attitude and work days missed will be measured. These are both reasonable objectives. Attitude is measured by the Attitude Toward Work survey (a fictitious title but you get the idea), and absenteeism (the number of days away from work) is an easily recorded and unambiguous measure. Think how much harder it would be if the hypothesis were stated as "Parents who enroll their children in after-school care feel better about their job." While you might get the same message, the results might be more difficult to interpret given the ambiguous nature of words such as *feel better.*

In sum, hypotheses should

- be stated in declarative form,
- posit a relationship between variables,
- reflect a theory or a body of literature that they are based on,
- be brief and to the point, and
- be testable.

When a hypothesis meets each of these five criteria, you know that it is good enough to continue with a study that will accurately test the general question from which the hypothesis was derived.

SUMMARY

A central component of any scientific study is the hypothesis, and the different types of hypotheses (null and research) help form a plan for answering the questions asked by the purpose of our research. The starting point and benchmark that characterize the null hypothesis let us use it as a comparison as we evaluate the acceptability of the research hypothesis. Now let's move on to how those null hypotheses are actually tested.

TIME TO PRACTICE

1. Go to the library and select five research articles from your area of interest. For each one, list the following.

    a. What is the null hypothesis (implied or explicitly stated)?

    b. What is the research hypothesis (implied or explicitly stated)?

    c. In your own area of interest, create a null and a research hypothesis.

2. For the following research questions, create one null hypothesis, one directional research hypothesis, and one nondirectional research hypothesis.

    a. What are the effects of attention on out-of-seat classroom behavior?

    b. What is the relationship between the quality of a marriage and the quality of the spouse's relationships with siblings?

    c. What's the best way to treat an eating disorder?

3. Go back to the five hypotheses that you found in Question 1 above and evaluate each using the five criteria that were discussed at the end of the chapter.

ANSWERS TO PRACTICE QUESTIONS

Questions 1 and 3 are specific to your own interests. So while there are no right answers, there are plenty of wrong ones!

2a. Null: Children with short attention spans as measured by the Attention Span Observation Scale will have the same frequency of out-of-seat behavior as those with long attention spans.

   Directional: Children with short attention spans as measured by the Attention Span Observation Scale will have a higher frequency of out-of-seat behavior than those with long attention spans.

   Nondirectional: Children with short attention spans as measured by the Attention Span Observation Scale differ in the frequency of out-of-seat behavior from those with long attention spans.

2b. Null: There is no relationship between overall quality of marriage and spouse's relationships with siblings.

   Directional: There is a positive relationship between overall quality of marriage and spouse's relationships with siblings.

   Nondirectional: There is a relationship between overall quality of marriage and spouse's relationships with siblings.

2c. Null: Pharmacological treatment combined with traditional psychotherapy has the same effect in treating anorexia nervosa as does traditional psychotherapy alone.

   Directional: Pharmacological treatment combined with traditional psychotherapy is more effective in treating anorexia nervosa than is traditional psychotherapy alone.

   Nondirectional: Pharmacological treatment combined with traditional psychotherapy is different from treating anorexia nervosa with traditional psychotherapy alone.

Are Your Curves Normal?

Probability and Why It Counts

Difficulty Scale ☺☺☺ (not too easy and not too hard, but very important)

- Why understanding probability is basic to the understanding of statistics
- What the normal, or bell-shaped, curve is and what its characteristics are
- How to compute and interpret *z* scores

WHY PROBABILITY?

And here you thought this was a statistics class! Ha! Well, as you will learn in this chapter, the study of probability is the basis for the normal curve (much more on that later) and the foundation for inferential statistics.

Why? First, the normal curve provides us with a basis for understanding the probability associated with any possible outcome (such as the odds of getting a certain score on a test or the odds of getting a head on one flip of a coin).

Second, the study of probability is the basis for determining the degree of confidence we have in stating that a particular finding or outcome is "true." Or, better said, that an outcome (like an average score) may not have occurred due to chance alone. For example, let's compare Group A (which participates in 3 hours of extra swim practice each week) and Group B (which has no extra swim practice each week). We find that Group A differs from Group B on a test of fitness, but can we say that the difference is due to the extra practice or due to something else? The tools the study of probability provides allow us to determine the exact mathematical likelihood that the difference is due to practice versus something else (such as chance).

All that time we spent on hypotheses in the last chapter is time well spent. Once we put together our understanding of what a null hypothesis and a research hypothesis are with the ideas that are the foundation of probability, we'll be in the position to discuss how likely certain outcomes (formulated by the research hypothesis) are.

THE NORMAL CURVE (AKA THE BELL-SHAPED CURVE)

What is a normal curve? Well, the **normal curve** (also called a **bell-shaped curve,** or bell curve) is a visual representation of a distribution of scores that has three characteristics. Each of these characteristics is illustrated in Figure 8.1.

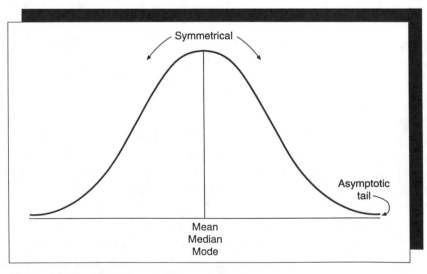

Figure 8.1. The Normal, or Bell-Shaped, Curve

The normal curve represents a distribution where the mean, median, and mode are equal to one another. You probably remember from Chapter 4 that if the median and the mean are different, then the distribution is skewed in one direction or the other. The normal curve is not skewed. It's got a nice hump (only one), and that hump is right in the middle.

Second, the normal curve is perfectly symmetrical about the mean. If you fold one half of the curve along its center line, the two halves would fit perfectly on each other. They are identical. One-half of the curve is a mirror image of the other.

Finally (and get ready for a mouthful), the tails of the normal curve are **asymptotic**—a big word. What it means is that they come closer and closer to the horizontal axis, but never touch.

The normal curve's shape of a bell also gives the graph its other name, the bell-shaped curve.

**TECH
TALK**

When your devoted author was knee-high, he always wondered how the tail of a normal curve can approach the horizontal or X-axis yet never touch it. Try this. Place two pencils one inch apart and then move them closer (by half) so they are one-half inch apart, and then closer (one-quarter inch apart), and closer (one-eighth inch apart). They continually get closer, right? But, they never (and never will) touch. Same thing with the tails of the curve. The tail slowly approaches the axis on which the curve "rests," but they can never really touch.

Why is this important? As you will learn later in this chapter, the fact that the tails never touch means that there is an infinitely small likelihood that a score can be obtained that is very extreme (way out in the left or right tail of the curve). If the tails did touch, then the likelihood that a very extreme score could be obtained would be nonexistent.

Hey, That's Not Normal!

We hope your next question is, "But there are plenty of sets of scores where the distribution is not normal or bell shaped, right?"

Yes (and here comes the big *but*). When we deal with large sets of data (more than 30), and as we take repeated samples of the data from a population, the values in the curve closely approximate the shape of a normal curve. This is very important because lots of what we do when we talk about inferring from a sample to a population is based on the assumption that what is taken from a population is distributed normally.

And as it turns out, in nature in general, many things are distributed with the characteristics of what we call normal. That is, there are lots of events or occurrences right in the middle of the distribution, but relatively few on each end, as you can see in Figure 8.2, which shows the distribution of IQ and height in the general population.

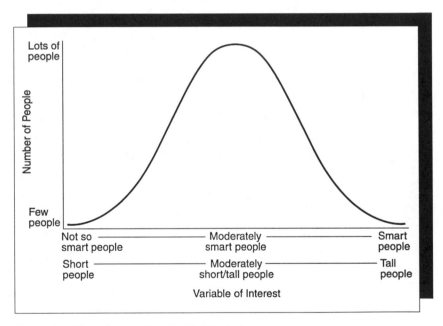

Figure 8.2. How Scores Can Be Distributed

For example, there are very few people who are brilliant and very few who are intellectually or cognitively at the absolute bottom of the group. There are lots who are right in the middle and fewer as we move toward the tails of the curve. There are relatively few tall people and relatively few short people, but lots of people right in the middle. In both of these examples, the distribution of intellectual skills and height approximate a normal distribution.

Consequently, those events that tend to occur in the extremes of the normal curve have a smaller probability associated with each occurrence. We can say with a great deal of confidence that the odds on any one person (whose height we do not know beforehand) being very tall (or very short) are just not very great. But we know that the odds of any one person being average in height, or right around the middle, are pretty good. Those events that tend to occur in the middle of the normal curve have a higher probability of occurring than those in the extreme.

More Normal Curve 101

You already know the three main characteristics that make a curve normal or make it appear bell shaped, but there's more to it than that. Take a look at the curve in Figure 8.3.

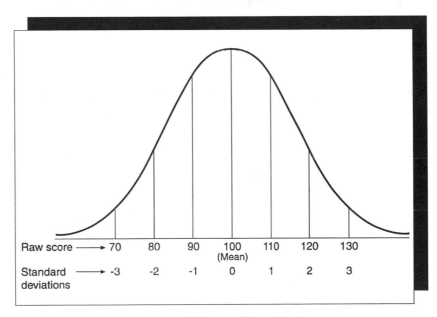

Figure 8.3. A Normal Curve Divided Into Different Sections

The distribution represented here has a mean of 100 and a standard deviation of 10. We've added numbers across the X-axis that represent the distance in standard deviations from the mean for this distribution. You can see that the X-axis (representing the scores in the distribution) is marked from 70 through 130 in increments of 10 (which is the standard deviation for the distribution), the value of 1 standard deviation. We made up these numbers (100 and 10), so don't go nuts trying to find out where we got them from.

So a quick review tells us that this distribution has a mean of 100 and a standard deviation of 10. Each vertical line within the curve separates the curve into a section, and each section is bound by particular scores. For example, the first section to the right of the mean of 100 is bound by the scores 100 and 110 representing 1 standard deviation from the mean (which is 100).

And below each raw score (70, 80, 90, 100, 110, 120, and 130), you'll find a corresponding standard deviation (–3, –2, –1, 0, +1, +2, and +3). As you may have figured out already, each standard deviation in our example is 10 points. So 1 standard deviation from the mean (which is 100) is the mean plus 10 points or 110. Not so hard, is it?

If we extend this argument further, then you should be able to see how the range of scores represented by a normal distribution with a mean of 100 and a standard deviation of 10 is 70 through 130 (which includes –3 to +3 standard deviations).

Now here's a big fact that is always true about normal distributions, means, and standard deviations: For any distribution of scores (regardless of the value of the mean and standard deviation), if the scores are distributed normally, almost 100% of the scores will fit between –3 and +3 standard deviations from the mean. This is very important, since it applies to all normal distributions. Since the rule does apply (once again, regardless of the value of the mean or standard deviation), distributions can be compared with one another. We'll get to that later.

With that said, we'll extend our argument a bit more. If the distribution of scores is normal, we can also say that between different points along the X-axis (such as between the mean and 1 standard deviation) a certain percentage of cases will fall. In fact, between the mean (which in this case is 100—got that yet?) and 1 standard deviation above the mean (which is 110), about 34% (actually 34.13%) of all cases in the distribution of scores will fall. This is a fact you can take to the bank since it will always be true.

Want to go further? Take a look at Figure 8.4. Here you can see the same normal curve in all its glory (the mean equals 100 and the standard deviation equals 10)—and the percentage of cases that we would expect to fall within the boundaries defined by the mean and standard deviation.

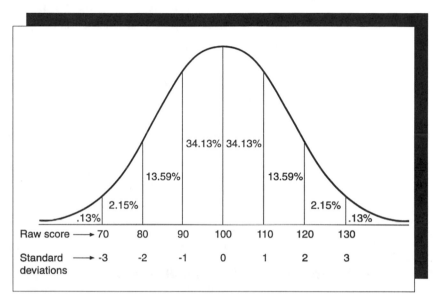

Figure 8.4. Distribution of Cases Under the Normal Curve

Here's what we can conclude.

The distance between	Includes	And the scores that are included (if the mean = 100 and the standard deviation = 10) are from
The mean and 1 standard deviation	34.13% of all the cases under the curve	100 to 110
1 and 2 standard deviations	13.59% of all the cases under the curve	110 to 120
2 and 3 standard deviations	2.15% of all the cases under the curve	120 to 130
3 standard deviations beyond the mean	0.13% of all the cases under the curve	Above 130

If you add up all the values in either half of the normal curve, guess what you get? That's right, 50%. Why? The distance between the mean and all the scores to the right of the mean underneath the normal curve includes 50% of all the scores.

And since the curve is symmetrical about its central axis (each half is a mirror image of the other), the two halves together represent 100% of all the scores. Not rocket science, but important to point out, nonetheless.

Now let's extend the same logic to the scores to the left of the mean of 100.

The distance between	Includes	And the scores that are included (if the mean = 100 and the standard deviation = 10) are from
The mean and −1 standard deviation	34.13% of all the cases under the curve	90 to 100
−1 and −2 standard deviations	13.59% of all the cases under the curve	80 to 90
−2 and −3 standard deviations	2.15% of all the cases under the curve	70 to 80
−3 standard deviations beyond the mean	0.13% of all the cases under the curve	Below 70

Now, be sure to keep in mind that we are using a mean of 100 and a standard deviation of 10 only as sample figures for a particular example. Obviously, not all distributions have a mean of 100 and a standard deviation of 10.

All of this is pretty neat, especially when you consider that the values of 34.13% and 13.59% and so on are absolutely independent of the actual values of the mean and the standard deviation. This, roughly, is 34% because of the shape of the curve, not because of the value of any of the scores in the distribution or the value of the mean or standard deviation. In fact, if you actually drew a normal curve on a piece of cardboard and then cut out the area between the mean and +1 standard deviation and then weighed it, it would tip the scale at exactly 34.13% of the entire piece of cardboard from which the curve was cut. (Try it—it's true).

In our example, this means that (roughly) 68% (34.13% doubled) of the scores fall between the values of 90 and 110. What about the other 32%? Good question. One-half (16%, or 13.59% + 2.15% + 0.13%) falls above (to the right of) 1 standard deviation above the mean and one-half falls below (to the left of) 1 standard deviation below the mean. And since the curve slopes, and the amount of area decreases as you move farther away from the mean, it is no surprise that the likelihood that a score will fall more toward the extremes of the distribution is less than the likelihood it will fall toward the middle. That's why the curve has a bump in the middle and is not skewed in either direction.

OUR FAVORITE STANDARD SCORE: THE Z SCORE

You have read more than once how distributions differ in their central tendency and variability.

But in the general practice of research, we will find ourselves working with distributions that are indeed different, yet we will be required to compare them with one another. And to do such a comparison, we need some kind of a standard.

Say hello to **standard scores**. These are scores that are comparable since they are standardized in units of standard deviations. For example, a standard score of 1 in a distribution with a mean of 50 and a standard deviation of 10 means the same as a standard score of 1 from a distribution with a mean of 100 and a standard deviation of 5; they both represent 1 standard score and are an equivalent distance from their respective means. Also, we can use our knowledge of the normal curve and assign a probability to the occurrence of a value that is 1 standard deviation from the mean. We'll do that later.

Although there are other types of standard scores, the one that you will see the most frequently in your study of statistics is called a **z score**. This is the result of dividing the amount that a raw score differs from the mean of the distribution by the standard deviation. See Formula 8.1.

$$z = \frac{(X - \overline{X})}{s} \qquad (8.1)$$

where

z   is the z score

X   is the individual score

$\overline{X}$ is the mean of the distribution

s   is the distribution standard deviation

For example, in Formula 8.2, you can see how the z score is calculated if the mean is 100, the raw score is 110, and the standard deviation is 10.

$$z = \frac{(110 - 100)}{10} = +1.0 \qquad (8.2)$$

It's just as easy to compute a raw score given a z score as the other way around. You already know the formula for a z score given the raw score, mean, and standard deviation. But if you know only the z score and the mean and standard deviation, then what's the corresponding raw score? Easy, just use the formula X = z(s) + $\overline{X}$. You can easily convert raw scores to z scores and back again if necessary.

For example, a z score of −.5 in a distribution with a mean of 50 and an s of 5 would equal a raw score of X = (−.5)(5) + 50, or 47.5.

The following data show the original raw scores plus the z scores for a sample of 10 scores that has a mean of 12 and a standard deviation of 2. Any raw score above the mean will have a corresponding z score that is positive, and any raw score below the mean will have a corresponding z score that is negative. For example, a raw score of 15 has a corresponding z score of +1.5, and a raw score of 8 has a corresponding z score of −2. And of course, a raw score of 12 (or the mean) has a z score of 0 (which it must be since it is no distance from the mean).

X	X − $\bar{X}$	z Score
12	0	0
15	3	1.5
11	−1	−0.5
13	1	0.5
8	−4	−2
14	2	1
12	0	0
13	1	0.5
12	0	0
10	−2	−1

Below are just a few observations about these scores, as a little review.

First, those scores below the mean (such as 8 and 10) have negative z scores, and those scores above the mean (such as 13 and 14) have positive z scores.

Second, positive z scores always fall to the right of the mean and are in the upper half of the distribution. And negative z scores always fall to the left of the mean and are in the lower half of the distribution.

Third, when we talk about a score being located 1 standard deviation above the mean, it's the same as saying that the score is 1 z score above the mean. For our purposes, when comparing scores across distributions, z scores and standard deviations are equivalent. In other words, a z score is simply the number of standard deviations from the mean.

Finally, (and this is very important), z scores across different distributions are comparable. Here's another table, similar to the one above, that will illustrate that last point. These 10 scores were selected from a set of 100 scores, with the scores having a mean of 59 and a standard deviation of 14.5.

Raw Score	$X - \bar{X}$	z Score
67	8	0.62
54	−5	−0.21
65	6	0.49
33	−26	−1.56
56	−3	−0.08
76	17	1.20
65	6	0.49
33	−26	−1.56
48	−11	−0.60
76	17	1.20

In the first distribution you saw earlier with a mean of 12 and a standard deviation of 2, a raw score of 12.8 has a corresponding z score of +.4, which means that a raw score of 12.8 is .4 standard deviations from the mean. In the second distribution with a mean of 59 and a standard deviation of 14.5, a raw score of 64.8 has a corresponding z score of +.4 as well. A miracle? No—just a good idea.

Both raw scores of 12.8 and 64.8, *relative to one another,* are equal distances from the mean. When these raw scores are represented as standard scores, then they are directly comparable to one another in terms of their relative location in their respective distributions.

What z Scores Represent

You already know that a particular z score represents a raw score but also represents a particular location along the x-axis of a distribution. And the more extreme the z score (such as −2 or +2.6), the further it is from the mean.

Since you already know the percentage of area that falls between certain points along the x-axis (such as 34% between the mean and a standard deviation of +1, for example, or about 14% between a standard deviation of +1 and a standard deviation of +2), we can make the following statements that will be true as well.

- 84% of all the scores fall below a *z* score of +1 (the 50% that falls below the mean plus the 34% that fall between the mean and +1 *z* score)
- 16% of all the scores fall above a *z* score of +1 (since the total area under the curve has to equal 100%, and 84% of the scores fall below score of +1.0)

Think about both of these for a moment. All we are saying is that, given the normal distribution, different areas of the curve are encompassed by different numbers of standard deviations or *z* scores.

OK—here it comes. These percentages or areas can also easily be seen as representing *probabilities* of a certain score occurring. For example, here's the big question (drumroll, please):

> In a distribution with a mean of 100 and a standard deviation of 10, what is the probability that any one score will be 110 or above?

The answer? 16% or 16 out of 100 or .16. How did we get this?

First, we computed the corresponding *z* score, which is +1 (110 – 100/10). Then, given the knowledge we already have (see Figure 8.4), we know a *z* score of 1 represents a location on the X-axis below which 84% (50% plus 34%) of all the scores in the distribution fall. Above that is the 16% of the scores or a probability of .16. Since we already know the areas between the mean and 1, 2, or 3 standard deviations above or below the mean, we can easily figure out the probability that the value of any one *z* score has of occurring.

But the method we just went through is fine for *z* values of 1, 2, and 3. But what if the value of the *z* score is not a whole number like 2, but 1.23 or –2.01. We need to find a way to be more precise.

How do we do that? Simple, learn calculus and apply it to the curve to compute the area underneath it at almost every possible point along the x-axis, or (and we like this alternative much more) use Table B1 found in Appendix B (the normal distribution table). This is a listing of all the values (except the very most extreme) for the area under a curve that corresponds to different z scores. This table has two columns. The first column, labeled z Score, is simply the z score that has been computed. The second column, Area Between the Mean and the z Score, is the exact area underneath the curve that is contained between the two points.

For example, if we wanted to know the area between the mean and a z score of +1, find the value 1.00 in the first column and read across to the second where you find the area between the mean and a z score of 1.00 to be 34.13. Seen that before?

Why aren't there any plus or minus signs in this table (such as −1.00)? Because the curve is symmetrical and it does not matter if the value of the z score is positive or negative. The area between the mean and 1 standard deviation in any direction is always 34.13%

Here's the next step. Let's say that for a particular z score of 1.38, you want to know the probability associated with that z score. If you wanted to know the percentage of the area between the mean and a z score of 1.38, you would find the corresponding area for the z score in Table B1 of 1.38, which is 41.62, indicating that more than 41% of all the cases in the distribution fall within a z score of 0 and 1.38 and that about 92% (50% plus 41.62%) will fall at or below a z score of 1.38. Now you should notice that we did this last example without any raw scores at all. Once you get to this table, they are just no longer needed.

But are we always interested only in the amount of area between the mean and some other z score? What about between two z scores, neither of which is the mean? For example, what if we were interested in knowing the amount of area between a z score of 1.5 and a z score of 2.5, which translates to a probability that a score falls between the two z scores? How can we use the table to compute these outcomes? It's easy. Just find the corresponding amount of area each z score encompasses and subtract one from the other. Often, drawing a picture helps, as in Figure 8.5.

For example, let's say that we want to find the area between a raw score of 110 and 125 in a distribution with a mean of 100 and a standard deviation of 10. Here are the steps we would take.

1 Compute the z score for a raw score of 110, which is 110 – 100/10, or +1.

2 Compute the z score for a raw score of 125, which is 125 – 100/10, or +2.5.

3 Using Table B1 in Appendix B, find the area between the mean and a z score of +1, which is 34.13%.

4 Using the normal curve chart in Appendix B, find the area between the mean and a z score of +2.5, which is 49.38%.

5 Since you want to know the distance *between* the two, subtract the smaller from the larger: 49.38 – 34.13, or 15.25%. Here's the picture that's worth a thousand words, in Figure 8.5.

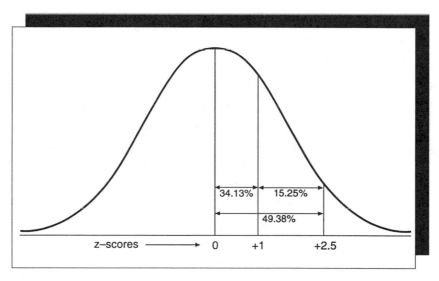

Figure 8.5. Using a Drawing to Figure Out the Difference in Area Between Two z Scores

OK—so we can be pretty confident that the probability of a particular score occurring can be best understood by examining where that score falls in a distribution relative to other scores. In this example, the probability of a score occurring between a z score of +1 and a z score of +2.5 is about 15%.

Here's another example. In a set of scores with a mean of 100 and a standard deviation of 10, a raw score of 117 has a corresponding z score of 1.17. This z score corresponds to an area under the curve of 87.9% (50% + 37.9%), meaning that the probability of this score occurring between a score of 0 and a score of 117 is 87.9% or 87.9 out of 100 or .879.

TECH TALK

Just two things about standard scores. First, even though we are focusing on z scores, there are other types of standard scores as well. For example, a T score is a type of standard score that is computed by multiplying the z score times 10 and adding 50. One advantage of this type of score is that you rarely have a negative T score. As with z scores, T scores allow you to compare standard scores from different distributions.

Second, a standard score is a whole different animal from a standardized score. A standardized score is one that comes from a distribution with a predefined mean and standard deviation. Standardized scores from tests such as the SATs and GREs (Graduate Record Exams) are used so that comparisons can easily be made between scores where the same mean and standard deviation are being used.

What z Scores Really Represent

The name of the statistics game is being able to estimate the probability of an outcome. If we take what we have talked about and done so far in this chapter one step further, it is deciding the probability of some event occurring. Then we will use some criterion to judge whether we think that event is as likely, more likely, or less likely than what we would expect by chance. The research hypothesis presents a statement of the expected event, and we use our statistical tools to evaluate how likely that event is.

That's the 20-second version of what statistics is, but that's a lot. So let's take everything from this paragraph and go through it again with an example.

Let's say that your lifelong friend, trusty Lew, gives you a coin and asks you to determine if it is a "fair" one—that is, if you flip it 10 times you should come up with 5 heads and 5 tails. We would expect 5 heads (or 5 tails) since the probability is .5 of any one head or tail on any one flip. On 10 independent flips (meaning that one flip does not affect another), we should get 5 heads, and so on. Now the question is, how many heads would disqualify the coin as being fake or rigged?

Let's say the criterion for fairness that we will use is if in flipping the coin 10 times we get heads (or heads turn up) less than 5% of the time we'll say the coin is rigged and call the police on Lew (who, incidentally, is already on parole). This 5% is a standard that is used by statisticians. If the probability of the event (be it the number of heads or the score on a test or the difference between the average scores for two groups) occurs in the extreme (and we're saying the extreme is defined as less than 5% of all such occurrences), it's an unlikely, or in this case, an unfair, outcome.

Here's the distribution of how many heads you can expect, just by chance alone on 10 flips. All the possible combinations are 2^{10}, or 1,024, possible outcomes such as 9 heads and 1 tail, 7 heads and 3 tails, and 10 heads and 0 tails, and on and on. For example, the probability associated with getting 6 heads in 10 flips is about 21%.

Number of Heads	Probability
0	0.00
1	0.01
2	0.04
3	0.12
4	0.21
5	0.25
6	0.21
7	0.12
8	0.04
9	0.01
10	0.00

So the likelihood of any particular outcome, such as 6 heads on 10 tosses, is about .21, or 21%. Now it's decision time. Just how many heads would one have to get on 10 flips to conclude that the coin is fixed, biased, busted, broken, or loony?

Well, as all good statisticians, we'll define the criterion as 5%, which we did earlier. If the probability of the observed outcome (the results of all our flips) is less than 5%, we'll conclude that it is so unlikely that something other than chance must be responsible—and our conclusion will be that the "something other than chance" is a bogus coin.

If you look at the table, you can see that 8, 9, or 10 heads all represent outcomes that are less than 5%. So if the result of 10 coin flips was 8, 9, or 10 heads, the conclusion would be that the coin is not a fair one. (Yep—you're right, 0, 1, and 2 qualify for the same decision. Sort of the other side of the coin—groan.)

The same logic applies to our discussion of z scores earlier. Just how extreme a z score would we expect before we could proclaim that an outcome is not just due to chance, but to some other factor? If you look at the normal curve table in Appendix B, you'll see that the cutoff point for a z score of 1.65 includes about 45% of the area under the curve. If you add that to the other 50% of the area on the other side of the curve, you come up with a total of 95%. That leaves just 5% above that point on the x-axis. Any score that represents a z score of 1.65 or above is then into pretty thin air—or at least in a location that has a much smaller chance of occurring than others.

Hypothesis Testing and z Scores: The First Step

What we showed you here is that any event can have a probability associated with it. And we use those probability values to make decisions as to how unlikely we think an event might be. For example, it's highly unlikely to get only 1 head and 9 tails in 10 tosses of a coin. And we also said that if an event seems to occur only 5 out of 100 times (5%), we will deem that event to be rather *unlikely* relative to all the other events that could occur.

It's much the same with any outcome related to a research hypothesis. The null hypothesis, which you learned about in Chapter 7, claims that there is no difference between groups (or variables) and that the likelihood of that occurring is 100%. We try to test the armor of the null for any chinks that might be there.

In other words, if through the test of the research hypothesis we find that the likelihood of an event that occurred is somewhat extreme, then the research hypothesis is a more attractive explanation than would be the null. So if we find a z score that is extreme (how extreme?—less than a 5% chance of occurring), we like to say that the reason for the extreme score is something to do with treatments or relationships and not just chance. We'll go into much greater detail on this point in the following chapter.

USING THE COMPUTER TO COMPUTE Z SCORES

 SPSS does lots of really cool things, but it's the little treats like the one you'll see here that make the program such a great time saver. Now that you know how to compute z scores by hand, let's let SPSS do the work.

To have SPSS compute z scores for the set of data you see in the first column in Figure 8.6 on page 166, follow these steps.

1. Enter the data in a new SPSS window.
2. Click Analyze → Descriptive Statistics → Descriptives
3. Double-click on the variable to move it to the Variable(s) box.
4. Click Save standardized values as variables in the Descriptives dialog box.
5. Click OK.

You can see in Figure 8.6 how SPSS computes the corresponding z scores.

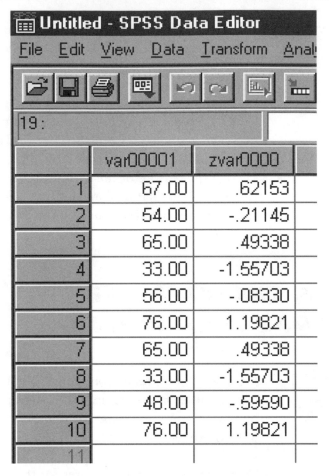

Figure 8.6. Having SPSS Compute z Scores for You

SUMMARY

Being able to figure out a z score, and being able to estimate how likely it is to occur in a sample of data, is the first and most important skill in understanding the whole notion of inference. Once we know how likely a test score or a difference between groups is, we can then compare that likelihood to what we would expect by chance and then make informed decisions. Now as we start Part IV of *Statistics for People Who (Think They) Hate Statistics,* we'll apply this model to specific examples of testing questions about the difference.

TIME TO PRACTICE

1. Normal curves:

   a. What are the characteristics of the normal curve?

   b. What human behavior, trait, or characteristic can you think of that is distributed normally?

2. Why is a z score a standard score, and why is it that z scores can be used to compare scores from different distributions with one another?

3. Compute the z scores for the following raw scores where $\overline{X} = 50$ and the standard deviation = 5.

   a. 55

   b. 50

   c. 60

   d. 57.5

   e. 46

4. Questions 4a though 4d are based on a distribution of scores with $\overline{X} = 75$ and the standard deviation = 6.38. Draw a small picture to help you see what's required.

   a. What is the probability of a score falling between a raw score of 70 and 80?

   b. What is the probability of a score falling above a raw score of 80?

   c. What is the probability of a score falling between a raw score of 81 and 83?

   d. What is the probability of a score falling below a raw score of 63?

ANSWERS TO PRACTICE QUESTIONS

1. a. In a normal curve, the mean, median, and mode are equal to one another; the curve is symmetrical about the mean; and the tails are asymptotic.

    b. Height and weight are examples as are intelligence and problem-solving skills.

2. A z score is a standard score (and comparable to others of the same type of score) since it is based on the degree of variability within its respective distribution of scores. Since a z score is always a measure of the distance between the mean and some point on the X-axis (regardless of the mean and standard deviation differences from one distribution to the next), the same units are used (units of standard deviations) and they can be compared to one another.

3. a. $z = (55 - 50)/5 = +1.00$.

    b. $z = (50 - 50)/5 = 0$.

    c. $z = (60 - 50)/5 = +2.00$.

    d. $z = (57.5 - 50)/5 = +1.5$.

    e. $z = (46 - 50)/5 = -0.8$.

4. a. The probability of a score falling between a raw score of 70 and a raw score of 80 is .5646. A z score for a raw score of 70 is –.78, and a z score for a raw score of 80 is .78. The area from the mean to a z score of .78 is 28.23%. The area between the two scores is 28.23 times 2, or 56.46%.

    b. The probability of a score falling above a raw score of 80 is .2177. A z score for a raw score of 80 is .78. The area between the mean and a z score of .78 is 28.23%. The area below a z score of .78 is .50 + .2828, or .7828. The difference between 1 (the total area under the curve) and .7828 is .2177.

    c. The probability of a score falling between a raw score of 81 and a raw score of 83 is .068. A z score for a raw score of 81 is .94, and a z score for a raw score of 83 is 1.25. The area from the mean to a z score of .94 is 32.64%. The area between the mean to a z score of 1.25 is 39.44. The difference between the two is .3944 – .3264 = .068, or 6.8%.

    d. The probability of a score falling below a raw score of 63 is .03. A z score for a raw score of 63 is 1.88. The area between the mean and a z score of –1.88 is 46.99%. The area below a z score of 1.88 is 1 – (.50 + .4699) = .03.

PART IV

Significantly Different

Using Inferential Statistics

SNAPSHOTS

"If it isn't Mr. Greater-Than-Thou..."

You've gotten this far and you're still alive and kicking, so congratulate yourself. By this point, you should have a good understanding of what descriptive statistics is all about, how chance figures as a factor in making decisions about outcomes, and how likely outcomes are to have occurred due to chance or some treatment.

You're an expert on creating and understanding the role that hypotheses play in social and behavioral science research. Now it's time for the rubber to meet the road. Let's see what you're made of in the next part of *Statistics for People Who (Think They) Hate Statistics*. Best of all, the hard work you've put in will shortly pay off with an understanding of applied problems!

This part of the book deals exclusively with understanding and applying certain types of statistics to answer certain types of research questions. We'll cover the most common statistical tests, and even some that are a bit more sophisticated. At the end of this section, we'll show you some of the more useful software packages that can be used to compute the same values that we'll do using a good old-fashioned calculator.

Let's start with a brief discussion of what the concept of significance is and go through the steps for performing an inferential test. Then we'll go on to examples of specific tests. We'll have lots of hands-on work here, so let's get started.

Significantly Significant

What It Means for You and Me

Difficulty Scale ☺☺ (somewhat thought provoking and key to it all!)

What you'll learn about in this chapter

- What the concept of significance is and why it is important
- The importance of and difference between Type I and Type II errors
- How inferential statistics works
- How to select the appropriate statistical test for your purposes

THE CONCEPT OF SIGNIFICANCE

There is probably no term or concept that represents more confusion for the beginning statistics student than the concept of statistical significance. But that doesn't mean it has to be that way for you. While it's a powerful idea, it is also relatively straightforward and can be understood by anyone in a basic statistics class.

We need an example of a study to illustrate the points we want to make. Let's take E. Duckett and M. Richards's *Maternal Employment and Young Adolescents' Daily Experiences in Single-Mother Families* (paper presented at the Society for Research in Child Development, Kansas City, MO, 1989). These two authors examined the attitudes of 436 fifth- through ninth-grade adolescents toward maternal employment.

Specifically, the two researchers investigated whether differences are present between the attitudes of adolescents whose mothers work and the attitudes of adolescents whose mothers do not work. They also examined some other factors, but for this example, we'll stick with the mothers-who-work and mothers-who-don't-work groups. One more thing. Let's add the word *significant* to our discussion of differences, so we have a research hypothesis something like this:

> There is a significant difference in attitude toward maternal employment by adolescents whose mothers work and adolescents whose mothers do not work as measured by a test of emotional state.

What we mean by the word *significant* is that any difference between the attitudes of the two groups is due to some systematic influence and not due to chance. In this example, that influence is whether or not mothers work. We assume that all the other factors that might account for any differences between groups were controlled. Thus, the only thing left to account for the differences between adolescents' attitudes is whether or not mothers work. Right? Yes. Finished? Not quite.

If Only We Were Perfect

Since our world is not a perfect one, we must allow for some leeway in how confident we are that only those factors we identify could cause any difference between groups. In other words, you need to be able to say that while you are pretty sure the difference between the two groups of adolescents is due to maternal employment, you cannot be absolutely, 100%, positively, unequivocally, indisputably (get the picture?) sure. There's always a chance, no matter how small, that you are wrong.

Why? Many reasons. For example, you could (horrors) just be plain ol' wrong. Maybe during this one experiment, differences between adolescents' attitudes were not due to whether mothers worked or didn't work, but were due to some other factor that was inadvertently not accounted for, such as a speech given by the local Mothers Who Work Club that several students attended. How about if the people in one group were mostly adolescent males and the people in the other group were mostly adolescent females? That could be the source of a difference as well. If you are a good researcher and do your homework, you can account for such differences, but it's always possible that you can't. And as a good researcher, you have to take that possibility into account.

So what do you do? In most scientific endeavors that involve testing hypotheses (such as the group differences example here), there is bound to be a certain amount of error that cannot be controlled—this is the chance factor that we have been talking about in the past few chapters. The level of chance or risk you are willing to take is expressed as a significance level, a term that unnecessarily strikes fear in the hearts of even strong men and women.

Significance level (here's the quick-and-dirty definition) is the risk associated with not being 100% confident that what you observe in an experiment is due to the treatment or what was being tested—in our example, whether or not mothers worked. If you read that significant findings occurred at the .05 level (or $p < .05$ in tech talk and what you regularly see in professional journals), the translation is that there is 1 chance in 20 (or .05 or 5%) that any differences found were not due to the hypothesized reason (whether mom works) but to some other, unknown reason or reasons. Your job is to reduce this likelihood as much as possible by removing all the competing reasons for any differences that you observed. Since you cannot fully eliminate the likelihood (since no one can control every potential factor), you assign some level of probability and report your results with that caveat.

In sum (and in practice), the researcher defines a level of risk that he or she is willing to take. If the results fall within the region that says, "This could not have occurred by chance alone—something else is going on," the researcher knows that the null hypothesis (which states an equality) is not the most attractive explanation for the observed outcomes. Instead, the research hypothesis (that there is an inequality or a difference) is the favored explanation.

Let's take a look at another example, this one being hypothetical.

A researcher is interested in seeing whether there is a difference in the academic achievement of children who participated in a preschool program and of children who did not participate. The null hypothesis is that the two groups are equal to each other on some measure of achievement.

The research hypothesis is that the mean score for the group of children who participated in the program is higher than the mean score for the group of children who did not participate in the program.

As a good researcher, your job is to show (as best you can—and no one is so perfect that they can account for everything) that *any* difference that exists between the two groups is due only to the effects of the preschool experience and no other factor or combination of factors. However, through a variety of techniques (that you'll learn about in your Stat II class!), you control or eliminate all the possible sources of difference, such as the influence of parents' education, number of children in the family, and so on. Once these other potential explanatory variables are removed, the only remaining alternative explanation for differences is the effect of the preschool experience itself.

But can you be absolutely (which is pretty darn) sure? No, you cannot. Why? First, because you can never be sure that you are testing a sample that identically reflects the profile of the population. And even if the sample perfectly represents the population, there are always other influences, which might affect the outcome, that you inadvertently missed when designing the experiment. There's always the possibility of error.

By concluding that the differences in test scores are due to differences in treatment you accept some risk. This degree of risk is, in effect (drumroll, please), the level of statistical significance at which you are willing to operate.

Statistical significance (here's the formal definition) is the degree of risk you are willing to take that you will reject a null hypothesis when it is actually true. For our example above, the null says that there is no difference between the two sample groups (remember, the null is always a statement of equality). In your data, however, you did find a difference. That is, given the evidence you have so far, group membership seems to have an effect on achievement scores. Maybe in reality, however, there is no difference. If you reject the null you stated, you would be making an error. The risk you take in making this kind of error (or the level of significance) is also known as a Type I error.

The World's Most Important Table (for This Semester Only)

Here's what it all boils down to.

A null hypothesis can be true or false. Either there is no difference between groups or there is really and truly an inequality (such as the difference between two groups). But remember, you'll never know this true state since the null cannot be directly tested (remember that the null applies only to the population).

And, as a crackerjack statistician, you can choose to either reject or accept the null hypothesis. Right? These four different conditions create the table you see here in Table 9.1.

Let's look at each cell.

More About Table 9.1

Table 9.1 has four important cells that describe the relationship between the nature of the null (whether it's true or not) and your action (accept or reject the null hypothesis). As you can see, the null can be either true or false and you can either reject or accept it.

The most important thing about understanding this table is the fact that the researcher never really knows the true nature of the null hypothesis and whether there *really* is or is not a difference between groups. Why? Because the population (which the null represents) is never directly tested. Why? Because it's impractical to do such, and that's why we have inferential statistics.

TABLE 9.1   Different Types of Errors

		Action You Take	
		Accept the Null Hypothesis	Reject the Null Hypothesis
True nature of the null hypothesis	The null hypothesis is really true.	**1** ☺ Bingo, you accepted a null when it is true and there is really no difference between groups.	**2** Oops—you made a Type I error and rejected a null hypothesis when there really is no difference between groups. Type I errors are also represented by the Greek letter alpha, or α.
	The null hypothesis is really false.	**3** Uh-oh—you made a Type II error and accepted a false null hypothesis. Type II errors are also represented by the Greek letter beta, or β.	**4** ☺ Good job, you rejected the null hypothesis when there really are differences between the two groups. This is also called power, or $1 - \beta$.

So

- Cell 1 in Table 9.1 represents a situation where the null hypothesis is really true (there's no difference between groups) and the researcher made the correct decision accepting it. No problem here. In our example, our results would show that there is no difference between the two groups of children, and we have acted correctly by accepting the null that there is no difference.

- Oops. Cell 2 represents a serious error. Here, we have rejected the null hypothesis (that there is no difference) when it is really true (and there is no difference). Even though there is no difference between the two groups of children, we will conclude there is and that's an error. Clearly a boo-boo called a **Type I error**, also known as the level of significance.

- Uh-oh, another type of error. Cell 3 represents a serious error as well. Here, we have accepted the null hypothesis (that there is no difference) when it is really false (and, indeed, there is a difference). We have said that even though there is a difference between the two groups of children, we will conclude there is not. Clearly a boo-boo, also known as a **Type II error**.

- Cell 4 in Table 9.1 represents a situation where the null hypothesis is really false and the researcher made the correct decision in rejecting it. No problem here. In our example, our results show that there is a difference between the two groups of children and we have acted correctly by rejecting the null that states there is no difference.

TECH TALK

So, if .05 is good and .01 is even better, why not set your Type I level of risk at .000001? For every good reason that you will be so rigorous in your rejection of false null hypotheses that you may miss a true one every now and then. Such a stringent Type I error rate allows for little leeway—indeed, the research hypothesis might be true but the associated probability might be .015—still quite rare, but missed with the too rigid Type I level of error.

Back to Type I Errors

Let's focus a bit more on cell 2 where a Type I error was made, since this is the focus of our discussion.

This Type I error, or level of significance, has certain values associated with it that define the risk you are willing to take in any test of the null hypothesis. The conventional levels set are between .01 and .05.

For example, if the level of significance is .01 it means that on any one test of the null hypothesis, there is a 1% chance you will reject the null hypothesis when the null is true and conclude that there is a group difference when there really is no group difference at all.

If the level of significance is .05, it means that on any one test of the null hypothesis, there is a 5% chance you will reject it when the null is true (and conclude that there is a group difference) when there really is no group difference at all. Notice that the level of significance is associated with an independent test of the null, and it is not appropriate to say that "on 100 tests of the null hypothesis, I will make an error on only 5, or 5% of the time."

In a research report, statistical significance is usually represented as $p < .05$, read as "the probability of observing that outcome is less than .05," often expressed in a report or journal article simply as "significant at the .05 level."

TECH TALK

With the introduction of fancy schmancy statistical analysis software, there's no longer the worry about the imprecision of such statements as "$p < .05$" or "$p < .01$"—$p < .05$ can mean anything from .000 to .049999, right? Instead, software such as SPSS gives you the *exact probability* such as $p = .013$ or $p = .158$ of the risk you are willing to take that you will commit a Type I error. So when you see in a research article the statement that "$p < .05$" it means that the value of p is equal to anything from .00 to .05. Likewise, when you see "$p > .05$" or "$p =$ n.s." (for nonsignificant), it means that the probability of rejecting a true null exceeds .05 and in fact can range from .0500001 to 1.00.

So, it's actually terrific when we know the exact probability of an outcome since we can more precisely measure the risk we are willing to take.

There is another kind of error you can make, which along with the Type I error is shown in Table 9.1. A Type II error (cell 3 in the chart) is when you inadvertently accept a false null hypothesis.

TECH TALK

When talking about the significance of a finding, you might hear the word *power* used. Power is a construct that has to do with how well a statistical test can detect and reject a null hypothesis when it is true. Mathematically, it's calculated by subtracting the value of the Type II error from 1. A more powerful test is always more desirable than a less powerful test, since the more powerful one lets you get to the heart of what's false and what's not.

For example, there may really be differences between the populations represented by the sample groups, but you mistakenly conclude there are not.

Ideally, you want to minimize both Type I and Type II errors, but it is not always easy or under your control. You have complete control over the Type I error level or the amount of risk that you are willing to take (since you actually set the level itself). Type II errors are not as directly controlled but instead are related to factors such as sample size. Type II errors are particularly sensitive to the number of subjects in a sample, and as that number increases Type II error decreases. In other words, as the sample characteristics more closely match that of the population (achieved by increasing the sample size), the likelihood that you will accept a false null hypothesis decreases as well.

SIGNIFICANCE VERSUS MEANINGFULNESS

What an interesting situation for the researcher when discovering that the results of an experiment indeed are statistically significant. You know technically what statistical significance means—that the research was a technical success and the null hypothesis is not a reasonable explanation for what was observed. Now if your experimental design and other considerations were well taken care of, statistically significant results are unquestionably the first step toward making a contribution to the literature in your field. However, the value of statistical significance and its importance or meaningfulness must be kept in perspective.

For example, let's take the case where a very large sample of illiterate adults (say, 10,000) is divided into two groups. One group receives intensive training to read using computers, and the other receives intensive training to read using classroom teaching. The average score for Group 1 (who learned in the classroom) is 75.6 on a reading test, the dependent variable. The average score on the reading test for Group 2 (who learned using the computer) is 75.7. The amount of variance in both groups is about equal. As you can see, the difference in score is only 1/10 of 1 point (75.6 vs. 75.7), yet when a t test for the significance between independent means is applied, the results are significant at the .01 level, indicating that computers work better than classroom teaching. (The next two chapters discuss t tests.)

The difference of .01 is indeed statistically significant, but is it meaningful? Does the improvement in test scores (by such a small margin) provide sufficient rationale for the $300,000 it costs to equip the program with computers? Or is the difference negligible enough that it can be ignored, even if it is statistically significant?

Here are some conclusions about the importance of statistical significance we can reach given this and the countless other possible examples.

- Statistical significance in and of itself is not very meaningful unless the study that is conducted has a sound conceptual base that lends some meaning to the significance of the outcome.
- Statistical significance cannot be interpreted independently of the context within which it occurs. For example, if you are the superintendent in a school system, are you willing to retain children in Grade 1 if the retention program significantly raises their standardized test scores by one-half point?
- While statistical significance is important as a concept, it is not the end-all and certainly should not be the only goal of scientific research. That is the reason why we set out to *test* hypotheses rather than *prove* them. If our study is designed correctly, then even null results tell you something very important. If a particular treatment does not work, it is important information that others need to know about. If your study is designed well, then you should know why the treatment does not work, and the next person down the line can design his or her study taking into account the valuable information you provided.

AN INTRODUCTION TO INFERENTIAL STATISTICS

Where descriptive statistics are used to describe a sample's characteristics, inferential statistics are used to infer something about the population based on the sample's characteristics.

At several points throughout the first half of *Statistics for People Who (Think They) Hate Statistics,* we have emphasized that a hallmark of good scientific research is choosing a sample in such a way that it is representative of the population from which it was selected. The process then becomes an inferential one, where you infer from the smaller sample to the larger population based on the results of tests (and experiments) conducted using the sample.

Before we start discussing individual inferential tests, let's go through the logic of how the inferential method works.

How Inference Works

Here are the general steps of a research project to see how the process of inference might work. We'll stay with adolescents' attitudes toward mothers working as an example.

Here's the sequence of events that might happen.

1. The researcher selects representative samples of adolescents who have mothers who work and adolescents who have mothers who do not work. These are selected in such a way that the samples represent the populations from which they are drawn.

2. Each adolescent is administered a test to assess his or her attitude. The mean scores for groups are computed and compared using some test.

3. A conclusion is reached as to whether or not the difference between the scores is the result of chance (meaning some factor other than moms working is responsible for the difference), or the result of "true" and statistically significant differences between the two groups (meaning the results are due to moms working).

4. A conclusion is reached as to the relationship between maternal employment and adolescents' attitudes in the population from which the sample was originally drawn. In other words, an inference, based on the results of an analysis of the sample data, is made about the population of all adolescents.

How to Select What Test to Use

Step 3 above brings us to ask the question, "How do I select the appropriate statistical test to determine if a difference between groups exists?" Heaven knows, there are plenty of them and you have to decide which one to use and when to use it. Well, the best way to learn which test to use is to be an experienced statistician who has taken lots of courses in this area and participated in lots of research. Experience is still the greatest teacher. In fact, there's no way you can really *learn* what to use and when to use it unless you've had the real-life, applied opportunity to actually use these tools. And as a result of taking this course, you are learning how to use these very tools.

So, for our purposes and to get started, we've created this nice little flow chart (aka cheat sheet) of sorts that you see in Figure 9.1. You have to have some idea what you're doing, so selecting the correct statistical test is not entirely autopilot, but it certainly is a good place to get started.

Don't think for a second that Figure 9.1 takes the place of your need to learn about when these different tests are appropriate. The flow chart is here only to help you get started.

Here's How to Use the Chart

1 Assume that you're very new to this statistics stuff (which you are) and that you have some idea what these tests of significance are, but you're pretty lost as far as deciding which one to use when.

2 Answer the question at the top of the flow chart.

3 Proceed down the chart by answering each of the questions until you get to the end of the chart. That's the statistical test you should use. This is not rocket science, and with some practice (which you'll will get throughout this part of *Statistics for People*), you'll be able to quickly and reliably select the appropriate test. Each of the chapters in this part of the book will begin with a chart like the one you see in Figure 9.1 and take you through the specific steps for the test statistic you should use.

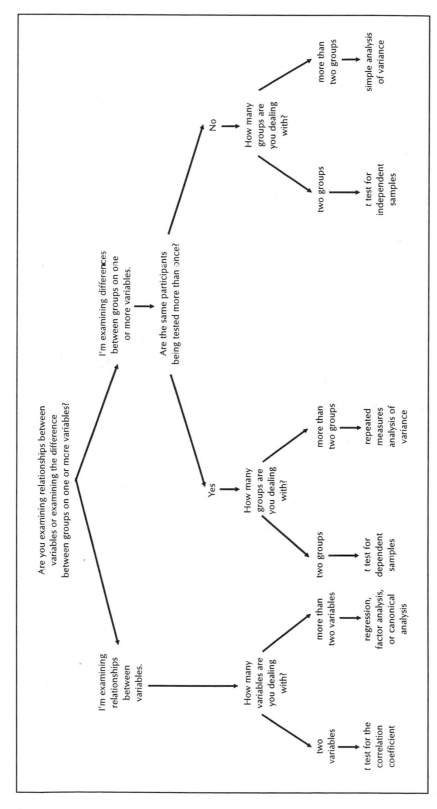

Figure 9.1. A Quick (but not always great) Approach to Determining What Type of Statistical Test to Use

Does the cute flow chart in Figure 9.1 contain all the statistical tests there are? Not by a long shot. There are hundreds, but the ones in Figure 9.1 are the ones used most often. And if you are going to become familiar with the research in your own field, you are bound to run into these.

AN INTRODUCTION TO TESTS OF SIGNIFICANCE

What inferential statistics does best is that it allows decisions to be made about populations based on the information about samples. One of the most useful tools for doing this is a test of statistical significance that can be applied to different types of situations, depending on the nature of the question being asked and the form of the null hypothesis.

For example, do you want to look at the difference between two groups, such as whether boys score significantly differently from girls on some test? Or the relationship between two variables, such as number of children in a family and average score on intelligence tests? The two cases call for different approaches, but both will result in a test of a null hypothesis using a specific test of statistical significance.

How a Test of Significance Works: The Plan

Tests of significance are based on the fact that each type of null hypothesis has associated with it a particular type of statistic. And each of the statistics has associated with it a special distribution you compare with the sample data. A comparison between the characteristics of your sample and the characteristics of the test distribution allows you to conclude if the sample characteristics are different from what you would expect by chance.

Here are the general steps to take in the application of a statistical test to any null hypothesis. These steps will serve as a model for each of the chapters in Part IV.

1. *A statement of the null hypothesis.* Do you remember that the null hypothesis is a statement of equality? The null hypothesis is the "true" state of affairs given no other information on which to make a judgment.

2. *Setting the level of risk (or the level of significance or Type I error) associated with the null hypothesis.* With any research hypothesis comes a certain degree of risk that you are wrong. The smaller this error is (such as .01 compared with .05), the less risk you are willing to take. No test of a hypothesis is completely risk free because you never really know the "true" relationship between variables. Remember that it is traditional to set the Type I error rate at .01 or .05. And SPSS and other programs specify the exact level.

3. *Selection of the appropriate test statistic.* Each null hypothesis has associated with it a particular test statistic. You can learn what test is related to what type of question in this part of *Statistics for People . . .*

4. *Computation of the test statistic value.* The **test statistic value** (called the **obtained value**) is the result of a specific statistical test. For example, there are test statistics for the significance of the difference between the averages of two groups, for the significance of the difference of a correlation coefficient from 0, and for the significance of the difference between two proportions. You'll actually compute the test statistic and come up with a numerical value.

5. *Determination of the value needed for rejection of the null hypothesis using the appropriate table of critical values for the particular statistic.* Each test statistic (along with group size and the risk you are willing to take) has a **critical value** associated with it.

This is the value you would expect the test statistic to yield if the null hypothesis is indeed true.

6. *Comparison of the obtained value to the critical value.* This is the crucial step. Here the value you obtained from the test statistic (the one you computed) is compared with the value (the critical value) you would expect to find by chance alone.

7. *If the obtained value is more extreme than the critical value, the null hypothesis cannot be accepted.* That is, the null hypothesis' statement of equality (reflecting chance) is not the most attractive explanation for differences that were found. Here is where the real beauty of the inferential method shines through. Only if your obtained value is more extreme than chance (meaning that the result of the test statistic is not a result of some chance fluctuation) can you say that any differences you obtained are not due to chance and that the equality stated by the null hypothesis is not the most attractive explanation for any differences you might have found. Instead, the differences must be due to the treatment.

8. *If the obtained value does not exceed the critical value, the null hypothesis is the most attractive explanation.* If you cannot show that the difference you obtained is due to something other than chance (such as the treatment), then the difference must be due to chance or something you have no control over. In other words, the null is the best explanation.

Here's the Picture That's Worth a Thousand Words

What you see in Figure 9.2 represents the eight steps that we just went through. This is a visual representation of what happens when the obtained and critical values are compared. In this example, the significance level is set at .05, or 5%. It could have been set at .01, or 1%.

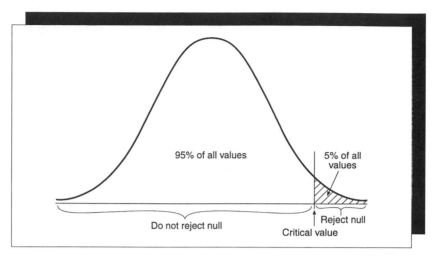

Figure 9.2. Comparing Obtained Values to Critical Values and Making Decisions About Rejecting or Accepting the Null Hypothesis

In examining Figure 9.2, note the following.

1. The entire curve represents all the possible outcomes based on a specific null hypothesis such as the difference between two groups or the significance of a correlation coefficient.

2. The critical value is the point beyond which the obtained outcomes are judged to be so rare that the conclusion is that the obtained outcome is not due to chance, but to some other factor. In this example, we define rare as having a less than 5% chance of occurring.

3. If the outcome representing the obtained value falls to the left of the critical value (it is less extreme), the conclusion is that the null hypothesis is the most attractive explanation for any differences that are observed. In other words, the obtained value falls in the region (95% of the area under the curve) where we only expect outcomes due to chance to occur.

4. If the obtained value falls to the right of the critical value (it is more extreme), the conclusion is that the research hypothe-

sis is the most attractive explanation for any differences that are observed. In other words, the obtained value falls in the region (5% of the area under the curve) where we would only expect outcomes due to something other than chance to occur.

SUMMARY

So now you know exactly how the concept of significance works, and all that is left is applying it to a variety of different research questions. That's what we'll start with in the next chapter and continue with through most of this part of the book.

TIME TO PRACTICE

1. Why is significance an importance construct in the study and use of inferential statistics?

2. What's wrong with the following statements?

   a. A Type I error of .05 means that 5 times out of 100, I will reject a true null hypothesis.

   b. It is possible to set the Type I error rate to 0.

   c. The smaller the Type I error rate, the better the results.

3. What does chance have to do with testing the research hypothesis for significance?

ANSWERS TO PRACTICE QUESTIONS

1. The concept of significance is crucial to the study and use of inferential statistics since significance (reflected in the idea of a significance level) sets the level at which we can be confident that the outcomes we observe are "truthful" and to what extent these outcomes can be generalized to the larger population from which the sample was selected.

2. a. Level of significance refers only to a single, independent test of the null hypothesis and not to multiple tests.

   b. It is impossible to set the error rate to 0 since it is not possible that we might not reject a null hypothesis when it is actually true. There's always that chance.

   c. The level of risk that you are willing to take to reject the null hypothesis when it is true has nothing to do with the meaningfulness of the outcomes of your research. You can have a highly significant outcome that is meaningless, or have a relatively high Type I error rate (.10) and have a very meaningful finding.

3. Chance is reflected in the degree of risk (Type I error) that we are willing to take in the possible rejection of a true null hypothesis.

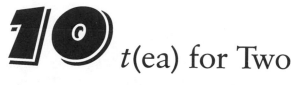

t(ea) for Two

Tests Between the Means of Different Groups

Difficulty Scale ☺☺☺ (not too hard—this is the first one of this kind, but you know more than enough to master it)

What you'll learn about in this chapter

- When the *t* test for independent means is appropriate to use
- How to compute the observed *t* value
- Interpreting the *t* value and understanding what it means

INTRODUCTION TO THE T TEST FOR INDEPENDENT SAMPLES

Even though eating disorders are recognized for their seriousness, little research has been done that compares the prevalence and intensity of symptoms across different cultures. John P. Sjostedt, John F. Shumaker, and S. S. Nathawat undertook this comparison with groups of 297 Australian and 249 Indian university students. Each student was tested on the Eating Attitudes Test and the Goldfarb Fear of Fat Scale. The groups' scores were compared with one another. On a comparison of means between the Indian and the Australian participants, Indian students scored higher on both of the tests. The results for the Eating Attitudes Test were $t_{(524)} = -4.19$, $p < .0001$, and the results for the Goldfarb Fear of Fat Scale were $t_{(534)} = -7.64$, $p < .0001$.

Now just what does all this mean? Read on.

Why was the *t* test for independent samples used? Sjostedt and his colleagues were interested in finding out if there was a difference on the average scores of one (or more) variable(s) between the two groups that were independent of one another. By *independent* we mean the two groups were not related in any way. Each participant in the study was tested only once. The researchers applied a *t* test for independent means, arriving at the conclusion that for each of the outcome variables, the differences between the two groups were significant at or beyond the .0001 level. Such a small Type I error means that there is very little chance that the difference in scores between the two groups was due to something other than group membership, in this case representing nationality, culture, or ethnicity.

Want to know more? Check out Sjostedt, J. P., Shumaker, J. F., and Nathawat, S. S. (1998). Eating disorders among Indian and Australian university students. *Journal of Social Psychology, 138*(3), 351-357.

The Path to Wisdom and Knowledge

Here's how you can use Figure 9.1, the flow chart introduced in Chapter 9, to select the appropriate test statistic, the *t* test for independent means. Follow along the highlighted sequence of steps in Figure 10.1.

1 The differences between the groups of Australian and Indian students are being explored.

2 Participants are being tested only once.

3 There are two groups.

4 The appropriate test statistic is *t* test for independent means.

TECH TALK

Almost every statistical test has certain assumptions that underlie the use of the test. For example, the *t* test has a major assumption that the amount of variability in each of the two groups is equal. This is the homogeneity of variance assumption. While this assumption can be violated if the sample size is big enough, small samples and a violation of this assumption can lead to ambiguous results and conclusions. Don't knock yourself out worrying about these assumptions since they are beyond the scope of this book. However, you should know that such assumptions are rarely violated, but it is worth knowing that they do exist.

COMPUTING THE TEST STATISTIC

The formula for computing the *t* value for the *t* test for independent means is shown in Formula 10.1. The difference between the means makes up the numerator of the following formula used to compute the *t* value or the test statistic of the obtained value. The amount of variation within and between each of the two groups makes up the denominator.

$$ t = \frac{\overline{X}_1 - \overline{X}_2}{\left[\sqrt{\frac{(n_1 - 1)s_1^2 + (n_2 - 1)s_2^2}{n_1 + n_2 - 2} \left[\frac{n_1 + n_2}{n_1 n_2} \right]} \right]} \tag{10.1} $$

where

$\overline{X}_1$ is the mean for Group 1

$\overline{X}_2$ is the mean for Group 2

n_1 is the number of participants in Group 1

n_2 is the number of participants in Group 2

s_1^2 is the variance for Group 1

s_2^2 is the variance for Group 2

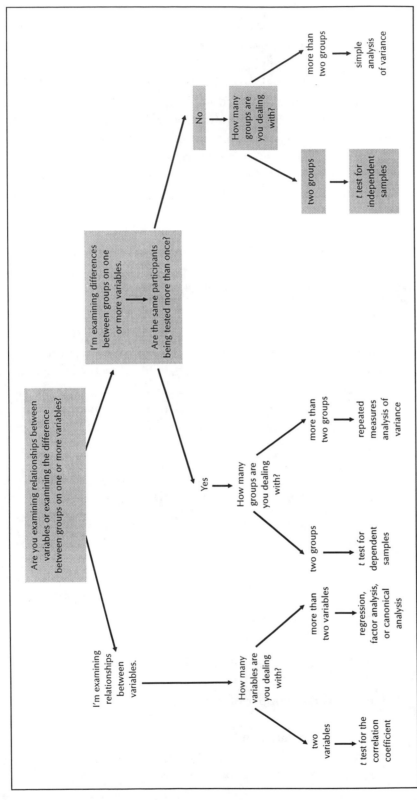

Figure 10.1. Determining That a *t* Test Is the Correct Test Statistic

Nothing new here at all. It's just a matter of plugging in the correct values.

Here are some data reflecting the number of words remembered following a program designed to help Alzheimer's patients remember the order of daily tasks. Group 1 was taught using visuals, and Group 2 was taught using visuals and intense verbal rehearsal. We'll use the data to compute the test statistic in the following example.

Group 1			Group 2		
7	5	5	5	3	4
3	4	7	4	2	3
3	6	1	4	5	2
2	10	9	5	4	7
3	10	2	5	4	6
8	5	5	7	6	2
8	1	2	8	7	8
5	1	12	8	7	9
8	4	15	9	5	7
5	3	4	8	6	6

Here are the famous eight steps and the computation of the t test statistic.

1. *A statement of the null and research hypotheses.*

As represented by Formula 10.2, the null hypothesis states that there is no difference between the means for Group 1 and Group 2. For our purposes, the research hypothesis (shown as Formula 10.3) states that there is a difference between the means of the two groups. The research hypothesis is a two-tailed, nondirectional research hypothesis since it posits a difference, but in no particular direction.

The null hypothesis is

$$H_0: \mu_1 = \mu_2 \qquad (10.2)$$

The research hypothesis is

$$H_1: \overline{X}_1 \neq \overline{X}_2 \qquad (10.3)$$

2. *Setting the level of risk (or the level of significance or Type I error) associated with the null hypothesis.*

The level of risk or Type I error or level of significance (any other names?) is .05, totally the decision of the researcher.

3. *Selection of the appropriate test statistic.*

Using the flow chart shown in Figure 10.1, we determined that the appropriate test is a *t* test for independent means. It is not a *t* test for dependent means (a common mistake beginning students make) since the groups are independent of one another.

4. *Computation of the test statistic value (called the obtained value).*

Now's your chance to plug in values and do some computation. The formula for the *t* value was shown in Formula 10.1. When the specific values are plugged in, we get the equation shown in Formula 10.4. (We already computed the mean and standard deviation.)

$$t = \frac{5.43 - 5.53}{\left[\sqrt{\frac{(30-1)3.42^2 + (30-1)2.06^2}{30+30-2}} \left[\frac{30+30}{30 \bullet 30} \right] \right]} \tag{10.4}$$

With the numbers plugged in, Formula 10.5 shows how we got the final value of −.14. The value is negative since a larger value (the mean of Group 2, which is 5.53) is being subtracted from a smaller number (the mean of Group 1, which is 5.43). Remember, though, that since the test is nondirectional and any difference is hypothesized, the sign of the difference is meaningless.

$$t = \frac{.1}{\left[\sqrt{\frac{339.01 + 122.96}{58}} \left[\frac{60}{900} \right] \right]} = -.14 \tag{10.5}$$

5. *Determination of the value needed for rejection of the null hypothesis using the appropriate table of critical values for the particular statistic.*

Here's where we go to Table B2 in Appendix B, which lists the critical values for the *t* test.

We can use this distribution to see if two independent means differ from one another by comparing what we would expect by chance (the tabled or critical value) to what we observe (the obtained value).

Our first task is to determine the **degrees of freedom** (*df*), which approximates the sample size. For this particular test statistic, the degrees of freedom are $n_1 - 1 + n_2 - 1$. So for each group, add the size of the two samples and subtract 2. In this example, $30 + 30 - 2 = 58$. These are the degrees of freedom for this test statistic and not necessarily for any other.

Using this number (58), the level of risk you are willing to take (earlier defined as .05), and a two-tailed test (since there is no direction to the research hypothesis), you can use the *t* test table to look up the critical value. At the .05 level, with 58 degrees of freedom for a two-tailed test, the value needed for rejection of the null hypothesis is . . . Oops! there's no 58 degrees of freedom in the table! What do you do? Well, if you select the value that corresponds to 55, you're being conservative in that you are using a value for a sample smaller than what you have (and the critical *t* value will be smaller).

If you go for 60 degrees of freedom (the closest to your value of 58), you will be closer to the size of the population, but a bit liberal in that 60 is larger than 58. Although statisticians differ in their viewpoint, let's always go with the value that's closest to the actual sample size. So the value needed to reject the null hypothesis with 58 degrees of freedom at the .05 level of significance is 2.001.

6. *A comparison of the obtained value and the critical value.*

The obtained value is –.14, and the critical value for rejection of the null hypothesis that Group 1 and Group 2 performed differently is 2.001. The critical value of 2.00 represents the value at which chance is the most attractive explanation for any of the observed differences between the two groups given 30 participants in each group and the willingness to take a .05 level of risk.

7. and 8. *Decision time!*

Now comes our decision. If the obtained value is more extreme than the critical value (remember Figure 9.2), the null hypothesis cannot be accepted. If the obtained value does not exceed the critical value, the null hypothesis is the most attractive explanation. In this case, the obtained value (−.14) does not exceed the critical value (2.001)—it is not extreme enough for us to say that the difference between Groups 1 and 2 occurred by anything other than chance. If the value were greater than 2.001, it would represent a value that is just like getting 8, 9, or 10 heads—too extreme for us to believe that something else other than chance is not going on. In the case of the coin, it's a unfair coin—in this example it would be that there is a better way to teach memory skills to these older people.

So what's the small difference between the two groups due to? If we stick with our current argument, then we could say the difference is due to anything from sampling error to rounding error, to simple variability in participants' scores. Most important, we're pretty sure (but, of course, not 100% sure) that the difference is not due to anything in particular that one group or the other experienced to make its scores better.

So How Do I Interpret $t_{(58)} = -.14$, $p > .05$?

- t represents the test statistic that was used
- 58 is the number of degrees of freedom
- −.14 is the value obtained using the formula we showed you earlier in the chapter
- $p > .05$ (the really important part of this little phrase) indicates that the probability is greater than 5% on any one test of the null hypothesis that the two groups differ from one another

USING THE COMPUTER
TO PERFORM A T TEST

SPSS is willing and ready to help you perform these inferential tests. Here's how to perform the one that we just did and interpret the output. We are using the data set named Chapter 10 Data Set 1. From your examination of the data, you can see how the grouping variable (Group 1 or Group 2) is in column 1 and the test variable (memory) is in column 2.

1. Enter the data in the Data Editor or download the file. Be sure that there is a column for group and that you have no more than two groups represented in that column.

2. Click Analyze → Compare Means → Independent-Samples T test and you will see the Independent-Samples T test dialog box shown in Figure 10.2.

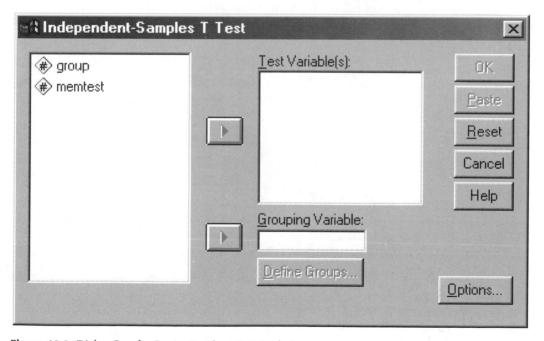

Figure 10.2. Dialog Box for Beginning the *t* Test Analysis

Notice how SPSS uses a capital T to represent this test while we have been using a small t. This difference is strictly a matter of personal preference and, more often than not, reflects what people were taught way back when. What's important for you is to know that there is a difference in letter only—it's the same exact test.

3. Click on the variable named group, and click ▶ to place it in the Grouping Variable(s): box.

4. Click on the variable named memtest, and click ▶ to place it in the Test Variable(s) box.

5. SPSS will not allow you to continue until you define the grouping variable. This basically means telling SPSS how many levels of the group variable there are (wouldn't you think that a program this smart could figure that out?). In any case, click Define Groups and enter the values 1 for Group 1 and 2 for Group 2 as shown in Figure 10.3. The name of the grouping variable (in this case group) has to be highlighted before you can define it.

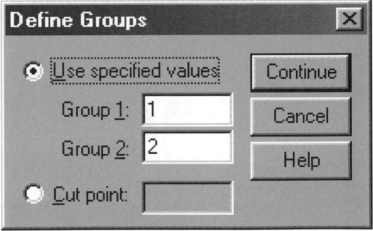

Figure 10.3. Define Groups Dialog Box

6. Click Continue, and then click OK and SPSS will conduct the analysis and produce the output you see in Figure 10.4.

Group Statistics

	GROUP	N	Mean	Std. Deviation	Std. Error Mean
MEMTEST	Group 1	30	5.43	3.42	.62
	Group 2	30	5.53	2.06	.38

Independent Samples Test

		Levene's Test for Equality of Variances		t-test for Equality of Means					95% Confidence Interval of the Difference	
		F	Sig.	t	df	Sig. (2-tailed)	Mean Difference	Std. Error Difference	Lower	Upper
MEMTEST	Equal variances assumed	4.994	.029	-.137	58	.891	-1.00E-01	.73	-1.56	1.36
	Equal variances not assumed			-.137	47.635	.891	-1.00E-01	.73	-1.57	1.37

Obtained value

Degrees of freedom

The exact probability that the t value of −.137 is due to chance

Figure 10.4. Copy of SPSS Output for a t Test Between Independent Means

What the SPSS Output Means

There's a ton of SPSS output from this analysis, and for our purposes, we'll deal only with selected output shown in Figure 10.4. There are three things to note.

1. The obtained t value is $-.137$, very close to what we got when we computed the value by hand earlier in this chapter ($-.14$) but not the same due to rounding error.

2. The number of degrees of freedom is 58 (which you already know is computed using the formula $n_1 + n_2 - 2$).

3. Here's the really important result. The significance of this finding is .891, or $p = .891$, which means that on one test of this null hypothesis, the likelihood of rejecting the hypothesis when it is true is pretty high (89 out of 100)! So the Type I error is certainly greater than .05, which allowed us to conclude earlier when we did the same analysis using the formula that $p > .05$.

SUMMARY

The t test is your first introduction to performing a real statistical test and trying to understand this whole matter of significance from an applied point of view. Be sure that you understand what was in this chapter before you move on. And be sure you can do by hand the few things that were asked for. Next, we move on to using another form of the same test, only this time, there are two measures taken from one group of participants rather than one measure taken from two separate groups.

TIME TO PRACTICE

1. Using the data in the file named Chapter 10 Data Set 2, test the research hypotheses at the .05 level of significance that boys raise their hand in class more often than girls. Do this practice problem by hand using a calculator. What is your conclusion regarding the research hypothesis? Remember to first decide whether this is a one- or two-tailed test.

2. Using the same data set (Chapter 10 Data Set 2), test the research hypothesis at the .01 level of significance that there is a difference between boys and girls in the number of times they raise their hands in class. Do this practice problem by hand using a calculator. What is your conclusion regarding the research hypothesis? You used the same data for this problem as for Question 1, but you have a different hypothesis (one is directional and the other is nondirectional). How do the results differ and why?

3. Using the data in the file named Chapter 10 Data Set 3, test the null hypothesis that urban and rural residents both have the same attitude toward gun control. Use SPSS to complete the analysis for this problem.

Instridal Sample-files

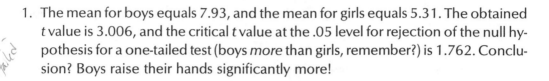

1. The mean for boys equals 7.93, and the mean for girls equals 5.31. The obtained *t* value is 3.006, and the critical *t* value at the .05 level for rejection of the null hypothesis for a one-tailed test (boys *more* than girls, remember?) is 1.762. Conclusion? Boys raise their hands significantly more!

2. Now this is very interesting. We have the same exact data, of course, but a different hypothesis. Here, the hypothesis is that the number of times is *different* (not just more or less) necessitating a two-tailed test. So using Table B2 and at the .01 level for a two-tailed test, the critical value is 2.977. The obtained value of 1.809 does not exceed what we would expect by chance, and given this hypothesis, there is no difference. So in comparison with one another, a one-tailed finding (see Question 2 above) need not be as extreme as a two-tailed finding given the same exact findings.

3. You can see the SPSS output in Figure 10.5, where there is no significant difference (*p* = .253) between urban and rural dwellers in their attitude toward gun control.

Group Statistics

	GROUP	N	Mean	Std. Deviation	Std. Error Mean
ATTITUDE	1.00	16	6.5112	1.7722	.4431
	2.00	14	5.3979	3.3144	.8858

Independent Samples Test

		Levene's Test for Equality of Variances		t-test for Equality of Means					95% Confidence Interval of the Difference	
		F	Sig.	t	df	Sig. (2-tailed)	Mean Difference	Std. Error Difference	Lower	Upper
ATTITUDE	Equal variances assumed	4.463	.044	1.168	28	.253	1.1134	.9531	-.8390	3.0658
	Equal variances not assumed			1.124	19.273	.275	1.1134	.9904	-.9576	3.1844

Figure 10.5. SPSS Output for a *t* Test of Independent Means

11 t(ea) for Two (Again)

Tests Between the Means of Related Groups

Difficulty Scale ☺☺☺ (hard—just like the one in Chapter 10, but a different question)

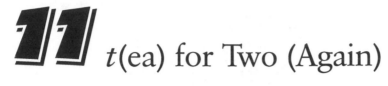

What you'll learn about in this chapter

- When the t test for dependent means is appropriate to use
- How to compute the observed t value
- Interpreting the t value and understanding what it means

INTRODUCTION TO THE T TEST FOR DEPENDENT SAMPLES

How best to educate children is clearly one of the most vexing questions that faces any society. Since children are so different from one another, a balance needs to be found between meeting the basic needs of all while ensuring that special children (on either end of the continuum) get the opportunities they need. An obvious and important part of education is reading, and three professors at the University of Alabama studied the effects of resource and regular classrooms on the reading achievement of learning disabled children. Renitta Goldman, Gary L. Sapp, and Ann Shumate Foster found that in general, one year of daily instruction in both settings resulted in no difference in overall reading achievement scores. On one specific comparison between the pretest and the posttest of the resource group, they found that $t_{(34)} = 1.23$, $p > .05$. At the beginning of the program, reading achievement scores for children in the resource room were 85.8. At the end of the program, reading achievement scores for children in the resource room were 88.5—a difference, but not a significant one.

So why a test of dependent means? A *t* test for dependent means indicates that a single group of the same subjects is being studied under two conditions. In this example, the conditions are before the start of the experiment and after its conclusion. Primarily, it is because the same children were tested at two times, before the start of the one-year program and at the end of the one-year program, that we use the *t* test for dependent means. As you can see by the above result, there was no difference in scores at the beginning and the end of the program. The very small *t* value (1.23) is not near extreme enough to fall outside the region where we would reject the null hypothesis. In other words, there is far too little change for us to say that this difference occurred by something other than chance. The small difference of 2.7 (88.5 – 85.8) is probably due to sampling error or variability within the groups.

Want to know more? Check out Goldman, R., Sapp, G. L., and Foster, A. S. (1998). Reading achievement by learning disabled students in resource and regular classes. *Perceptual and Motor Skills, 86,* 192-194.

The Path to Wisdom and Knowledge

Here's how you can use the flow chart to select the appropriate test statistic, the *t* test for dependent means. Follow along the highlighted sequence of steps in Figure 11.1.

1   The difference between the students' scores on the pretest and on the posttest is the focus.

2   Participants are being tested more than once.

3   There are two groups.

4   The appropriate test statistic is *t* test for dependent means.

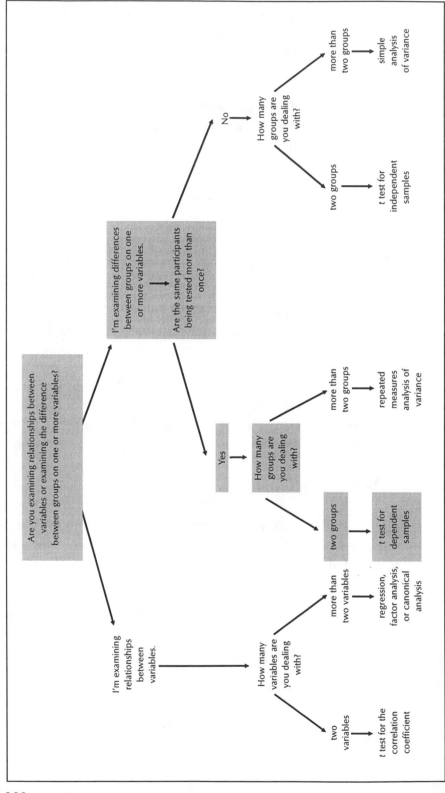

Figure 11.1. Determining That a *t* Test for Dependent Samples Is the Correct Test Statistic

COMPUTING THE TEST STATISTIC

The t test for dependent means involves a comparison of means from each group and focuses on the differences between the scores. As you can see in Formula 11.1, the sum of the differences between the two tests forms the numerator and reflects the difference between groups.

$$t = \frac{\Sigma D}{\sqrt{\dfrac{n\Sigma D^2 - (\Sigma D)^2}{(n-1)}}}$$ (11.1)

where

ΣD is the sum of all the differences between groups

ΣD^2 is the sum of the differences squared between groups

n is the number of pairs of observations

Here are some data to illustrate how the t value is computed. Just like in the above example, there is a pretest and a posttest, and for illustration's sake, assume that these are before and after scores from a reading program.

Pretest	Posttest	Difference	D^2
3	7	4	16
5	8	3	9
4	6	2	4
6	7	1	1
5	8	3	9
5	9	4	16
4	6	2	4
5	6	1	1
3	7	4	16
6	8	2	4
7	8	1	1
8	7	-1	1
7	9	2	4
6	10	4	16
7	9	2	4
8	9	1	1

(continued)

	Pretest	Posttest	Difference	D^2
	8	8	0	0
	9	8	−1	1
	9	4	−5	25
	8	4	−4	16
	7	5	−2	4
	7	6	−1	1
	6	9	3	9
	7	8	1	1
	8	12	4	16
Sum	158	188	30	180
Mean	6.32	7.52	1.2	7.2

Here are the famous eight steps and the computation of the *t* test statistic.

1. *A statement of the null and research hypotheses.*

The null hypothesis states that there is no difference between the means for the pretest and the posttest scores on reading achievement. The research hypothesis is a one-tailed, directional research hypothesis since it posits that the posttest score will be higher than the pretest score.

The null hypothesis is

$$H_0: \mu_{\text{posttest}} = \mu_{\text{pretest}} \qquad (11.2)$$

The research hypothesis is

$$H_1: \overline{X}_{\text{posttest}} > \overline{X}_{\text{pretest}} \qquad (11.3)$$

2. *Setting the level of risk (or the level of significance or Type I error) associated with the null hypothesis.*

The level of risk or Type I error or level of significance is .05, totally the decision of the researcher.

3. *Selection of the appropriate test statistic.*

Using the flow chart shown in Figure 11.1, we determined that the appropriate test is a *t* test for dependent means. It is not a *t* test for independent means since the groups are not independent of each other. In fact, they're not groups of participants, but groups of scores for the same participants. The groups are dependent on one another. Another name for the t test for dependent means is the t test for paired samples or the t test for correlated samples. You'll see in Chapter 13 that there is a very close relationship between a test of the significance of the correlation between these two sets of scores (pre and post) and the t value we are computing here.

4. *Computation of the test statistic value (called the obtained value).*

Now's your chance to plug in values and do some computation. The formula for the t value was shown above. When the specific values are plugged in, we get the equation shown in Formula 11.4. (We already computed the means and standard deviations for the pretest and posttest scores.)

$$t = \frac{30}{\sqrt{\dfrac{(25 \bullet 180) - 30^2}{(25 - 1)}}} \tag{11.4}$$

With the numbers plugged in, we have the following equation with a final obtained t value of 2.45. The mean score for pretest performance was 6.32, and the mean score for posttest performance was 7.52.

$$t = \frac{30}{\sqrt{150}} = 2.45 \tag{11.5}$$

5. *Determination of the value needed for rejection of the null hypothesis using the appropriate table of critical values for the particular statistic.*

Here's where we go Table B2 that specifically lists the critical values for the t test. Once again, we have a t test and we'll use the same table we used in Chapter 10 to find out the critical value for rejection of the null hypothesis.

Our first task is to determine the degrees of freedom (df), which approximates the sample size. For this particular test statistic, the degrees of freedom are $n_1 - 1$, or $25 - 1 = 24$. These are the degrees of freedom for this test statistic only and not necessarily for any other.

Using this number (24), the level of risk you are willing to take (earlier defined as .05), and a one-tailed test (since there is a direction to the research hypothesis—the posttest score will be larger than the pretest score), the value needed for rejection of the null hypothesis is 1.711.

6. *A comparison of the obtained value and the critical value and a decision.*

The obtained value is 2.45, larger than the critical value needed for rejection of the null hypothesis.

7. and 8. *Time for a decision.*

Now comes our decision. If the obtained value is more extreme than the critical value, the null hypothesis cannot be accepted. If the obtained value does not exceed the critical value, the null hypothesis is the most attractive explanation. In this case, the obtained value does exceed the critical value—it is extreme enough for us to say that the difference between the pretest and the posttest did occur by something other than chance. And if we did our experiment correctly, then what could the factor be that affected the outcome? Easy—the introduction of the daily reading program. We know the difference is due to a particular factor. The difference between the pretest and the posttest groups could not have occurred by chance, but instead is due to the treatment.

So How Do I Interpret $t_{(24)} = 2.45$, $p < .05$?

- t represents the test statistic that was used
- 24 is the number of degrees of freedom
- 2.45 is the obtained value using the formula we showed you earlier in the chapter
- $p < .05$ (the really important part of this little phrase) indicates that the probability is less than 5% on any one test of the null

hypothesis that the average of posttest scores is greater than the average of pretest scores. Since we defined .05 as our criterion for the research hypothesis being more attractive than the null hypothesis, our conclusion is that there is a significant difference between the two sets of scores.

USING THE COMPUTER TO PERFORM A T TEST

 SPSS is willing and ready to help you perform these inferential tests. Here's how to perform the one that we just did and interpret the output. We are using the data set named Chapter 11 Data Set 1, which was also used in the earlier example.

1. Enter the data in the Data Editor. Be sure that there is a separate column for pretest and posttest scores. Unlike a *t* test for independent means, there are no groups to identify. In Figure 11.2, you can see how the cell entries are labeled pretest and posttest.

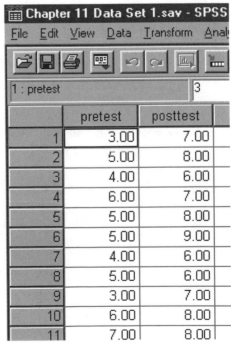

Figure 11.2. Data From Chapter 11 Data Set 1

2. Click Analyze → Compare Means → Paired-Samples T test, and you will see the dialog box shown in Figure 11.3.

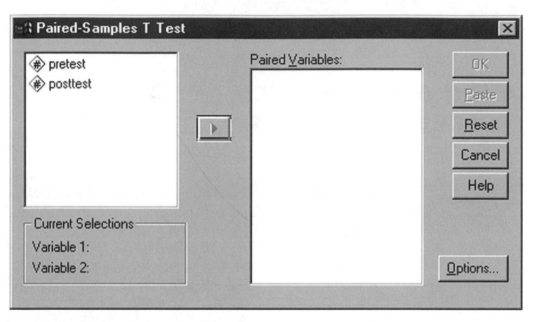

Figure 11.3. Paired-Samples T Test Dialog Box

3. Click on the variable named pretest.

4. Click on the variable named posttest.

5. Click ▶ to move the highlighted variables to the Paired Variables text box.

6. Click OK

7. SPSS will conduct the analysis and produce the output you see in Figure 11.4.

☞ T-Test

Paired Samples Statistics

		Mean	N	Std. Deviation	Std. Error Mean
Pair 1	PRETEST	6.3200	25	1.7253	.3451
	POSTTEST	7.5200	25	1.8285	.3657

Paired Samples Correlations

		N	Correlation	Sig.
Pair 1	PRETEST & POSTTEST	25	.051	.810

Paired Samples Test

		Paired Differences							
					95% Confidence Interval of the Difference				
		Mean	Std. Deviation	Std. Error Mean	Lower	Upper	t	df	Sig. (2-tailed)
Pair 1	PRETEST - POSTTEST	-1.2000	2.4495	.4899	-2.2111	-.1889	-2.449	24	.022

Figure 11.4. SPSS Output for a *t* Test Between Dependent Means

215

What the SPSS Output Means

This SPSS output is rather straightforward. Here's a description of the various components and once again, we're focusing only on those that we think are within the scope of this book and most relevant to your understanding of the test we're discussing.

First, for both the pretest and the posttest, there are the reported means, sample size, standard deviations, and the standard error of the mean (a measure of sampling error). From this information, you can immediately see that the posttest score (7.52) is larger than the pretest score (6.32). At least this far into the analysis, it appears that the results are supporting the research hypothesis that the children scored higher on the posttest than the pretest.

Now for the results of interest—the actual values associated with the t test. The difference between the means of the pretest and posttest groups is –1.2, which is negative since the posttest mean was subtracted from the pretest mean. And the exact probability that a t score of –2.449 was obtained by chance is .022—very unlikely. But we cannot yet reach a conclusion regarding the research hypothesis being supported. Read on.

Notice anything different between the results we have here and the results from the analysis done by hand in Formula 11.5? The difference in the SPSS output (Figure 11.4) is negative. But when we computed the value manually, it was positive. Know why? Because SPSS (believe it or not) cannot do a one-tailed test between means and always subtracts the second variable (in this case, the posttest scores) from the first variable (in this case, the pretest scores). When we did it by hand, we did it the other way around, consistent with the research hypothesis (see Formula 11.3). SPSS just does not support that type of analysis. So what do we do?

Well, we go back to the table we used in Chapter 10 and figure out if the results are significant. Using Table B2 in Appendix B, we find that for a one-tailed test, with 24 degrees of freedom at the .05 level of significance, the critical value for rejection of the null hypothesis is 1.71. So while SPSS will give us the specific t value, it will not give us the probability of that value for a one-tailed test. It does for two-tailed, but not for one-tailed. For that, we have to rely on our own skills and approximate it as we did here (or use a software program that can do one-tailed tests (see Chapter 16 for more about this).

Believe it or not, way back in the olden days, when your author and perhaps your instructor were graduate students, there were only huge mainframe computers and not a hint of such marvels as we have today on our desk tops. In other words, everything that was done in our statistics class was done only by hand. The great benefit of that is, first, it helps you to better understand the process. Second, should you be without a computer, you can still do the analysis. So if the computer does not spit out all of what you need, use some creativity. As long as you know the basic formula for the critical value and have the appropriate tables, you'll do fine.

SUMMARY

That's it for means. You've just learned how to compare data from independent (Chapter 10) and dependent (Chapter 11) groups, and now it's time to move on to another class of significance tests that deals with more than two groups (be they independent or dependent). This class of techniques, called analysis of variance, is very powerful and popular and will be a valuable tool in your war chest!

TIME TO PRACTICE

1. What is the difference between a test of independent means and a test of dependent means, and when is each appropriate?

2. For Chapter 11 Data Set 2, compute the *t* value manually and write a conclusion as to whether there was a change in tons of paper used as a function of the recycling program in 25 different districts. (Hint: before and after become the two levels of treatment). Test the hypothesis at the .01 level.

3. For Chapter 11 Data Set 3, compute the *t* value and write a conclusion whether there is a difference in satisfaction level between a group of families' use of service centers following a social service intervention. Do this exercise using SPSS, and report the exact probability of the outcome.

ANSWERS TO PRACTICE QUESTIONS

1. A *t* test for independent means tests two distinct groups of participants, each of whom is tested once. A *t* test for dependent means tests one group of participants, each of whom is tested twice.

2. The mean for before the recycling program was 34.44, and the mean for after was 34.84. There is an increase in recycling. Is the difference across the 25 districts significant? The obtained value is –.262, and with 24 degrees of freedom, the difference is not significant at the .01 level—the level at which the research hypothesis is being tested. Conclusion: The recycling program does not result in an increase in paper recycled.

3. There was a slight increase in level of satisfaction, from 6.37 to 7.60, resulting in a *t* value of –.495. This difference has an associated probability level of .626. It's unlikely that this difference was due to anything other than chance.

ANSWERS

Two Groups Too Many?

Try Analysis of Variance

Difficulty Scale ☺ (longer and harder than the others, but a very interesting and useful procedure—worth the work!)

What you'll learn about in this chapter

- What analysis of variance is and when it is appropriate to use
- How to compute and interpret the F statistic
- How to use SPSS to complete an analysis of variance

INTRODUCTION TO ANALYSIS OF VARIANCE

One of the upcoming fields in the area of psychology is the psychology of sports. While the field focuses mostly on enhancing performance, there are many aspects of sports that receive special attention. One aspect focuses on what psychological skills are necessary to be a successful athlete. With this question in mind, Marious Goudas, Yiannis Theodorakis, and Georgios Karamousalidis have tested the usefulness of the Athletic Coping Skills Inventory.

As part of their research, they used a simple analysis of variance (or ANOVA) to test the hypothesis that number of years of experience in sports is related to coping skill (or an athlete's score on the Athletic Coping Skills Inventory). ANOVA was used since more than two groups were being tested and these groups were compared on their average performance. In particular, Group 1 included athletes with 6 years of experience or less, Group 2 included athletes with 7 to 10 years of experience, and Group 3 included athletes with more than 10 years of experience.

The test statistic for ANOVA is the F test (named for R. A. Fisher, the creator of the statistic), and the results showed that $F_{(2, 110)} = 13.08, p < .01$. The means of the three groups did differ from one another in their score on the Peaking Under Pressure subscale of the test. In other words, any difference in test score is due to number of years of experience in athletics rather than some chance occurrence of scores.

Want to know more? Check out the original reference: Goudas, M., Theodorakis, Y., and Karamousalidis, G. (1998). Psychological skills in basketball: Preliminary study for development of a Greek form of the Athletic Coping Skills Inventory. *Perceptual and Motor Skills, 86,* 59-65.

The Path to Wisdom and Knowledge

Here's how you can use the flow chart shown in Figure 12.1 to select ANOVA as the appropriate test statistic. Follow along the highlighted sequence of steps.

1 We are testing for differences between scores of the different groups, in this case the difference between the peaking scores of athletes.

2 The athletes are not being tested more than once.

3 There are three groups (less than 6 years, 7-10 years, and more than 10 years of experience).

4 The appropriate test statistic is simple analysis of variance.

Different Flavors of ANOVA

ANOVA comes in many different flavors. The simplest kind, and the focus of this chapter, is the **simple analysis of variance,** where

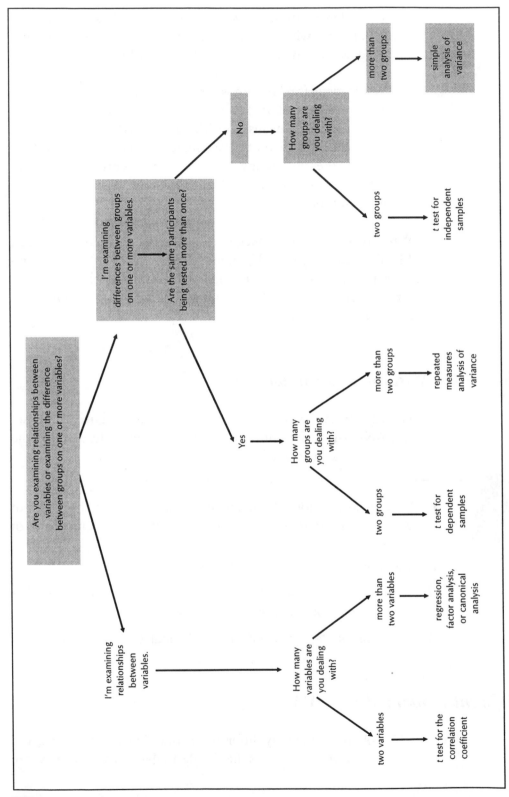

Figure 12.1. Determining That Analysis of Variance Is the Correct Test Statistic

there is one factor or one treatment variable (such as group membership) being explored and there are more than two groups within this factor. Simple ANOVA is also called **one-way analysis of variance** since there is only one grouping dimension. The technique is called **analysis of variance** because the variance due to differences in performance are separated into variance that's due to differences between individuals *within* groups and variance due to differences *between* groups. Then the two types of variance are compared with one another.

In fact, ANOVA is in many ways similar to a *t* test. In both procedures, differences between means are computed. But with ANOVA, there are more than two means.

For example, let's say we were investigating the effects on language development of being in preschool for 5, 10, or 20 hours per week. The group the children belong to is the treatment variable, or the grouping factor. Language development is the dependent variable, or the outcome. The experimental design looks something like this.

Group 1 (5 hours per week)	Group 2 (10 hours per week)	Group 3 (20 hours per week)
Language development test score	Language development test score	Language development test score

The more complex type of ANOVA is called a **factorial design,** where there is more than one treatment factor being explored. Here's an example where the effect of number of hours of preschool participation is being examined, but the effects of gender differences are being examined as well. The experimental design can look something like this.

	Number of Hours of Preschool Participation		
Gender	Group 1 (5 hours per week)	Group 2 (10 hours per week)	Group 3 (20 hours per week)
Male	Language development test score	Language development test score	Language development test score
Female	Language development test score	Language development test score	Language development test score

This factorial design is described as a 3×2 factorial design. The 3 indicates that there are three levels of one grouping factor (Group 1, Group 2, and Group 3). The 2 indicates that there are two levels of the other grouping factor (male and female). In combination, there are 6 different possibilities (males who spend 5 hours per week in preschool, females who spend 5 hours per week in preschool, males who spend 10 hours a week in preschool, etc.).

These factorial designs follow the same basic logic and principles of simple ANOVA, but they are just more ambitious in that they can test the influence of more than one factor at a time as well as a combination of factors.

COMPUTING THE TEST STATISTIC

Simple ANOVA involves testing the difference between the means of more than two groups on one factor or dimension. For example, you might want to know whether four groups of people (20, 25, 30, and 35 years of age) differ in their attitude toward public support of private schools. Or you might be interested in determining whether five groups of children from different grades (2nd, 4th, 6th, 8th, and 10th) differ in the level of parental participation in school activities.

Any analysis where

- there is only one dimension or treatment,
- there are more than two levels of the grouping factor, and
- one is looking at differences across groups in averages scores

requires that simple ANOVA be used.

The formula for the computation of the F value, which is the test statistic needed to evaluate the hypothesis that there are overall differences between groups, is shown in Formula 12.1. It is simple at this level, but it takes a bit more effort to compute than some of the other test statistics you have worked with in earlier chapters.

$$F = \frac{MS_{between}}{MS_{within}} \qquad (12.1)$$

TECH TALK

The logic behind this ratio goes something like this. If there was absolutely no variability within each group (all the scores were the same), then any difference between groups would be meaningful, right? Probably so. The ANOVA formula (which is a ratio) compares the amount of variability between groups (which is due to the grouping factor) to the amount of variability within groups (which is due to chance). If that ratio is 1, then the amount of variability due to within-group differences is equal to the amount of variability due to between-group differences, and any difference between groups would not be significant. As the average difference between groups gets larger (and the numerator of the ratio increases in value), the *F* value increases as well. As the *F* value increases, it becomes more extreme in relation to the distribution of all *F* values and is more likely due to something other than chance. Whew!

Here are some data and some preliminary calculations to illustrate how the *F* value is computed. For our example, let's assume these are three groups of preschoolers and their language scores.

Group 1 Scores	Group 2 Scores	Group 3 Scores
87	87	89
86	85	91
76	99	96
56	85	87
78	79	89
98	81	90
77	82	89
66	78	96
75	85	96
67	91	93

Here are the famous eight steps and the computation of the *F* test statistic.

1. *A statement of the null and research hypotheses.*

The null hypothesis, shown in Formula 12.2, states that there is no difference between the means for the three different groups. ANOVA, also called the F test (since it produces an F statistic or an F ratio), is also known as a robust test since all it looks for is an overall difference between groups.

It does not look at pairwise differences such as the difference between Group 1 and Group 2. For that, we have to use another technique, which we will discuss later in the chapter.

$$H_0: \mu_1 = \mu_2 = \mu_3 \qquad (12.2)$$

The research hypothesis, shown in Formula 12.3, states that there is an overall difference between the means of the three groups. Note that there is no direction to the difference as all F tests are nondirectional.

$$H_1: \overline{X}_1 \neq \overline{X}_2 \neq \overline{X}_3 \qquad (12.3)$$

Up to now, we've talked about one- and two-tailed tests. No such thing when talking about ANOVA. Since more than two groups are being tested, and since the F test is an omnibus (how's that for a word?) test (meaning that it tests for an overall difference between means), talking about the direction of specific differences does not make any sense.

2. *Setting the level of risk (or the level of significance or Type I error) associated with the null hypothesis.*

The level of risk or Type I error or level of significance (any other names?) is .05. Once again, the level of significance used is totally at the discretion of the researcher.

3. *Selection of the appropriate test statistic.*

Using the flow chart shown in Figure 12.1, we determined that the appropriate test is a simple ANOVA.

4. *Computation of the test statistic value (called the obtained value).*

Now's your chance to plug in values and do some computation. There's a good deal of computation to do.

- The *F* ratio is a ratio of variability between groups to variability within groups. To compute these values, we first have to compute what is called the sums of squares for each source of variability—between groups, within groups, and the total.
- The between-group sum of squares is equal to the sum of the differences between the mean of all scores and the mean of each group's score, which is then squared. This gives us an idea of how different each group's mean is from the overall mean.
- The within-group sum of squares is equal to the sum of the differences between each individual score in a group and the mean of each group, which is then squared. This gives us an idea how different each score in a group is from the mean of that group.
- The total sum of squares is equal to the sum of the between-group and within-group sum of squares. OK—let's figure these values.

Here are the practice data you saw above with all the calculations you need to compute the between-group, within-group, and total sum of squares.

First, let's look at what we have in this expanded table. Starting down the left of the table:

Group	Test Score	X^2	Group	Test Score	X^2	Group	Test Score	X^2
1	87	7,569	2	87	7,569	3	89	7,921
1	86	7,396	2	85	7,225	3	91	8,281
1	76	5,776	2	99	9,801	3	96	9,216
1	56	3,136	2	85	7,225	3	87	7,569
1	78	6,084	2	79	6,241	3	89	7,921
1	98	9,604	2	81	6,561	3	90	8,100
1	77	5,929	2	82	6,724	3	89	7,921
1	66	4,356	2	78	6,084	3	96	9,216
1	75	5,625	2	85	7,225	3	96	9,216
1	67	4,489	2	91	8,281	3	93	8,649
n	10			10		10		
ΣX	766			852			916	
$\overline{X}$	76.60			85.20			91.60	
$\Sigma(X^2)$	59,964			72,936			84,010	
$(\Sigma X)^2/n$	58,675.60			72,590.40			83,905.60	

$N = 30$

$\Sigma\Sigma X = 2,534$

$(\Sigma\Sigma X)^2/N = 214,038.53$

$\Sigma\Sigma(X^2) = 216,910.00$

$\Sigma(\Sigma X)^2/n = 215,171.60$

Figure 12.1.

n is the number of participants in each group (such as 10)

ΣX is the sum of the scores in each group (such as 766)

$\overline{X}$ is the mean of each group (such as 76.60)

$\Sigma(X^2)$ is the sum of each score squared (such as 59,964)

$(\Sigma X)^2/n$ is the sum of the scores in each group squared and then divided by the size of the group (such as 58,675.60)

Second, let's look at the right-most column:

N is the total number of participants (such as 30)

$\Sigma\Sigma X$ is the sum of all the scores across groups

$(\Sigma\Sigma X)^2/N$ is the sum of all the scores across groups squared divided by N

$\Sigma\Sigma(X^2)$ is the sum of all the sums of squared scores

$\Sigma(\Sigma X)^2/n)$ is the sum of the sum of each group's scores squared divided by n

That is a load of computation to carry out, and we are almost finished.

First, we compute the sum of scores for each source of variability. Here are the calculations:

Between sum of squares	$\Sigma(\Sigma X)^2/n - (\Sigma\Sigma X)^2/N$ or 215,171.60 – 214,038.53	= 1,133.07
Within sum of squares	$\Sigma\Sigma X^2 - \Sigma(\Sigma X)^2/n$ or 216,910 – 215,171.6	= 1,738.40
Total sum of squares	$\Sigma\Sigma X^2 - (\Sigma\Sigma X)^2/N$ or 216,910 – 214,038.53	= 2,871.47

Second, we need to compute the mean sum of squares, which is simply an average sum of squares. These are the variance estimates that we need to eventually compute the all-important F ratio.

We do that by dividing each sum of squares by the appropriate number of degrees of freedom (*df*). Remember, degrees of freedom are an approximation of the sample or group size. We need two sets of degrees of freedom for ANOVA. For the between-group estimate, it is $k - 1$, where k equals the number of groups (in this case there are 3 groups and 2 degrees of freedom), and for the within-group estimate, we need $n - k$, where n equals the total sample size (which means that the number of degrees of freedom is $30 - 3$, or 27). And the F ratio is simply a ratio of the mean sums of squares due to between-group differences over the mean sums of squares due to within-group differences, or $566.54/64.39 = 8.799$. This is the obtained F value.

Here's a summary table of the variance estimates used to compute the F ratio.

Source	Sums of Squares	df	Means Sums of Squares	F
Between groups	1,133.07	2	566.54	8.799
Within groups	1,738.40	27	64.39	
Total	2,871.47	29		

All that trouble for one little F ratio. But as we have said earlier, it's essential to do these procedures at least once by hand. It gives you the important appreciation of where the numbers come from and some insight into what they mean.

Since you already know about t tests, you might be wondering how a t value (which is always used for the test between the difference of the means for two groups) and an F value (which is always more than two groups) might be related. Interestingly enough, an F value for two groups is equal to a t value for two groups squared, or $F = t^2$. Handy trivia question, right? But also useful if you know one and need to know the other.

5. *Determination of the value needed for rejection of the null hypothesis using the appropriate table of critical values for the particular statistic.*

As we have done before, we have to compare the obtained and critical values. We now need to turn to the table that lists the critical values for the F test, Table B3 in Appendix B. Our first task is to determine the degrees of freedom for the numerator, which is $k - 1$, or $3 - 1 = 2$. Then determine the degrees of freedom for the denominator, which is $n - k$, or $30 - 3 = 27$. Together, they are represented as $F_{(2, 27)}$.

The obtained value is 8.80, or $F_{(2, 27)} = 8.80$. The critical value at the .05 level with 2 degrees of freedom in the numerator (represented by columns in Table B3) and 27 degrees of freedom in the denominator (represented by rows in Table B3) is 3.36. So at the .05 level, with 2 and 27 degrees of freedom for an omnibus test between the means of the three groups, the value needed for rejection of the null hypothesis is 3.36.

6. *A comparison of the obtained value and the critical value and a decision.*

The obtained value is 8.80, and the critical value for rejection of the null hypothesis at the .05 level that the three groups are different from one another (without concern for where the difference lies) is 3.36.

7. and 8. *Decision time.*

Now comes our decision. If the obtained value is more extreme than the critical value, the null hypothesis cannot be accepted. If the obtained value does not exceed the critical value, the null hypothesis is the most attractive explanation. In this case, the obtained value does exceed the critical value—it is extreme enough for us to say that the difference between the three groups is not due to chance. And if we did our experiment correctly, then what could the factor be that affected the outcome? Easy—the number of hours of preschool. We know the difference is due to a particular factor since the difference between the groups could not have occurred by chance, but instead is due to the treatment.

So How Do I Interpret $F_{(2, 27)} = 8.80$, $p < .05$?

- F represents the test statistic that was used
- 2, 27 are the numbers of degrees of freedom for the between-group and within-group estimates

- 8.80 is the obtained value using the formula we showed you earlier in the chapter
- $p < .05$ (the really important part of this little phrase) indicates that the probability is less than 5% on any one test of the null hypothesis that the average scores of each group's language skills differ. Since we defined .05 as our criterion for the research hypothesis being more attractive than the null hypothesis, our conclusion is that there is a significant difference between the three sets of scores.

TECH TALK

(Really Important) Tech Talk

Imagine this scenario. You're a high-powered researcher at an advertising company, and you want to see if color makes a difference in sales. And you'll test this at the .05 level. So you put together a brochure that is all black and white, one that is 25% color, the next 50%, then 75%, and finally, 100% color, for five different levels. You do an ANOVA and find out that there is a difference. But since ANOVA is an omnibus test, you don't know where the source of the significant difference lies. So you take two groups at time (such as 25% color and 75% color) and test them against each other. In fact, you test every combination of 2 against each other. Kosher? No way. This is called performing multiple *t* tests, and it is actually against the law in some jurisdictions.

When you do this, the Type I error rate (which you set at .05) balloons depending on the number of tests you want to conduct. There are 10 possible comparisons (no color vs. 25%, no color vs. 50%, no color vs. 75%, etc.), and the real Type I error rate is $1 - (1 - \alpha)^k$, where

α is the Type I error rate, which is .05 in this example

k is the number of tests

So, instead of .05, the actual error rate that each comparison is being tested at .22, or

$$1 - (1 - .05)^5 = .22$$

Quite a difference, no?

USING THE COMPUTER
TO COMPUTE THE F RATIO

The *F* ratio is not an easy value to compute by hand. That's all there is to it. Using the computer is much easier and more accurate because it eliminates any computational errors. That said, you should be glad you have seen the value computed manually since it's an important skill to have. But also be glad that there are tools such as SPSS.

We'll use the data found in Chapter 12 Data Set 1, which was used in the above preschool example.

1. Enter the data in the Data Editor. Be sure that there is a column for group and that you have three groups represented in that column. In Figure 12.2, you can see how the cell entries are labeled group and lang_sc.

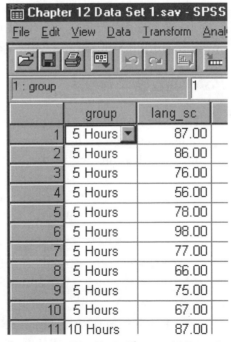

Figure 12.2. Data From Chapter 12 Data Set 1

2. Click Analyze → Compare Means → One-Way ANOVA and you will see the One-Way ANOVA dialog box shown in Figure 12.3.

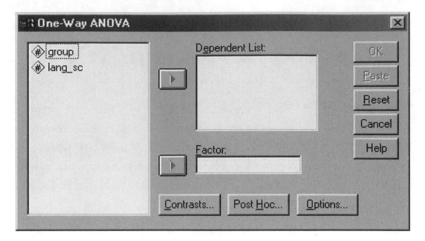

Figure 12.3. One-Way ANOVA Dialog Box

3. Click on the variable named group, and then click ▶ to move it to the Factor box.

4. Click on the variable named lang_sc, and then click ▶ to move it to the Dependent List box.

5. Click Options and then Descriptives and then Continue.

6. Click OK. SPSS will conduct the analysis and produce the output you see in Figure 12.4.

What the SPSS Output Means

This SPSS output is straightforward and looks just like the table that we created earlier to show you how to compute the F ratio along with some descriptive statistics. Here's what we have.

1. The source of the variance as between-group, within-group, and total is identified.

2. Next, we have the respective sum of squares for each source.

3. The degrees of freedom follow, then followed by the mean square, which is the sum of squares divided by the degrees of freedom.

4. Finally, there's the obtained value and the associated level of significance.

Keep in mind that this hypothesis was tested at the .05 level. The SPSS output provides the exact probability of the outcome, .001—much more accurate and much more unlikely than .05.

Descriptives

LANG_SC

	N	Mean	Std. Deviation	Std. Error	95% Confidence Interval for Mean		Minimum	Maximum
					Lower Bound	Upper Bound		
5 Hours	10	76.6000	11.9648	3.7836	68.0409	85.1591	56.00	98.00
10 Hours	10	85.2000	6.1968	1.9596	80.7671	89.6329	78.00	99.00
20 Hours	10	91.6000	3.4059	1.0770	89.1636	94.0364	87.00	96.00
Total	30	84.4667	9.9507	1.8167	80.7510	88.1823	56.00	99.00

ANOVA

LANG_SC

	Sum of Squares	df	Mean Square	F	Sig.
Between Groups	1133.067	2	566.533	8.799	.001
Within Groups	1738.400	27	64.385		
Total	2871.467	29			

Figure 12.4 SPSS Output for a One-Way Analysis of Variance

**TECH
TALK**

OK, so you've run an ANOVA and you know that there is an overall difference between the means of three or four or more groups. But where does that difference lie? You already know not to perform multiple *t* tests.

You need to perform what are called **post hoc,** or after-the-fact, comparisons. Here's where each mean is compared to each other mean and you can see where the difference lies, but what's most important is that the Type I error for each comparison is controlled at the same level as you set. There are a bunch of these different comparisons, among them being the Bonferroni (your dear author's favorite statistical term). To complete this specific analysis using SPSS, you click the Post Hoc option you see in the ANOVA dialog box (Figure 12.3), then click Bonferroni, then Continue, and so on, and you'll see output something like that shown in Figure 12.5.

It's really simple to see how this analysis tells you that the significant pairwise differences between the groups contributing to the overall significant difference between all three groups lies between Groups 1 and 3 and there is no pairwise difference between Groups 1 and 2 or Group 3. This pairwise stuff is very important since it allows you to understand the source of the difference between more than two groups.

SUMMARY

Analysis of variance (ANOVA) is the most complex of all the inferential tests you will learn in *Statistics for People Who (Think They) Hate Statistics*. It takes a good deal of concentration to perform the manual calculations, and even when you use SPSS, you have to be on your toes to understand this is an overall test and one part will not give you information about differences between pairs of treatments. If you chose to go on and do post hoc analysis, you're really completing all the tasks that go along with the powerful tool. Now that we are done, done, done with testing differences between means, we'll move on to examine the significance of correlations, or the relationship between two variables.

Multiple Comparisons

Dependent Variable: LANG_SC

Bonferroni

(I) GROUP	(J) GROUP	Mean Difference (I-J)	Std. Error	Sig.	95% Confidence Interval	
					Lower Bound	Upper Bound
5 Hours	10 Hours	-8.6000	3.5885	.071	-17.7594	.5594
	20 Hours	-15.0000*	3.5885	.001	-24.1594	-5.8406
10 Hours	5 Hours	8.6000	3.5885	.071	-.5594	17.7594
	20 Hours	-6.4000	3.5885	.257	-15.5594	2.7594
20 Hours	5 Hours	15.0000*	3.5885	.001	5.8406	24.1594
	10 Hours	6.4000	3.5885	.257	-2.7594	15.5594

* The mean difference is significant at the .05 level.

Figure 12.5. Post Hoc Comparisons After a One-Way ANOVA

TIME TO PRACTICE

1. Using the following table, provide three examples of a simple one-way ANOVA, two examples of a two-factor ANOVA, and one example of a three-factor ANOVA. We show you some examples. Be sure to identify the grouping and the test variable as we have done here.

Design	Grouping Variable(s)	Test Variable
Simple ANOVA	Three levels of hours of training— 2, 4, 6, and 8 hours	Typing accuracy
	Enter Your Example Here	Enter Your Example Here
	Enter Your Example Here	Enter Your Example Here
	Enter Your Example Here	Enter Your Example Here
Two-factor ANOVA	Two levels of training and gender (2 × 2 design)	Typing accuracy
	Enter Your Example Here	Enter Your Example Here
	Enter Your Example Here	Enter Your Example Here
Three-factor ANOVA	Two levels of training and two of gender and three of income	Voting attitudes
	Enter Your Example Here	Enter Your Example Here

2. Using the data in Chapter 12 Data Set 2 and SPSS, compute the *F* ratio for a comparison between the three levels representing the average amount of time that swimmers practice weekly (<15, 15-25, and >25) and the outcome is their time for the 100-yard freestyle. Answer the question whether practice time makes a difference. Don't forget to use the Options feature to get the means for the groups.

ANSWERS TO PRACTICE QUESTIONS

1.

Design	Grouping Variable(s)	Test Variable
Simple ANOVA	Three levels of hours of training—2, 4, 6, and 8 hours	Typing accuracy
	Four age groups—20, 25, and 30-year-olds	Strength
	Six levels of job types	Job performance
Two-factor ANOVA	Two levels of training and gender (2 × 2 design)	Typing accuracy
	Three levels of age (5, 10, and 15 years	Social skills
Three-factor ANOVA	Curriculum type (Type 1 or Type 2)	year in school (junior high or high school)

2. The means for the three groups are 58.05 seconds, 57.96 seconds, and 59.03 seconds and the probability of this F value ($F_{2, 33}$ = .160) occurring by chance is .853, far above what we would expect due to the treatment. Our conclusion? The number of hours of practice makes no difference in how fast you swim!

13 Cousins or Just Good Friends?

Testing Relationships Using the Correlation Coefficient

Difficulty Scale ☺☺☺☺ (easy—you don't even have to figure anything out!)

INTRODUCTION TO TESTING THE CORRELATION COEFFICIENT

In his research article on the relationship between the quality of a marriage and the quality of the relationship between the parent and the child, Daniel Shek tells us that there are at least two possibilities. First, a poor marriage might enhance parent-child relationships. This is because parents who are dissatisfied with their marriage would substitute their relationship with their children for emotional gratification. Or, according to the spillover hypothesis, a poor marriage might damage the parent-child relationship. This is because a poor marriage might set the stage for increased difficulty in parenting children.

Shek examined the link between marital quality and parent-child relationships in 378 Chinese married couples over a two-year period. He found that higher levels of marital quality are related to higher levels of parent-child relationships. And this was found for concurrent measures (at the present time) as well as longitudinal measures (when the relationships are looked at over time). He also found that the strength of the relationship between parents and children was the same for both mother and fathers. This is an obvious example of how the use of the correlation coefficient gives us the information we need about whether sets of variables are related to one another. Shek computed a whole bunch of different correlations across mothers and fathers as well at Time 1 and Time 2, but all with the same purpose: to see if there was a significant correlation between the variables. Remember that this does not say anything about the causal nature of the relationship, but only that they are associated with one another.

Want to know more? Check out Shek, D. T. L. (1998). Linkage between marital quality and parent-child relationship. *Journal of Family Issues, 19,* 687-704.

The Path to Wisdom and Knowledge

Here's how you can use the flow chart to select the appropriate test statistic, the test for the correlation coefficient. Follow along the highlighted sequence of steps in Figure 13.1.

1 The relationship between variables, and not the difference between groups, is being examined.

2 Only two variables are being used.

3 The appropriate test statistic to use is the *t* test for the correlation coefficient.

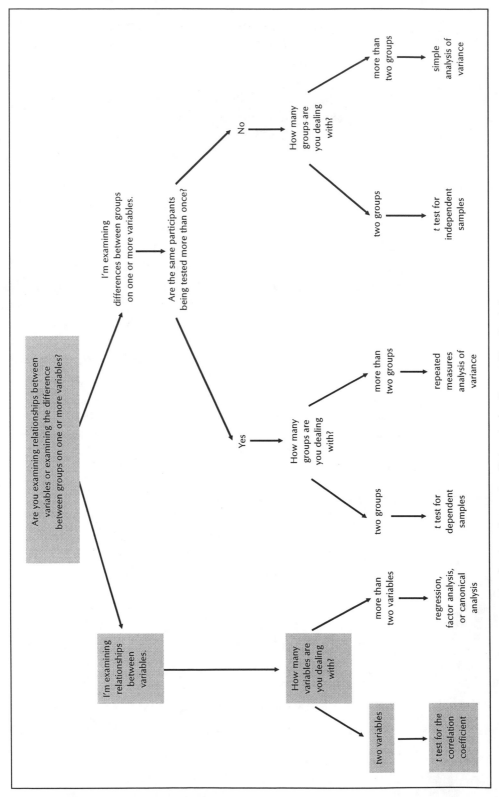

Figure 13.1. Determing That a *t* Test for the Correlation Coefficient is the Correct Test Statistic

COMPUTING THE TEST STATISTIC

Here's something you'll probably be pleased to read: The correlation coefficient can act as its own test statistic. This makes things much easier since you don't have to compute any test statistics, and examining the significance is very easy indeed.

Let's use, as an example, the following data that examine the relationship between two variables, the quality of marriage and the quality of parent-child relationships.

Quality of Marriage	Quality of the Parent-Child Relationship
76	43
81	33
78	23
76	34
76	31
78	51
76	56
78	43
98	44
88	45
76	32
66	33
44	28
67	39
65	31
59	38
87	21
77	27
79	43
85	46
68	41
76	41
77	48
98	56
99	55
98	45
87	68
67	54
78	33

You can use the sample formula from Chapter 5 to compute the Pearson correlation coefficient. When you do, you will find that $r = .393$. Now let's go through the steps of actually testing the value for significance and making a decision as to what the value means.

Here are the famous eight steps and the computation of the t test statistic.

1. *A statement of the null and research hypotheses.*

The null hypothesis states that there is no relationship between the quality of the marriage and the quality of the relationship between parents and children. The research hypothesis is a two-tailed, nondirectional research hypothesis since it posits that there is a relationship between the two variables, but the direction is not important. Remember that correlations can be positive (or direct) or negative (or indirect), and the most important characteristics of a correlation coefficient is its size and not its sign (positive or negative).

The null hypothesis is shown in Formula 13.1.

$$H_0: \rho_{xy} = 0 \qquad (13.1)$$

The Greek letter ρ, or rho, represents the population estimate of the correlation coefficient.

The research hypothesis (shown in Formula 13.2) states that there is a relationship between the two values and that the relationship differs from a value of 0.

$$H_1: r_{xy} \neq 0 \qquad (13.2)$$

One tail or two? It's pretty easy to conceptualize what a one-tailed versus a two-tailed test is when it comes to differences between means. And it may even be easy for you to understand a two-tailed test of the correlation coefficient (where any difference from zero is what's tested). But what about a one-tailed test? It's really just as easy. A directional

test of the research hypothesis that there is a relationship posits that relationship as being either direct (positive) or indirect (negative). So if you think that there is a positive correlation between two variables, then the test is one tailed. Similarly, if you think there is a negative correlation between two variables, the test is one tailed as well. It's only when you don't predict the direction of the relationship that the test is two tailed. Got it?

2. *Setting the level of risk (or the level of significance or Type I error) associated with the null hypothesis.*

The level of risk or Type I error or level of significance is .05.

3. and 4. *Selection of the appropriate test statistic.*

Using the flow chart shown in Figure 13.1, we determined that the appropriate test is for the correlation coefficient. In this instance, we do not need to compute a test statistic since the sample r value ($r_{xy} = .393$) is itself the test statistic.

5. *Determination of the value needed for rejection of the null hypothesis using the appropriate table of critical values for the particular statistic.*

Table B4 lists the critical values for the correlation coefficient.

Our first task is to determine the degrees of freedom (df), which approximates the sample size. For this particular test statistic, the degrees of freedom are $n - 2$, or $29 - 2 = 27$, where n is equal to the number of pairs used to compute the correlation coefficient. These are the degrees of freedom only for this test statistic and not necessarily for any other.

Using this number (27), the level of risk you are willing to take (.05), and a two-tailed test (since there is no direction to the research hypothesis), the critical value is .349 (using $df = 30$ since it's closest). So at the .05 level, with 28 degrees of freedom for a two-tailed test, the value needed for rejection of the null hypothesis is .349.

TECH TALK

OK, we cheated a little. Actually, you can compute a t value (just like for the test for the difference between means) for the significance of the correlation coefficient. The formula is not any more difficult than any you have dealt with up to now, but you won't see it here. The point is that some smart statisticians have computed the critical r value for different sample sizes (and likewise degrees of freedom) for one- and two-tailed tests at different levels of risk (.01, .05) as you see in Table B4. So if you are reading along in your journal and see that a correlation was tested using a t value, you'll now know why.

6. *A comparison of the obtained value and the critical value and a decision.*

The obtained value is .393, and the critical value for rejection of the null hypothesis that the two variables are not related is .349.

7. and 8. *Making a decision.*

Now comes our decision. If the obtained value (or the value of the test statistic) is more extreme than the critical value (or the tabled value), the null hypothesis cannot be accepted. If the obtained value does not exceed the critical value, the null hypothesis is the most attractive explanation.

In this case, the obtained value (.393) does exceed the critical value (.349)—it is extreme enough for us to say that the relationship between the two variables (quality of marriage and quality of parent-child relationships) did occur by something other than chance.

So How Do I Interpret $r_{(28)} = .393, p < .05$?

- r represents the test statistic that was used
- 28 is the number of degrees of freedom
- .393 is the obtained value using the formula we showed you in Chapter 5

- $p < .05$ (the really important part of this little phrase) indicates that the probability is less than 5% on any one test of the null hypothesis that the relationship between the two variables is due to chance alone. Since we defined .05 as our criterion for the research hypothesis being more attractive than the null hypothesis, our conclusion is that there is a significant relationship between the two variables. This means that as the level of marital quality increases, so does the level of quality of the parent-child relationship. Similarly, as the level of marital quality decreases, so does the level of quality of the parent-child relationship.

Correlation coefficients are used for lots of different purposes, and you're likely to read about them in journal articles being used to estimate the reliability of a test. There are several different types of reliabilities that use correlation coefficients such as test-retest (the correlation of scores at two points in time), parallel forms (the correlation between scores on different forms), and internal consistency (the intercorrelation between items). But any way you slice it, they're all just correlations.

Causes and Associations (Again!)

You'd have thought that you heard enough of this already, but this is so important that we really can't emphasize it enough. So we'll emphasize it again. Just because two variables are related to one another (as in the above example), it has no bearing on whether one causes the other. In other words, having a terrific marriage of the highest quality in no way ensures that the parent-child relationship will be of a high quality as well. These two variables may be correlated because they share some traits that might make a person a good husband or wife and also a good parent (patience, understanding, willingness to sacrifice), but it's certainly possible to see how someone can be a good husband or wife and have a terrible relationship with his or her children.

Remember the crimes and ice cream example from Chapter 5? It's the same here. Just because things are related and share something in common with one another has no bearing on whether there is a causal relationship between the two.

Significance Versus Meaningfulness (Again, Again!)

In Chapter 5, we reviewed the importance of the use of the coefficient of determination for understanding the meaningfulness of the correlation coefficient. You may remember that you square the correlation coefficient to determine the amount of variance accounted for by one variable in another variable. In Chapter 9, we also went over the general issue of significance versus meaningfulness.

But we should mention and discuss this topic again. Even if a correlation coefficient is significant (as was the case in the example in this chapter), it does not mean that the amount of variance accounted for is meaningful. For example, in this case, the coefficient of determination for a simple Pearson correlation value of .393 is equal to .154, indicating that 15.4% of the variance is accounted for and a whopping 84.6% of the variance is not. It leaves lots of room for doubt, doesn't it?

So, even though we know that there is a positive relationship between the quality of a marriage and the quality of a parent-child relationship and they tend to "go" together, the relatively small correlation of .393 indicates that there are lots of other things going on in that relationship that may be important as well. So if ever you wanted to apply a popular saying to statistics, "what you see is not always what you get."

USING THE COMPUTER TO COMPUTE A CORRELATION COEFFICIENT (AGAIN)

We did this once in Chapter 5, but we'll do it again here. We are using the data set named Chapter 13 Data Set 1, which was used in the example shown earlier in the chapter.

1. Enter the data in the Data Editor. Be sure you have two columns, each for a different variable. In Figure 13.2, you can see that the columns were labeled qual_mar (for Quality of Marriage) and qual_pc (Quality of Parent-Child Relationship).

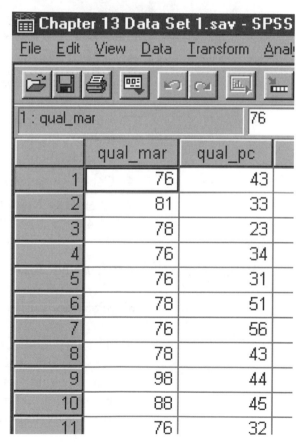

Figure 13.2. Chapter 13 Data Set 1

2. Click Analyze → Correlate → Bivariate, and you will see the Bivariate Correlations dialog box as shown in Figure 13.3.

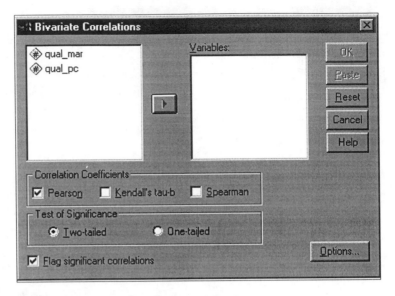

Figure 13.3. Bivariate Correlations Dialog Box

3. Double-click on the variable named qual_mar to move it to the Variable(s) box. Double-click on the variable named qual_pc to move it to the Variable(s) box.

4. Click Two-tailed for a two-tailed test.

5. Click OK. The SPSS output is shown in Figure 13.4.

What the SPSS Output Means

This SPSS output is simple and straightforward.

1. The correlation between the two variables of interest is .393, which is significant at the .05 level, but to be (much) more precise, the probability of committing a Type I error is .035. That means that the likelihood of rejecting the null when true (that the two variables are not related) is about 3.5%—not bad odds.

Correlations

Correlations

		QUAL_MAR	QUAL_PC
QUAL_MAR	Pearson Correlation	1.000	.393*
	Sig. (2-tailed)	.	.035
	N	29	29
QUAL_PC	Pearson Correlation	.393*	1.000
	Sig. (2-tailed)	.035	.
	N	29	29

*. Correlation is significant at the 0.05 level (2-tailed).

Figure 13.4. SPSS Output for Testing the Significance of the Correlation Coefficient

SUMMARY

Correlations are powerful tools that point out the direction of a relationship and help us to better understand what two different outcomes share with one another. Remember that correlations only work when you are talking about associations and never work when you are talking about causal effects.

TIME TO PRACTICE

1. Given the following information, use Table B4 in Appendix B to determine whether the correlations are significant and how you would interpret the results.

   a. The correlation between speed and strength for 20 women is .567. Test these results at the .01 hypothesis using a one-tailed test.

   b. The correlation between the number correct on a math test and the time it takes to complete the test is −.45. Test whether this correlation is significant for 80 children at the .05 level of significance. Choose either a one- or two-tailed test and justify your choice.

   c. The correlation between number of friends and grade point average (GPA) for 50 adolescents is .37. Is this significant at the .05 level for a two-tailed test?

2. Use the data in Chapter 13 Data Set 2 to answer the questions below. Do the analysis manually or using SPSS.

   a. Compute the correlation between motivation and GPA.

   b. Test for the significance of the correlation coefficient at the .05 level using a two-tailed test.

   c. True or false? The more highly you are motivated, the more you will study. Which did you select and why?

3. Discuss the general idea that just because two things are correlated, it does not mean that one causes the other. Provide an example (other than ice cream and crime!).

ANSWERS TO PRACTICE QUESTIONS

1. a. With 18 degrees of freedom ($df = n - 2$) at the .01 level, the critical value for rejection of the null hypothesis is .516. There is a significant correlation between speed and strength, and the correlation accounts for 32.15% of the variance.

   b. With 78 degrees freedom at the .05 level, the critical value for rejection of the null hypothesis is .183 for a one-tailed test. There is a significant correlation between number correct and time. A one-tailed test was used since the research hypothesis was that the relationship was indirect or negative, and approximately 20% of the variance is accounted for.

   c. With 48 degrees freedom at the .05 level, the critical value for rejection of the null hypothesis is .273 for a two-tailed test. There is a significant correlation between number of friends a child might have and GPA, and the correlation accounts for 13.69% of the variance.

2. a. and b. We used SPSS to compute the correlation as .434, significant at the .017 level using a two-tailed test. Figure 13.5 shows the final output from the analysis.

   c. True. The more motivated you are, the more you will study; and the more you study, the more you are motivated. But (and this is a bit "but") studying more does not cause you to be more highly motivated, nor does being more highly motivated cause you to study more.

Correlations

Correlations

		MOTIV	GPA
MOTIV	Pearson Correlation	1.000	.434*
	Sig. (2-tailed)	.	.017
	N	30	30
GPA	Pearson Correlation	.434*	1.000
	Sig. (2-tailed)	.017	.
	N	30	30

*. Correlation is significant at the 0.05 level (2-tailed).

Figure 13.5 SPSS Output for Chapter 13 Data Set 2

3. The example here is simply number of hours you study and your performance on your first test in statistics. These variables are not causally related. For example, you will have classmates who studied for hours and did poorly because they never understood the material, and classmates who did very well without any studying at all because they had some of the same material in another class. Just imagine if we forced someone to stay at his or her desk and study for 10 hours each of four nights before the exam. Would that ensure that he or she would get a good grade? Of course not. Just because they are related does not mean that one causes the other.

14 What to Do When You're Not Normal

Chi-Square and Some Other Nonparametric Tests

Difficulty Scale ☺☺☺☺ (easy)

What you'll learn about in this chapter

- A brief survey of nonparametric statistics and when and how they should be used

INTRODUCTION TO NONPARAMETRIC STATISTICS

Almost every statistical test that we've covered so far in *Statistics for People Who (Think They) Hate Statistics* assumes that the data set you are working with has certain characteristics. For example, one assumption underlying a *t* test between means (be the means independent or dependent) is that the variances of each group are homogeneous or similar. And the assumptions can be tested. Another assumption of many **parametric statistics** is that the sample is large enough to represent the population. Statisticians have found that it takes a sample size of about 30 to fulfill this assumption. Many of the statistical tests we covered so far are also robust, or powerful enough so that even if one of these assumptions is violated, the test is still valid.

But what do you do when the assumptions may be violated? The original research questions are certainly still worth asking and answering. That's when we use **nonparametric statistics** (also called distribution-free statistics). These tests don't follow the same "rules" (meaning they don't require the same assumptions as the parametric tests we've reviewed), but the nonparametrics are just as valuable. The use of nonparametric tests also allows us to analyze data that come as frequencies such as the number of children in different grades or the percentage of people receiving social security.

For example, if we wanted to know whether the number of people who voted for the school voucher in the most recent election is what we would expect by chance, or if there was really a pattern of preference, we would then use a nonparametric technique called chi-square.

In this chapter, we will cover chi-square, one of the most commonly used nonparametric tests, and provide a brief review of some others just so you can become familiar with some of the nonparametric tests that are available.

INTRODUCTION TO ONE-SAMPLE CHI-SQUARE

Chi-square is an interesting nonparametric test that allows you to determine if what you observe in a distribution of frequencies would be what you would expect to occur by chance. A one-sample chi-square includes only one dimension, such as the example you'll see here. A two-sample chi-square includes two dimensions, such as whether preference for the school voucher is independent of political party affiliation and gender.

For example, here are data from a sample selected at random from the 1990 census data collected in Sonoma County, California. As you can see, the table organizes information about level of education.

	Level of Education		
No College	Some College	College Degree	Total
25	42	17	84

The question of interest here is whether the number of respondents is equally distributed across all levels of education. To answer this question, the chi-square value was computed and then tested for significance. In this example, the chi-square value is equal to 11.643, which is significant beyond the .05 level. The conclusion is that the number of respondents at the various levels of education for this sample is not equally distributed. In other words, it's not what we would expect by chance.

The rationale behind the one-sample chi-square test is that in any set of occurrences, you can easily compute what you would expect by chance. You do this by dividing the total number of occurrences by the number of classes or categories. In our census example above, the observed total number of occurrences was 84. We would expect that by chance 84/3, or 28, respondents would fall into each of the three categories of level of education.

Then we look at how different what we expect by chance is from what we observe. If there is no difference between what we expect and what we observe, the chi-square value would be equal to zero.

Let's look more closely at how the chi-square value is computed.

COMPUTING THE CHI-SQUARE TEST STATISTIC

The chi-square test involves a comparison between what is observed and what would be expected by chance. The formula for computing the chi-square value for a one-sample chi-square test is shown in Formula 14.1.

$$\chi^2 = \Sigma \frac{(O - E)^2}{E} \qquad\qquad (14.1)$$

where

χ^2 is the chi-square value

Σ is the summation sign

O is the observed frequency

E is the expected frequency

Here are some data we'll use to compute the chi-square value.

Preference for School Voucher			
For	Maybe	Against	Total
23	17	50	90

Here are the famous eight steps to test this statistic.

1. *A statement of the null and research hypotheses.*

The null hypothesis shown in Formula 14.2 states that there is no difference in the frequency or the proportion of occurrences in each category.

$$H_0: P_1 = P_2 = P_3 \qquad\qquad (14.2)$$

The P in the null hypothesis represents the percentage of occurrences in any one category. This null hypothesis states that the percentage of cases in Category 1, Category 2, and Category 3 are equal. We are using only three categories, but the number could be extended as the situation fits as long as each of the categories is mutually exclusive, meaning that any one observation cannot be in more than one category. For example, you can't be both male and female, and so forth.

The research hypothesis shown in Formula 14.3 states that there is a difference in the frequency or proposition of occurrences in each category.

$$H_1: P_1 \neq P_2 \neq P_3 \qquad\qquad (14.3)$$

2. *Setting the level of risk (or the level of significance or Type I error) associated with the null hypothesis.*

The Type I error rate is set at .05.

3. *Selection of the appropriate test statistic.*

Any test between frequencies or proportions of mutually exclusive categories (such as For, Maybe, and Against) requires the use of chi-square. The flow chart we have used all along to select the type of statistical test to use is not applicable to nonparametric procedures.

4. *Computation of the test statistic value (called the obtained value).*

Let's go back to our voucher data from our earlier example and construct a worksheet that will help us compute the chi-square value.

Category	O (observed frequency)	E (expected frequency)	D (difference)	$(O-E)^2$	$(O-E)^2/E$
For	23	30	7	49	1.63
Maybe	17	30	13	169	5.63
Against	50	30	20	400	13.33
Total	90	90			

Here are the steps we took to prepare this worksheet.

1 Enter the categories (Category) of For, Maybe, and Against. Remember that these three categories are mutually exclusive. You can be in only one at a time.

2 Enter the observed frequency (O), which reflects the data that were collected.

3 Enter the expected frequency (E), which is the total of the observed frequency (90) divided by the number of categories (3), or 90/3 = 30.

4 For each cell, subtract the expected frequency from the observed frequency (D). It does not matter which is subtracted from the other since these values are squared in the next step.

5 Square the observed minus the expected value. You can see these values in the column named $(O - E)^2$.

6 Divide the difference between the observed and the expected frequencies that have been squared by the expected frequency. You can see these values in the column marked $(O - E)^2/E$.

7 Sum up this last column, and you have the total chi-square value of 20.6.

---

5. Determination of the value needed for rejection of the null hypothesis using the appropriate table of critical values for the particular statistic.

Here's where we go Table B5 for the list of critical values for the chi-square test.

Our first task is to determine the degrees of freedom (*df*), which approximates the number of categories in which data have been organized. For this particular test statistic, the degrees of freedom are $R - 1$, where R equals rows, or $3 - 1 = 2$.

Using this number (2) and the level of risk you are willing to take (earlier defined as .05), you can use the chi-square table to look up what the critical value is. It is 5.99. So at the .05 level, with 2 degrees of freedom, the value needed for rejection of the null hypothesis is 5.99.

6. A comparison of the obtained value and the critical value and a decision.

The obtained value is 20.6, and the critical value for rejection of the null hypothesis that the frequency of occurrences in Groups 1, 2, and 3 are equal is 5.99. Now comes our decision. If the obtained value is more extreme than the critical value, the null hypothesis cannot be accepted. If the obtained value does not exceed the critical value, the null hypothesis is the most attractive explanation.

7. and 8. *Decision time!*

In this case, the obtained value exceeds the critical value—it is extreme enough for us to say that the distribution of respondents across the three groups is not equal. Indeed, there is a difference in the number of people voting for, maybe, or against when it comes to preference for the school voucher.

TECH TALK

A commonly used name for the one-sample chi-square test is goodness of fit. This name suggests the question of how well a set of data "fits" an existing set. The "set" of data is, of course, what you observe. The "fit" part suggests that there is another set of data to which the observed set can be matched. This standard is the set of expected frequencies that are calculated in the course of computing the χ^2 value. If the observed data fit, it's just too close to what you would expect by chance and does not differ significantly. If the observed data do not fit, then what you observed is different from what you would expect.

So How Do I Interpret $\chi^2_{(2)} = 20.6$, $p < .05$?

- χ^2 represents the test statistic
- 2 is the number of degrees of freedom
- 20.6 is the obtained value using the formula we showed you earlier in the chapter
- $p < .05$ (the really important part of this little phrase) indicates that the probability is less than 5% on any one test of the null hypothesis that the frequency of votes is equally distributed across all categories. Since we defined .05 as our criterion for the research hypothesis being more attractive than the null hy-

pothesis, our conclusion is that there is a significant difference between the two sets of scores.

USING THE COMPUTER TO PERFORM A CHI-SQUARE TEST

Here's how to perform a simple, one-sample chi-square test using SPSS. We are using the data set named Chapter 14 Data Set 1, which was used in the school voucher example.

1. Open the data set. For a one-sample chi-square test, you need only enter the number of occurrences into each column, using a different value for each possible outcome. In this example, there would be a total of 90 data points in column 1; 23 would be entered as 1s (or For), 17 would be entered as 2s (or Maybe), and 50 would be entered as 3s (or Against).

2. Click Analyze → Nonparametric Tests → Chi-Square, and you will see the dialog box shown in Figure 14.1.

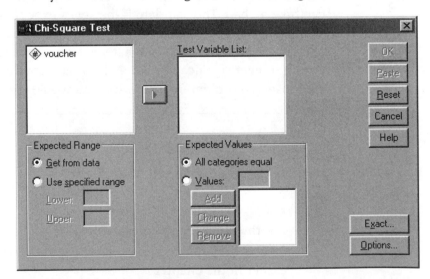

Figure 14.1. Chi-Square Test Dialog Box

3. Double-click on the variable named voucher.

4. Click OK. SPSS will conduct the analysis and produce the output you see in Figure 14.2.

NPar Tests

Chi-Square Test

Frequencies

SCH_BOND

	Observed N	Expected N	Residual
1.00	23	30.0	-7.0
2.00	17	30.0	-13.0
3.00	50	30.0	20.0
Total	90		

Test Statistics

	SCH_BOND
Chi-Square a	20.600
df	2
Asymp. Sig.	.000

a. 0 cells (.0%) have expected frequencies less than 5. The minimum expected cell frequency is 30.0.

Figure 14.2. SPSS Output for a Chi-Square Analysis

What the SPSS Output Means

The SPSS output for the chi-square test shows you exactly what we talked about earlier. We'll address only the output that is relevant our analysis.

1. The Categories 1 (For), 2 (Maybe), and 3 (Against) are listed along with their Observed N.

2. This is followed by the Expected N, which is this case is 90/3, or 30.

3. The chi-square value of 20.600 and degrees of freedom appear under the Test Statistics section of the output.

The exact level of significance is so small that SPSS computes it only as .000. A very unlikely outcome!

OTHER NONPARAMETRIC TESTS YOU SHOULD KNOW ABOUT

You may never need a nonparametric test to answer any of the research questions that you propose. On the other hand, you may very well find yourself dealing with samples that may be very small (or at least fewer than 30) or data that violate some of the important assumptions underlying parametric tests.

If that's the case, try nonparametrics on for size. Table 14.1 provides all you need to know about some other nonparametric tests including their name, what they are used for, and a research question that illustrates how each might be used. Keep in mind that the table represents only a few of the many different tests that are available.

SUMMARY

Chi-square is one of many different types of nonparametric statistics that help you answer questions based on data that violate the basic assumptions of the normal distribution or are just too small. These nonparametric tests are a very valuable tool, and even as limited an introduction as this will provide you with some assistance.

TABLE 14.1 Nonparametric Tests to Analyze Data in Categories and by Ranks

Test Name	When the Test Is Used	A Sample Research Question
To analyze data organized in categories		
McNemar test for significance of changes	To examine "before and after" changes	How effective is a phone call to undecided candidates on their voting for a particular issue?
Fisher's exact rest	Computes the exact probability of outcomes in a 2 × 2 table	What is the exact likelihood of getting six heads on a toss of six coins?
Chi-square one-sample test (just like we focused on earlier in this chapter)	To determine if the number of occurrences across categories is random	Did brands Fruities, Whammies, and Zippies each sell an equal number of units during the recent sale?
To analyze data organized by ranks		
Kolmogorov-Smirnov test	To see whether scores from a sample came from a specified population	How representative is a set of judgments of other children of the entire elementary school to which they go?
The sign test, or median test	Used to compare the medians from two samples	Is the median income of people who voted for Candidate A greater than the median income of people who voted for Candidate B?
Mann-Whitney U test	Used to compare two independent samples	Did the transfer of learning, measured by number correct, occur faster for Group A than for Group B?
Wilcoxon rank test	To compare the magnitude as well as the direction of differences between two groups	Is preschool twice as effective as no preschool experience for helping develop children's language skills?
Kruskal-Wallis one-way analysis of variance	Compares the overall difference between two or more independent samples	How do rankings of supervisors differ between four regional offices?
Friedman two-way analysis of variance	Compares the overall difference between two or more independent samples on more than one dimension	How do rankings of supervisors differ as a function of regional office and gender?
Spearman rank correlation coefficient	Computes the correlation between ranks	What is the correlation between rank in the senior year of high school and rank during the freshman year of college?

TIME TO PRACTICE

1. Using the following data, test the question that an equal number of Democrats, Republicans, and Independents voted during the last election. Test the hypothesis at the .05 level of significance. Do this by hand.

Political Affiliation		
Republican	Democrat	Independent
800	700	900

2. Using the following data, test the question that an equal number of boys and girls participate in soccer at the elementary level at the .01 level of significance. (The data are available as Chapter 14 Data Set 2.) Use SPSS or some other statistical program and compute the exact probability of the chi-square value. What's your conclusion?

Gender	
Boys	Girls
45	55

3. Of the following four research questions, which ones are appropriate for the chi-square test?

   a. The difference between the average scores of two math classes.

   b. The difference between the number of children who passed the math test in Class 1 and the number of children who passed the math test in Class 2.

   c. The number of cars that passed the CRASH Test this year versus last year.

   d. The speed with which a soccer player can run 100 yards compared to the speed of a football player.

ANSWERS TO PRACTICE QUESTIONS

1. Here's the worksheet for computing the chi-square value:

Category	O (observed frequency)	E (expected frequency)	D (difference)	$(O-E)^2$	$(O-E)^2/E$
Republican	800	800	0	0	0.00
Democrat	700	800	100	10,000	12.50
Independent	900	800	100	10,000	12.50

With 2 degrees of freedom at the .05 level, the critical value needed for rejection of the null hypothesis is 5.99. The obtained value of 25 allows us to reject the null and conclude that there is a significant difference in the numbers of people who voted as a function of political party.

2. Here's the worksheet for computing the chi-square value:

Category	O (observed frequency)	E (expected frequency)	D (difference)	$(O-E)^2$	$(O-E)^2/E$
Boys	45	50	5	25	0.50
Girls	55	50	5	25	0.50

With 1 degree of freedom at the .01 level of significance, the critical value needed for rejection of the null hypothesis is 6.64. The obtained value of 1.00 means that the null cannot be rejected and there is no difference between the number of boys and girls who play soccer.

3. Chi-square would be appropriate for Questions b and c since the data that are collected are categorical in nature. Questions a and d deal with data that are continuous (such as average scores and speed of running).

Some Other (Important) Statistical Procedures You Should Know About

Difficulty Scale ☺☺☺☺ (moderately easy—just an extension of what you already know)

What you'll learn about in this chapter

- An overview of more advanced statistical procedures and when and how they are used

Throughout *Statistics for People Who (Think They) Hate Statistics,* we covered only a small part of the whole body of statistics. We didn't have room, but more important, at the level at which you are beginning, it's important to keep things simple and direct.

However, that does not mean that in a research article you read or in some discussion in a class, you don't come across other analytical techniques that might be important for you to know about. So for your edification, here are seven of those techniques, what they do, and examples of studies that used the technique to answer a question.

MULTIVARIATE ANALYSIS OF VARIANCE

You won't be surprised to learn that there are many different renditions of analysis of variance (ANOVA), each one designed to fit a particular "more than two groups being compared" situation. One of these, multivariate analysis of variance (MANOVA), is used when there is more than one dependent variable. So instead of looking just at one outcome, more than one outcome or dependent variable is used. If the dependent or outcome variables are related to one another (which they usually are), it would be hard to determine clearly the effect of the treatment variable on any one outcome. Hence, MANOVA to the rescue.

For example, Jonathan Plucker from Indiana University examined gender, race, and grade differences in how gifted adolescents dealt with pressures at school. The MANOVA analysis that he used was a 2 (gender—male/female) × 4 (race—Caucasian, African American, Asian American, and Hispanic) × 5 (grade—8th through 12th) MANOVA. The *multivariate* part of the analysis was the five scales of the Adolescent Coping Scale. Using a multivariate technique, the effects of the independent variables (gender, race, and grade) can be estimated for each of the five scales, independent of one another.

Want to know more? Take a look at Plucker, J. A. (1998). Gender, race, and grade differences in gifted adolescents' coping strategies. *Journal for the Education of the Gifted, 21,* 423-436.

REPEATED MEASURES ANALYSIS OF VARIANCE

Here's another kind of analysis of variance. Repeated measures analysis of variance is very similar to analysis of variance where, if you recall (see Chapter 12), the means of two or more groups are tested for differences. In a repeated measures ANOVA, there is one factor on which participants are tested more than once.

For example, B. Lundy, T. Field, C. McBride, T. Field, and S. Largie examined same-sex and opposite-sex interaction with best friends using juniors and seniors in high school. One of their main analyses was ANOVA with three factors: gender (male or female), friendship (same-sex or opposite-sex), and year in high school (junior or senior year). The repeated measure is year in high school, since the measurement was repeated across the same subjects.

Want to know more? Take a look at Lundy, B., Field, T., McBride, C., Field, T., and Largie, S. (1998). Same-sex and opposite-sex best friend interactions among high school juniors and seniors. *Adolescence, 33,* 130, 280-289.

FACTOR ANALYSIS

Factor analysis is a technique based on how well various items are related to one another and form clusters or factors. Each factor represents several different variables, and factors turn out to be more efficient than individual variables to represent outcomes in certain studies. In using this technique, the goal is to represent those things that are related to one another by a more general name such as a factor.

For example, David Wolfe and his colleagues at the University of Western Ontario attempted to understand how experiences of maltreatment occurring before children were 12 years old affect peer and dating relationships during adolescence. To do this, the researchers collected data on many different variables and then looked at the relationship between all of them. Those that seemed to contain items that were related (and also belonged to a group that made theoretical sense) were deemed factors, such as the factor named Abuse/Blame in this study. Another factor was named Positive Communication and was made up of 10 different items, all of which were related to each other.

Want to know more? See Wolfe, D. A., Wekerle, C., Reitzel-Jaffe, D., and Lefebvre, L. (1968). Factors associated with abusive relationships among maltreated and non-maltreated youth. *Developmental Psychopathology, 10*, 61-85.

ANALYSIS OF COVARIANCE

Here's our last rendition of ANOVA. Analysis of covariance (ANCOVA) is particularly interesting since it basically allows you to equalize initial differences between groups. Let's say you are sponsoring a program to increase running speed and want to compare how fast two groups of athletes can run a 100-yard dash. Since strength is often related to speed, you have to make some correction so that strength does not account for any differences at the end of the program. Rather, you want to see the effects of training with strength removed. You would measure participants' strength before you started the training program and then use ANCOVA to adjust final speed based on initial strength.

Michaela Hynie, John Lyndon, and Ali Tardash from McGill University used ANCOVA in their investigation of the influence of intimacy and commitment on the acceptability of premarital sex and contraceptive use. They used ANCOVA with social acceptability as the dependent variable (in which they were looking for group differences) and ratings of a particular scenario as the covariate. ANCOVA would ensure that differences in social acceptability would be corrected using ratings, so this would be one difference that would be controlled.

Want to know more? See Hynie, M., Lyndon, J., and Tardash, A. (1997). Commitment, intimacy, and women's perceptions of premarital sex and contraceptive readiness. *Psychology of Women's Quarterly, 21*, 447-464.

MULTIPLE REGRESSION

You learned in Chapter 6 how the value of one variable can be used to predict the value of another. Often, social and behavioral sciences researchers look at how more than one variable can predict another. We touched on this in Chapter 6, and here's more about what is called multiple regression.

For example, it's fairly well established that parents' literacy behaviors (like having books in the home) are related to how much and how well their children read. So it would seem quite interesting to look at such variables as parents' age, educational level, literacy activities, and shared reading with children to see what they contribute to early language skills and interest in books. Paula Lyytinen, Marja-Leena Laakso, and Anna-Maija Poikkeus did exactly that and used stepwise regression analysis to examine the contribution of parental background variables to children's literacy. They found that mothers' literacy activities and mothers' level of education contributed significantly to children's language skills while mothers' age and shared reading did not.

Want to know more? Take a look at Lyytinen, P., Laakso, M. L., and Poikkeus, A. M. (1998). Parental contributions to child's early language and interest in books. *European Journal of Psychology of Education, 3*, 297-308.

PATH ANALYSIS

Here's another statistical technique that examines correlations but allows a bit of a suggestion as to the direction, or causality, in the relationship between factors. Path analysis basically examines the direction of relationships through the postulation of some theoretical relationship between variables and then a test to see if the direction of these relationships is substantiated by fact.

For example, A. Efklides, M. Papadaki, G. Papantonious, and G. Kiosseoglou examined individual feelings of difficulty experienced in the learning of mathematics. To do this, they administered several different types of tests (such as those in the area of cognitive ability) and found that feelings of difficulty are mainly influenced by cognitive (problem solving) rather than affective (emotional) factors. One of the most interesting uses of path analysis is that a technique called structural equation modeling is used to present the results in a graphical representation of the relationship between all the different factors under consideration. That way, you can actually see what relates to what and with what degree of strength. Then you can judge how well the data fit the model that was previously suggested. Cool.

Want to know more? Take a look at Efklides, A., Papadaki, M., Papantonious, G., and Kiosseoglou, G. (1998). Individual differences in feelings of difficulty: The case of school mathematics. *European Journal of Psychology of Education, 2, 207-226.*

INTERNAL CONSISTENCY

Internal consistency isn't an analytical technique—it's a goal that you might have when using an instrument to assess a particular outcome. It's a cousin to the correlation coefficient and mostly applies to testing or evaluation settings. You might develop a math test and you want the test to be internally consistent. This means that all the items on the test measure the same general phenomenon or outcome—which would be math in this situation. The internal consistency value is a correlation-like coefficient that you compute by comparing performance on each individual item with overall individual performance.

For example, researchers from Hadassah Medical School examined word association and psychosexual cues in their assessment of people with eating disorders. As part of their research, they used the Eating Attitudes Test, shown to have an internal consistency level (also called alpha or Cronbach's alpha) of .94, pretty high when you consider that the top of the range is 1.00.

Want to know more? See Berry, E. M., Kelly, D., Canetti, L., and Bachar, E. (1998). Word association test and psychological cues in assessing persons with eating disorders. *Perceptual and Motor Skills, 86,* 43-50.

SUMMARY

Just because you probably will not be using these more advanced procedures anytime soon, that's all the more reason to know at least something about them, since you will certainly see them mentioned in various research publications and may even hear them mentioned in another class you are taking. And combined with your understanding of the basics (all the chapters in the book up to this one), you can really be confident of having mastered a good deal of important information about basic (and even some intermediate) statistics.

16 A Statistical Software Sampler

Difficulty Scale ☺☺☺☺☺ (a cinch!)

What you'll learn about in this chapter

- All about other types of software that allow you to analyze, chart, and better understand your data

Y ou need not be a nerd or anything of the sort to appreciate and enjoy what the various computer programs can do for you in your efforts to learn and use basic statistics. The purpose of this chapter is to give you an overview of some of the more commonly used programs and some of their features and a quick look at how they work. But before we do go into these descriptions, here are some words of advice.

You can find a mega listing of software programs and links to the home pages of the companies that have created these programs at http://www.psychstat.smsu.edu/scripts/ dws148f/statisticsresourcesmain.asp. We couldn't possibly cover them all here, but you can at least look and see what you might find of interest.

SELECTING THE PERFECT
STATISTICS SOFTWARE

Here are some tried-and-true suggestions for making sure that you get what you want from a stat program.

1. Whether the software program is expensive (like SYSTAT) or not (like EcStatic), be sure you try it out before you buy it. Almost every one of the programs listed below has a demo that you can download, and in some cases you can even ask them to send you a demo version on disk or CD. These versions are often fully featured and last for up to 30 days, giving you plenty of time to try before you buy.

2. While we're mentioning price, buying it directly from the manufacturer might be the *most* expensive way to go. Rather, your school bookstore will certainly offer a discount, and a mail order company might have even a better deal. You can find these sellers' 800 phone numbers listed in any popular computer magazine.

3. Many of the vendors who produce statistical analysis software offer two flavors. The first is the commercial version and the second is the academic version. They are usually the same in content but may differ (sometimes dramatically) in price. If you are going for the academic version, be sure that it is the same as the fully featured commercial version, and if not, then ask yourself if you can live with the differences. Why is the academic version so much cheaper? The company hopes that if you are a student, when you graduate, you'll move into some fat-cat job and buy the full version!

4. It's hard to know exactly what you'll need before you get started, but some packages come in modules, and you don't have to buy all of them to get the tools you need for the job you have to do. Read the company's brochures and call and ask questions.

5. Shareware is another option, and there are plenty of such programs available. Shareware is a method of distributing software so you pay for it only if you like it. Sounds like the honor system, doesn't it? Well, it is. The prices are almost al-

ways very reasonable, often the shareware is better than the commercial product, and if you do pay, you help ensure that the clever author will continue his or her other efforts at delivering new versions that are even better than the one you have.

6. Don't buy any software that does not offer telephone technical support or, at the least, some type of email contact. To test this, call the tech support number (before you buy!) and see how long it takes for them to pick up the phone. If you're on hold for 20 minutes, that may indicate that they don't take tech support seriously enough to get to users' questions quickly. Or, if you email them and never hear back, look for another product.

7. Almost all the big stat packages do the same things—the difference is in the way that they do them. For example, SPSS, MiniTab, and JMP all do a nice job of analyzing data and are acceptable. But it's the little things that might make a difference. For example, MiniTab allows you to have more than one file open at once while SPSS does not. Go figure.

8. Make sure you have the hardware to run the program you want to use. For example, most software is not limited by the number of cases and variables you want to analyze. The only limit is usually the size of your hard drive, which you'll use to store the data files. And if you have a slow machine such as one with a 386 or a 486 processor and 8 or 16 megabytes of RAM (random access memory), then you're likely to be waiting around and watching that hourglass while your CPU does its thing. Be sure of the hardware you need to run a program before you download the demo.

WHAT'S OUT THERE

There are more statistical analysis programs available than you would ever need. Here's a listing of some of the most popular and their outstanding features. Remember that many of these do the same thing. If at all possible, as we emphasize in the preceding section, try before you buy.

JMP

JMP operates on Mac and Windows platforms and is billed as "statistical discovery software that can help you explore data, fit models, discover patterns, and discover points that don't fit patterns." One of the product's main selling points is that when graphics are used, discoveries and relationships between data are more likely to be revealed. With these discoveries, the results of your work are more easily understood.

One of JMP's features is to present a graph accompanying every statistic so you can always see the results of the analysis both as statistical text and as a graphic. And all this is done automatically without you requesting it.

Need more information? Try http://www.jmpdiscovery.com/ on the Internet.

Cost: $695 for the commercial version. The student version, named JMPIN, is $60 and is available from Duxberry Press, an ITP company.

Minitab

This is one of the first programs that was available for the personal computer and is now in Version 12, which means that it's seen its share of changes over the years in response to users' needs. Some of the more outstanding features of this new version are

- one file holds all the work created in a session, including data, results, graphs, and such;
- more than one worksheet can be open at the same time (an advantage over many other programs);
- graphs are OLE objects, which means they can be easily exported to other applications; and
- it includes Meet Minitab, an introductory book for beginners, plus many other features.

In Figure 16.1, you can see a sample of what Minitab output looks like for a correlation and a regression analysis—neat and nicely organized.

Regression Analysis

The regression equation is
Weight = - 205 + 5.09 Height

Predictor	Coef	StDev	T	P
Constant	-204.74	29.16	-7.02	0.000
Height	5.0918	0.4237	12.02	0.000

S = 14.79   R-Sq = 61.6%   R-Sq(adj) = 61.2%

Analysis of Variance

Source	DF	SS	MS	F	P
Regression	1	31592	31592	144.38	0.000
Residual Error	90	19692	219		
Total	91	51284			

Unusual Observations

Obs	Height	Weight	Fit	StDev Fit	Residual	St Resid
9	72.0	195.00	161.87	2.08	33.13	2.26R
25	61.0	140.00	105.86	3.62	34.14	2.38R
40	72.0	215.00	161.87	2.08	53.13	3.63R
84	68.0	110.00	141.50	1.57	-31.50	-2.14R

R denotes an observation with a large standardized residual

Figure 16.1. Sample Output From Minitab

Need more information? Try http://www.minitab.com/ on the Internet.

Cost: $975 for the commercial version and $295 for the academic version.

StatView

This statistical analysis program comes from people who bring you SAS and JMP (from the SAS Institute). StatView is a bit less ambitious than the monster SAS system, but still very comprehensive and designed for both the Mac and Windows operating systems.

StatView works like some other statistical software. It has two types of windows. In the dataset window you enter, manage, and transform data. In the view window you can analyze, examine results, and use the drawing tools to prepare a presentation. StatView offers several outstanding features such as its spreadsheet-like operation allowing for precise and powerful manipulation of data. For example, formulas are easy to create and are dynamic as well (when values change in the formula, so do connected cells).

In Figure 16.2, you can see numerous StatView windows and the spreadsheet-like data-entry system. There's also a sample correlation matrix that shows the correlation between the fat content and calories in candy bars (which is high—surprised?).

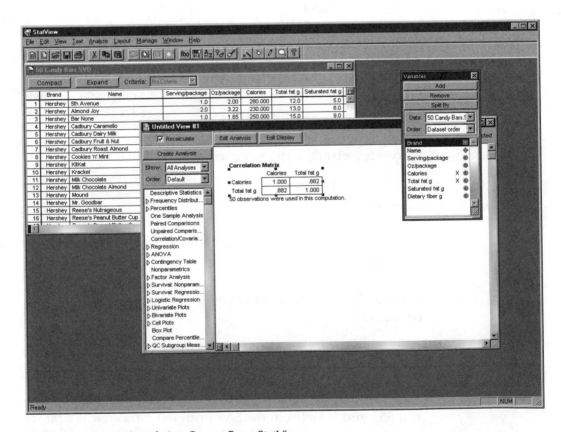

Figure 16.2. Some Correlation Output From StatView

Other nice features? Mac-Windows compatibility, lots of regression tools, and improved analysis of variance tools.

Need more information? Try http://www.sas.com/ on the Internet.

Cost: $695 for the commercial version and $350 for the academic version.

Statistica

StatSoft offers a collection of Statistica products for Windows as well as Statistica for the Mac. Some of the features that are particularly nice about this powerful program are the self-prompting dialog boxes (you click OK and Statistica tells you what to enter) and the ability to use macros to automate tasks. A nice bonus at the Web site is an Electronic Statistical Textbook, which you can download in its entirety (have patience since it can take up to 30 minutes depending on the speed of your Internet connection).

Need more information? Try http://www.statsoftinc.com/ on the Internet.

Cost: $995 for the commercial version and $200 for the academic version.

SPSS: Mac, Windows, MS-DOS, OS/2, UNIX, VMS, MVS-VM/CMS

SPSS may be the most popular big-time statistical package in use. It comes with a variety of different modules that cover all aspects of statistical analysis including both basic and advanced statistics, and a version exists for almost every platform.

One of the nicer new features included in Version 9 is that you can easily—with one mouse click—create a graph from any tabled data. Then you can use the Chart Editor to modify what you produced. Also featured is a powerful report writer. Figure 16.3 shows one such graph created with one right-click and the selection of the type of graph we wanted (in this case it was a line graph).

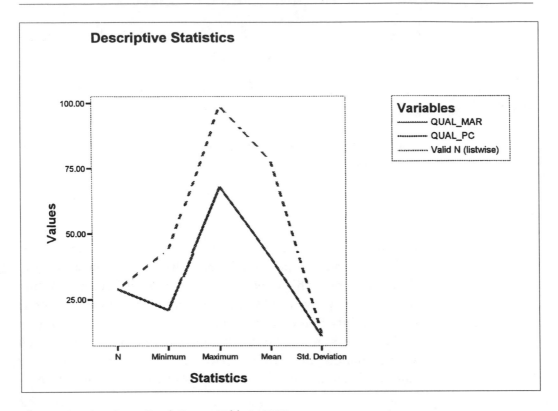

Figure 16.3. Creating a Graph From a Table in SPSS

Need more information? Try http://www.spss.com on the Internet.

Cost: $795 for the commercial version and $495 for the academic version.

SYSTAT

SYSTAT is also produced by the same company that offers SPSS and is just as powerful but tends to be used by researchers in biological and physical sciences, rather than social and behavioral sciences like SPSS. It's available for more operating systems than most other software packages, including DOS, Windows, OS/2, Mac, and Unix, and supports a strong command language so analysis can be fine-tuned to users' needs. The beginner can use this stuff, but it's more appropriate for the more advanced student or professional.

Need more information? Try http://www.spss.com/software/ science/systat/ on the Internet.

Cost: $1,299 for the commercial version and $799 for the academic version.

STATISTIX for Windows

STATISTIX is as powerful as the other programs described here but also offers publication-quality custom-titled and legend graphs that can be exported to bitmap, Postscript, and HPGL file formats. This is a big plus for those people interested in creating their own publications or reports based on STATISTIX output. Another nice feature is a 330-page (real paper, believe it or not) manual. And when you call technical support, you talk with the programmers, who should know what they're talking about. Figure 16.4 shows you some STATISTIX output from a one-tailed *t* test.

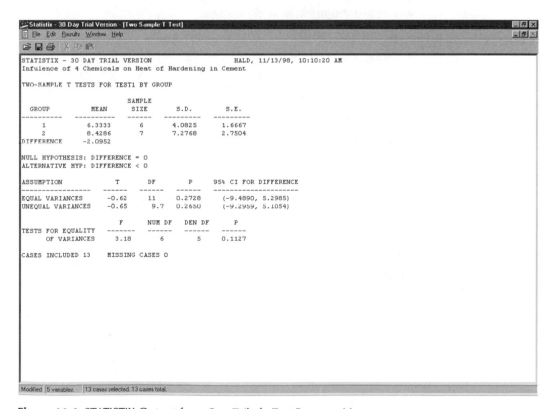

Figure 16.4. STATISTIX Output for a One-Tailed *t* Test Between Means

Need more information? Try http://www.sigma-research.com/ bookshelf/rtsxw.htm on the Internet.

Cost: $495 for the commercial version and $495 for the academic version.

EcStatic

Both the Windows and DOS versions of EcStatic are a steal for the money. They are by far the least expensive, and you certainly get much more than you pay for compared to the huge programs described above. And if you think that this program is missing anything, take a look at the following list of features it offers.

- Analysis of variance
- Breakdown
- Convert scores
- Correlation
- Cross-tabulation and chi-square
- Frequency distributions and histograms
- Nonparametric statistics
- Regression
- Scatterplot
- Summary statistics
- Transformations
- *t* test

Need more information? Try http://www.somewareinvt.com/ ecstatic.htm on the Internet.

Cost: $69.96, with a huge discount on 10 or more ($39.95)—tell your instructor!

AND THERE'S A LOT MORE . . .

What we described above are the so-called industry leaders. But that doesn't mean they are the best. There are literally hundreds of other programs available, some very powerful that do one thing very well and some that are more general. Here are some, with a brief description of what each does and how you can get in touch with the producer. Keep in mind that new software is being developed every day, so if you have an interest in this area, check with your teacher (and see our discussion in Chapter 17) to find out where to check for the most current information.

CoHort

This company produces a suite of helpful tools including CoPlot, which creates 2D and 3D scientific graphs; CoDraw, which helps you create publication-quality technical drawings; CoStat, which is an interactive, menu-driven, statistical program; and CoVis, which allows the animation of 2D and 3D scientific graphs.

Need more information? Try http://www.cohort.com/ on the Internet.

Cost: $159 for each module.

MacAnova

Here's some free software written for Macintosh, DOS, and Unix platforms that offers analysis of variance and related models, matrix algebra, time series, and some univariate and multivariate exploratory statistics.

Need more information? Try http://www.stat.umn.edu/ on the Internet.

Cost: Free.

Resampling Stats

This program is designed to use the "new statistics" of resampling and offers a set of 15 resampling commands to solve problems in probability and inferential statistics.

Need more information? Try http://www.statistics.com/brochure. html on the Internet.

Cost: $225 for the commercial version and $125 for the academic version.

Stat Ease Inc.

Stat Ease provides Design-Ease and Design-Expert for the analysis and graphical representation of data. Both Windows and Mac platforms are available.

Need more information? Try http://www.statease.com/ on the Internet.

Cost: $395 for Design-Ease and $995 for Design-Expert.

SUMMARY

That's the end of Part IV and just about the end of *Statistics for People Who (Think They) Hate Statistics*. But read on! The next chapter includes the best ten Internet sites in the universe for information about statistics, followed by Chapter 18, the ten commandments of data collection. Have fun with both of these.

PART V

Ten Things You'll Want to Know and Remember

SNAPSHOTS

"The Internet's got him... Pull the plug!
PULL THE PLUG!"

The Ten Best Internet Sites for Statistics Stuff

If you're not using the Internet in all your schoolwork, you are missing out on an extraordinary resource. What's on the Internet will not make up for a lack of studying or motivation—nothing will do that—but you can certainly find a great deal of information that will enhance your whole college experience. And this doesn't even begin to include all the fun you can have!

So now that you're a certified novice statistician, here are some Internet sites that you might find very useful should you want to learn more about statistics.

Tons and Tons of Resources

Here's the mother lode. Pages and pages of every type of statistical resource you can want has been creatively assembled by Professor David W. Stockburger at http://www.psychstat.smsu.edu/scripts/dws148f/statisticsresourcesmain.asp. This site receives the gold medal of statistics sites. Don't miss it.

For example, take a look at Berrie's page (at http://www.huizen.dds.nl/~berrie/) and see some QuickTime (short movies) of the effects of changing certain data points on the value of the mean and standard deviation. Or look at the different home pages that have been created by instructors for courses offered around the country. Or look at all the different software packages that can do statistical analysis (far more than we could mention in Chapter 16).

289

Who's Who and What's Happened

The History of Statistics page located at http://www.Anselm. edu/homepage/jpitocch/biostatshist.html contains portraits and bibliographies of famous statisticians and a timeline of important contributions to the field of statistics. So names like Bernoulli, Galton, Fisher, and Spearman pique your curiosity? How about the development of the first test between two averages during the early 20th century? It might seem a bit boring until you have a chance to read about the people who make up this field and their ideas.

It's All Here

Keith Dear, PhD, a faculty member at the University of Newcastle (Australia), has devoted hundreds of hours to the construction of a Web site named SurfStat Australia (at http://surfstat.newcastle. edu.au/surfstat/main/surfstat.html) that contains (among other things) a complete interactive statistics text. Besides the text, there are exercises, a list of other statistics sites on the Internet, and a collection of Java applets (cool little programs you can use to work with different statistical procedures).

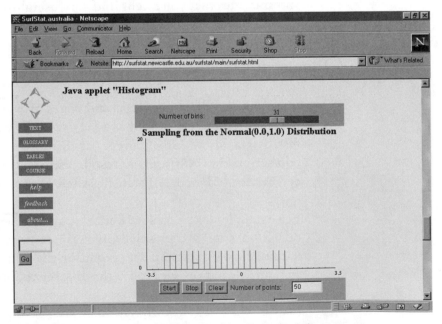

Figure 17.1. SurfStat's Approach to Teaching Basic Statistics

Data? You Want Data?

A Guide to the Web for Statisticians Data Sets (at http://www.maths.uq.edu.au/~gks/webguide/datasets.html) contain so much raw data that it will make your head spin and your calculator run out of power. Here's listing after listing of actual data sets that are available to you for use in your studying, papers, and even your teaching exercises (if you're the instructor).

For example, there's FEDSTATS (at http://www.fedstats.gov/) where more than 70 agencies in the U.S. federal government produce statistics of interest to the public. The Federal Interagency Council on Statistical Policy maintains this site to provide easy access to the full range of statistics and information produced by these agencies for public use. Here you can find country profiles contributed by the (boo!) CIA; public school student, staff, and faculty data (from the National Center for Education Statistics); and the Atlas of the United States Mortality (from the National Center for Health Statistics). What a ton of data!

How About Studying Statistics in Stockholm?

Statistics is the name of the page, but the one-word title is misleading since the site (from the good people at the University of Florida at http://www.stat.ufl.edu/vlib/statistics.html) includes information on just about every facet of the topic including data sources, job announcements, departments, divisions and schools of statistics (a huge description of programs all over the world), statistical research groups, institutes and associations, statistical services, statistical archives and resources, statistical software vendors and software, statistical journals, mailing list archives, and related fields. Tons of great information is available here. Make it a stop along the way.

More and More and More Resources

Statistics on the Web at http://www.maths.uq.edu.au/~gks/webguide/datasets.html is another location that's just full of information and references that you can easily access. Here, you'll find information on professional organizations, institutes and consulting groups, educational resources, Web courses, online textbooks, publications and publishers, statistics book list, software-oriented pages, mailing lists and discussion groups, and even information on statisticians and other statistical people.

Calculators Galore!

Want to draw a histogram? How about a table of random numbers? A sample size calculator? The Statistical Calculators page at http://www.stat.ucla.edu/calculators/ has just about every type of calculator and table you could need. Enough to carry you through any statistics course that you might take and even more.

For example, you can click on the Random Permutations link and complete the two boxes (as you see in Figure 17.2 for 2 random permutations of 100 integers) and you get the number of permutations you want. This is very handy when you need a table of random numbers for a specific number of participants so you can assign them to groups.

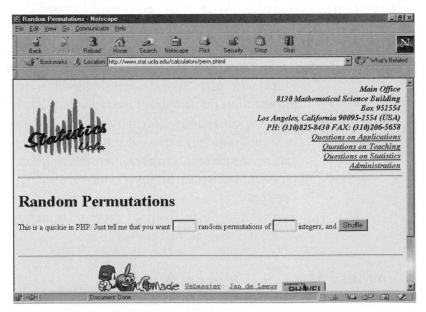

Figure 17.2. Generating a Set of Random Numbers

Online Statistical Teaching Materials

If you do ever have to teach statistics, or even tutor fellow students, this is one place you'll want to visit: http://www.helsinki. fi/~jpuranen/links.html. It contains hundreds of resources on every topic that was covered in *Statistics for People Who (Think They) Hate Statistics* and more. You name it and it's here: regression, demos, history, Sila (a demonstration of inference), an interactive online tutorial, statistical graphics, handouts to courses, teaching materials, journal articles, and even quizzes! Whew, what a deal. There tends to be a lot of material that may not be suited to what you are doing in this class, but this wide net has certainly captured some goodies.

HyperStat

This online tutorial with 18 lessons, at http://www.davidmlane. com/hyperstat/index.html, offers nicely designed and user-friendly coverage of the important basic topics. What we really liked about the site was the glossary, which uses hypertext to connect different concepts to one another. For example, in Figure 17.3, you can see the definition of descriptive statistics also linked to other glossary terms like mean, standard deviation, and box plot. Click on any of those and Zap! you're there.

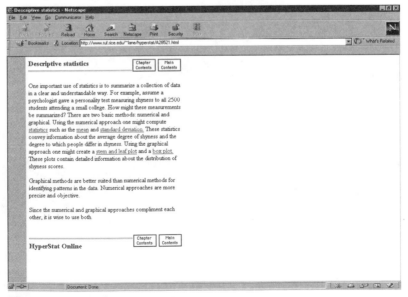

Figure 17.3. Sample HyperStat Screen

Take a Chance

And just for fun, try A Course Called Chance at http://www.dartmouth.edu/~chance/course/course.html, containing a database on courses that focus on the importance of chance, even in everyday encounters. This material is simply fascinating and given what we have said about the importance of chance in *Statistics for People,* you might want to visit here and see what's in store. You'll even find a Pepsi-Coke comparison. Try it. You'll like it.

18 The Ten Commandments of Data Collection

Now that you know how to analyze data, you would be well served to hear something about collecting them. The data collection process can be a long and rigorous one, even if it involves only a simple, one-page questionnaire given to a group of students, parents, patients, or voters. The data collection process may very well be the most time-consuming part of your project. But as many researchers do, this period of time is also used to think about the upcoming analysis and what it will entail.

Here they are: the ten commandments for making sure your data get collected in a way that they are usable. Unlike the original Ten Commandments, these should not be carved in stone (since they can certainly change), but if you follow them you can avoid lots of aggravation.

Commandment 1. As you begin thinking about a research question, begin thinking about the type of data you will have to collect to answer that question. Interview? Questionnaire? Paper and pencil? Find out how other people have done it in the past by reading the relevant journals in your area of interest and consider doing what they did.

Commandment 2. As you think about the type of data you will be collecting, think about where you will be getting the data. If you are using the library for historical data or accessing files of data that have already been collected such as census data (available through the U.S. Census Bureau and some online), you will have few logistical problems. But what if you want to assess the interaction between newborns and their parents? The attitude of teachers toward unionizing? The age at which people over 50 think they are old? All these questions involve needing people to provide the answers, and finding people can be tough. Start now.

Commandment 3. Make sure that the data collection forms you use are clear and easy to use. Practice on a set of pilot data so you can make sure it is easy to go from the original scoring sheets to the data collection form.

Commandment 4. Always make a duplicate copy of the data file, and keep it in a separate location. Keep in mind that there are two types of people: those who have lost their data and those who will. Keep a copy of data collection sheets in a separate location. If you are recording your data as a computer file, such as a spreadsheet, be sure to make a backup!

Commandment 5. Do not rely on other people to collect or transfer your data unless you have personally trained them and are confident that they understand the data collection process as well as you do. It is great to have people help you, and it helps keep the morale up during those long data collection sessions. But unless your helpers are competent beyond question, you could easily sabotage all your hard work and planning.

Commandment 6. Plan a detailed schedule of when and where you will be collecting your data. If you need to visit three schools and each of 50 children needs to be tested for a total of 10 minutes at each school, that is 25 hours of testing. That does not mean you can allot 25 hours from your schedule for this activity. What about travel from one school to another? What about the child who is in the bathroom when it is his turn, and you have to wait 10 minutes until he comes back to the classroom? What about the day you show up and Cowboy Bob is the featured guest . . . and on and on. Be prepared for anything, and allocate 25%-50% more time in your schedule for unforeseen happenings.

Commandment 7. As soon as possible, cultivate possible sources for your subject pool. Since you already have some knowledge in your own discipline, you probably also know of people who work with the type of population you want or who might be able to help you gain access to these samples. If you are in a university community, it is likely that there are hundreds of other people competing for the same subject sample that you need. Instead of competing, why not try a more out-of-the-way (maybe 30 minutes away) school district or social group or civic organization or hospital where you might be able to obtain a sample with less competition?

Commandment 8. Try to follow up on subjects who missed their testing session or interview. Call them back, and try to reschedule. Once you get in the habit of skipping possible participants, it becomes too easy to cut the sample down to too small a size. And you can never tell—the people who drop out might be dropping out for reasons related to what you are studying. This can mean that your final sample of people is qualitatively different from those who started.

Commandment 9. Never discard the original data, such as the test booklets, interview notes, and so forth. Other researchers might want to use the same database, or you may have to return to the original materials for further information.

And number 10? Follow the previous 9. No kidding!

SNAPSHOTS

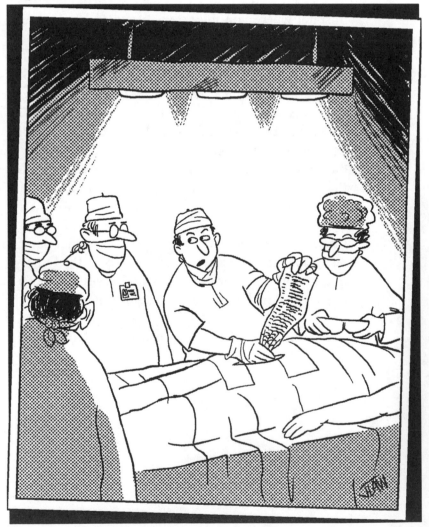

"Doctors, I think we've found the Appendix . . . "

Appendix A
SPSS *in Less Than 30 Minutes*

This appendix will teach you enough about SPSS to complete the exercises in *Statistics for People Who (Think They) Hate Statistics*. Learning SPSS is not rocket science—just take your time, work as slowly as you need, and ask a fellow student or your instructor for help if necessary.

You are probably familiar with other Windows applications, and you will find that many SPSS features operate exactly the same. We assume you know about dragging, clicking, double-clicking, and working with Windows. If you do not, you can refer to one of the many popular trade computer books that can help. Keep in mind that SPSS 10.0 is designed to work with the Windows 95/98 and higher operating systems and will not work with any earlier version of Windows. SPSS 10.0 takes advantage of Windows' special architecture as well as other features such as shortcuts, right-clicking, and multitasking.

This appendix is an introduction to SPSS and shows you just some of the things it can do. Throughout the examples in this appendix, we will use the data in Appendix C named Sample Data Set. You are welcome to enter those data manually or download them from the book's Internet site.

STARTING SPSS

Like other Windows-based applications, SPSS is organized as a group and is available on the Start menu. This group was created when you first installed SPSS. To start SPSS, follow these steps.

1. Click Start, then point to Programs.

2. Click the SPSS icon. When you do this, you will see the SPSS opening screen as shown in Figure A1. You should note that some computers are set up differently and your SPSS icon might be located on the desktop. In that case, to open SPSS, just double-click on the icon.

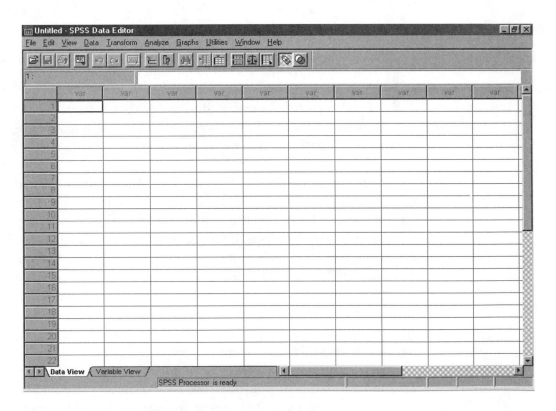

Figure A1. SPSS Opening Window

When you first open SPSS, you will be in the Data Editor. This is where you enter data that you want to analyze. If you think the Data Editor is similar to a spreadsheet in form and function, you are right. In form it is similar, since it consists of rows and columns just like Microsoft Excel or Lotus 1-2-3. The columns represent variables, and the rows represent cases. In function as well, the Data Editor is much like a spreadsheet. Values that are entered can be transformed, sorted, rearranged, and more.

THE SPSS TOOLBAR AND STATUS BAR

The use of the Toolbar, the set of icons that are underneath the menus, can greatly facilitate your SPSS activities. If you want to know what an icon on the Toolbar does, just place the mouse pointer on it, and you will see a tip telling you what the tool does. Some of the buttons on the Toolbar are dimmed, meaning they are not active.

The Status Bar, located at the bottom of the SPSS window, is another useful on screen tool. Here, you can see a one-line report as to what activity SPSS is currently involved in. Messages such as "SPSS for Windows processor is ready" tell you that SPSS is ready for your directions or input of data. Or, "Running Means . . . " tells you that SPSS is in the middle of the procedure named Means.

USING SPSS HELP

If you need help, you have come to the right place. SPSS offers help that is only a few mouse clicks away, and it is especially useful when you are in the middle of data file and need information about an SPSS feature. SPSS Help is so comprehensive that even if you are a new SPSS user, it can show you the way.

You can get help (see Figure A2) in SPSS by pressing the F1 function key or using the Help menu you see in Figure A3.

Figure A2 Various Help Options

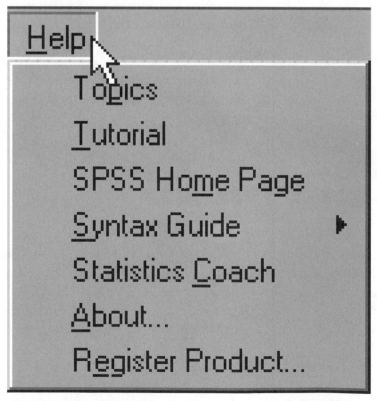

Figure A3. SPSS Help Menu

As you can see, there are seven options on the Help menu, greatly expanded from earlier versions of SPSS.

- Topics gives you a list of topics for which you can get help.
- Tutorial offers you a short tutorial on all aspects of using SPSS.
- SPSS Home Page takes you to the home page for SPSS on the Internet.
- Syntax Guide helps you to learn and use SPSS's programming language.
- Statistics Coach walks you through procedures step-by-step.
- About . . . tells you the version of SPSS that you are currently using.
- Register Product . . . allows you to register the current version of SPSS.

Using the F1 Function Key

Any time you need help on any feature of SPSS, there is a quick and easy way to get it. Press the F1 function key while you are working and you will see the Help dialog box shown in Figure A2.

The Contents Tab

The Contents tab describes the major headings for help. Double-clicking on any one heading provides a list of possible topics that you might want to consult for the help you need. For example, if you want help on how to edit output, you would follow these steps.

1. Press F1.
2. Click the Contents tab.
3. Double-click Output management, and you will see a list of topics within that general content area.
4. Double-click the topic labeled Editing Output.
5. Select the information you want.

The Index Tab

The Index tab in SPSS Help provides an alphabetical listing of help topics. To find help on a particular topic, follow these steps. For example, here is how you would use the Index option to find help on computing the mean of a set of numbers.

1. Press the F1 function key.
2. Click the Index tab.
3. Type mean. As you enter the letters of the term on which you need help, SPSS Help immediately tries to identify the topic listing. Double-clicking on the index entry mean or highlighting the topic and clicking the Display button produces the help that you are looking for.

The Find Tab

What if you cannot find a term in the Index, but you need help anyway? The Find option allows you to enter any words that may be part of a help screen. SPSS then searches for the word, rather than just presenting help on a topic. In effect, you are searching all the words in all the topics.

SPSS Find is very sensitive to what words you enter. For example, the word *mean* is general and will turn up lots of references. The word *Mean* is more specific, and the word *MEAN* (in all caps) even more so (since that is the specific procedure in SPSS syntax language). So if you know exactly what you want, you can be specific, but be careful since it can be at the expense of missing what you are looking for if you are not sure of what you want.

Using Help Options

Once you find help on what you want (such as information about the mean), you can click on the Options button in the Help window and perform a variety of tasks such as annotating the help screen so you can add your own information to what help already exists, copy the help contents to the Clipboard, print out the contents of the help menu, change the fonts of the help contents, change the position of help on the screen, and change colors. In a Help window, you can also click How To and have SPSS walk you through the steps of the procedure.

A BRIEF TOUR OF SPSS

Now sit back and enjoy a brief tour of what SPSS can do. Nothing fancy here, just some simple descriptions of data, a test of significance, and a graph or two. What we are trying to show you is how easy it is to use SPSS.

Opening a File

You can enter your own data to create a new SPSS data file, use an existing file, or even import data from such applications as Microsoft Excel into SPSS. Any way you do it, you need to have data to work with. Figure A4 shows the data contained in Appendix C, called Sample Data Set, which is also available on the Internet. Go to the Sage Web site at

www.sagepub.com

and search for

E-SalkindDataSets

then click on the book title.

	id	gender	group	test1	test2	var	var	var	var	var
1	1.00	Male	Control	98.00	32.00					
2	2.00	Female	Exp	87.00	33.00					
3	3.00	Female	Control	89.00	54.00					
4	4.00	Female	Control	88.00	44.00					
5	5.00	Male	Exp	76.00	64.00					
6	6.00	Male	Control	68.00	54.00					
7	7.00	Female	Control	78.00	44.00					
8	8.00	Female	Exp	98.00	32.00					
9	9.00	Female	Exp	93.00	64.00					
10	10.00	Male	Exp	76.00	37.00					
11	11.00	Female	Control	75.00	43.00					
12	12.00	Female	Control	65.00	56.00					
13	13.00	Male	Control	76.00	78.00					
14	14.00	Female	Control	78.00	99.00					
15	15.00	Female	Control	89.00	87.00					
16	16.00	Female	Exp	81.00	56.00					
17	17.00	Male	Control	78.00	78.00					
18	18.00	Female	Control	83.00	56.00					
19	19.00	Male	Control	88.00	67.00					
20	20.00	Female	Control	90.00	88.00					
21	21.00	Male	Control	93.00	81.00					
22	22.00	Male	Exp	89.00	93.00					

Figure A4. An Open SPSS File

A Simple Table and Graph

Now it is time to get to the reason why we are using SPSS in the first place: the various analytical tools that are available.

First, let's say we want to know the general distribution of males and females. That is all, just a count of how many males and how many females are in the total sample we are working with. We also want to create a simple bar graph of the distribution.

Figure A5 shows the output that provides exactly the information we asked for, which was the frequency of the number of males and females. We used the Frequencies option on the Descriptive Statistics (under the main menu Analyze) to compute these values.

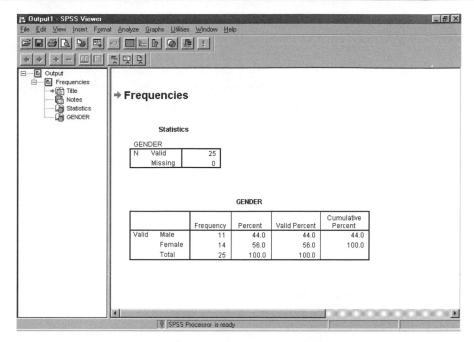

Figure A5. Results of a Simple Descriptive Analysis

Then we used the Graphs option to create a simple bar graph of the frequency, as you see in Figure A6.

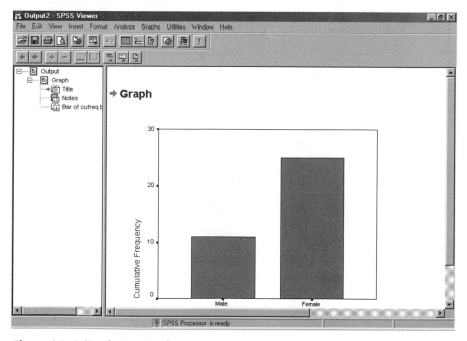

Figure A6. A Simple Bar Graph

A Simple Analysis

Let's see if males and females differ in their average test1 scores. This is a simple analysis requiring a *t* test for independent samples. The procedure is a comparison between males and females for the mean of test1.

In Figure A7, you can see a partial summary of the results of the *t* test. Notice that now the listing in the left pane (the outline view) of the SPSS Viewer shows the Frequencies, Graph, and *t* test procedures listed. To see any part of the output, all we need do is click on that element. Almost always when SPSS produces output in the Viewer, you will have to scroll to see the entire output.

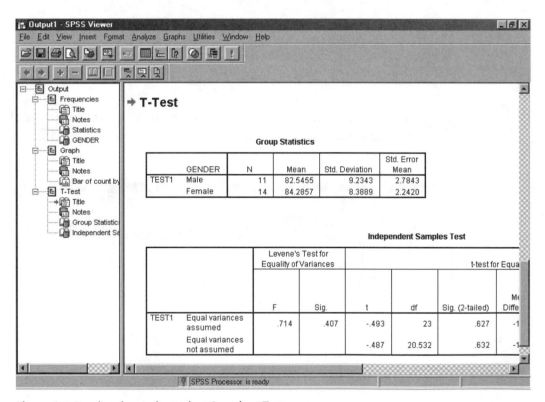

Figure A7. Results of an Independent-Samples *t* Test

CREATING AND EDITING A DATA FILE

As a hands-on exercise, let's create the beginning of the data file you see in the Sample Data Set in Appendix C on page 364. The first step is to define the variables in your data set and then to enter the data. You should have a new Data Editor window open (Click File → New → Data).

Defining Variables

SPSS cannot work unless variables are defined. You can have SPSS define the variables for you, or you can do the defining yourself, thereby having much more control over the way things look and work. SPSS will automatically name the first variable VAR00001. If you defined a variable in row 1, column 5, then SPSS would name the variable VAR00005 and also number the other columns sequentially. But you can also define variables, assigning a name of your choice.

Custom Defining Variables

When it comes to getting started with a new data file, custom defining variables should be your choice since it allows for much greater flexibility.

To define a variable name, follow these steps. You should be in a new data window.

1. Double-click on the dimmed *var* heading at the top of the column you want to define. You will see the Variable View screen as shown in Figure A8.

   As you can see, you can now define the variable according to a number of important characteristics such as Name, Type, Width, etc.

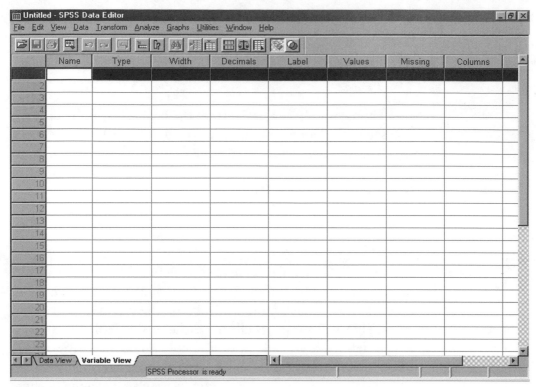

Figure A8. Define Variable Dialog Box

2. Enter a name for the variable. In our example, we are going to use id (variable 1 in the data set in the Sample Data Set). The name you assign to a variable must have no more than eight characters, and you cannot use spaces (too bad!).

3. Once the name is defined, use the down arrow key to move to the second column, which corresponds to the second variable, and enter the name of the second variable.

4. Repeat Steps 2 and 3 until the following variables are defined. For now, only worry about defining the variable name.

Row	Variable	Name
1	1	id
2	2	gender
3	3	group
4	4	test1
5	5	test2

5. Click the Data View tab at the bottom of the SPSS Data Editor and you will see all the variables named in a spreadsheet-like format as shown in Figure A9.

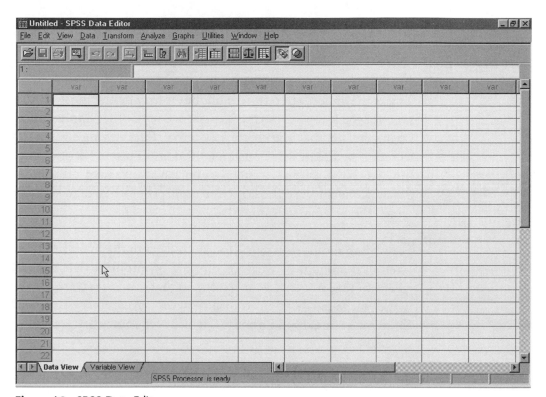

Figure A9. SPSS Data Editor.

Entering Data

Entering data into the Data Editor window and creating a data file is simple: Place the cursor in the cell where you want to enter data, click, and type. Let's enter data for the first case like this, and then the remaining Sample Data Set on page 364.

1. Click in row 1, column 1. The cell borders of the individual cell in the data file will be outlined.

2. Type the value 001 and press the Tab key to move to the next variable, named gender. If you want to move to the next case in the same column, press the Enter key. The value 1.00 will be entered since the default format is two decimal places. You should be in row 1, column 2.

3. Type 2 *(for male)* and press the Tab key.   *record*

4. Continue entering data into the Data Editor as you see in the same Data Set in Appendix C.

If you make an error, just backspace and retype your entry.

Saving a Data File

This is the easiest operation of all, but it may be the most important. As you know from your experience with other applications, saving the files that you create is essential. First, saving allows you to recall the file to work on at a later point in time. Second, it allows you to back up files. Finally, you can always save a file under a new name and use the copy for a purpose other than that for which the original was intended.

How often should you save? You should get in the habit of saving after a set amount of work or number of minutes. One general rule is to save as often as necessary so that you can re-create any work you might happen to lose between saves. Every time you finish a case or every 15 minutes (whichever comes first) is a good guideline.

To save data, follow these steps.

1. Click File → Save As. When you do this, you will see the Save Data As dialog box.

2. Select the directory in which you want to save the data. If you are working in a computer lab, be sure you have permission.

3. Enter the file name you want to use to save the data in the File Name text box. Notice that the .sav extension is already there.

4. Click Save.

The data you entered will then be saved as a data file, and the name of the file will appear in the title bar of the Data Editor window. The next time you select Save Data from the File menu, you will not see the Save Data As dialog box. SPSS will just save the changes under the name you originally assigned to the data file.

And remember, SPSS will save the data in the active directory. In most cases, that will be the same directory that contains SPSS, a situation you may or may not want.

Defining Variable Values

You can leave your data appearing as numerical values in the SPSS Data Editor, or you can have alphanumeric labels represent the numerical values.

Why would you want to assign a character-based value to a variable? You probably already know that, in general, it makes more sense to work with numbers (like 1 or 2) than with string or alphanumeric variables (such as male or female).

But it sure is a lot easier to look at a data file and see words rather than numbers. Just think about the difference between data files with numbers representing various levels (such as 1 and 2) of a variable and with the actual values (such as male and female). The Labels option in the Define Variable dialog box allows you to enter values in the cell, but what you will see are value labels.

Changing Variable Values

To assign or change a variable label, follow these steps. We assign the values of male and female to the 1 and 2 that have already been entered under the gender column.

1. Double-click the second column in the Data Editor named gender. You will be in the Variable view.
2. Under the Values column, click the cell in the gender row.
3. Click the three-dot ellipses. When you do this, you will see the Value Labels dialog box as shown in Figure A10 on page 314.
4. Enter a value in the Value box. In this example, the value 1 is being entered.
5. Enter a label in the Value Label box. In this case, the label is Male.
6. Click the Add button.

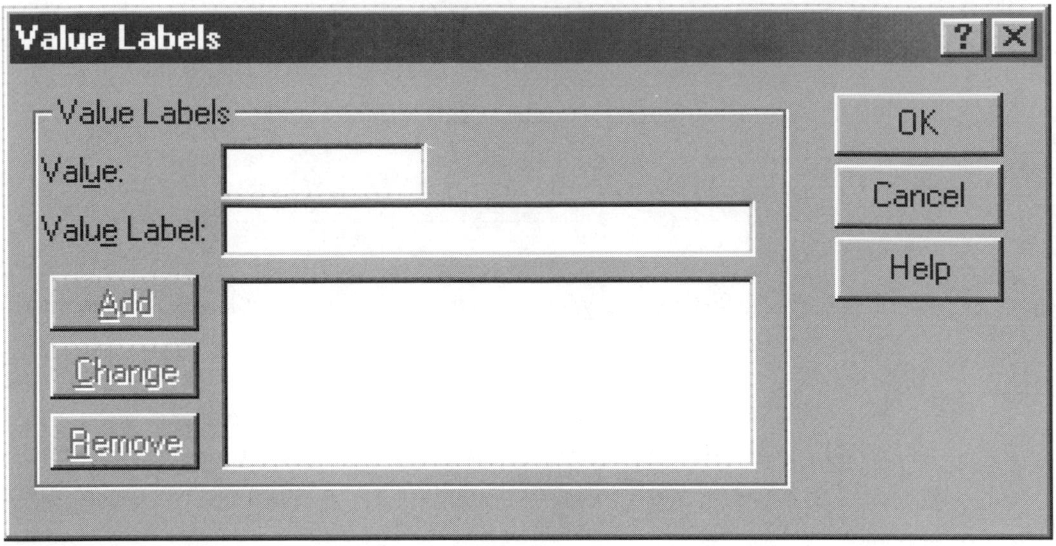

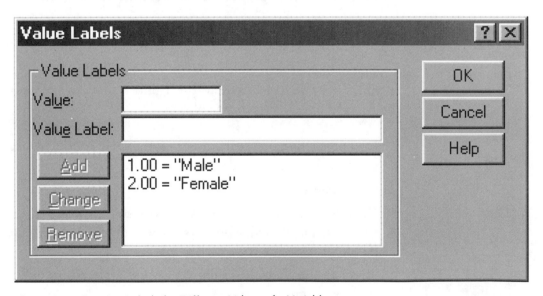

Figure A10. Define Labels Dialog Box

7. Repeat Steps 4 through 6 to enter the label of Female for the value 2.

8. The completed Value Labels dialog box should appear as shown in Figure A11.

Figure A11. Creating Labels for Different Values of a Variable

9. Click OK.

And when you select View → Value Labels from the main menu (in Data View), you will see the labels in the Data Editor as you do in Figure A12. Notice how the value of the entry in Figure A12 is actually 2, even though the label in cell reads Female.

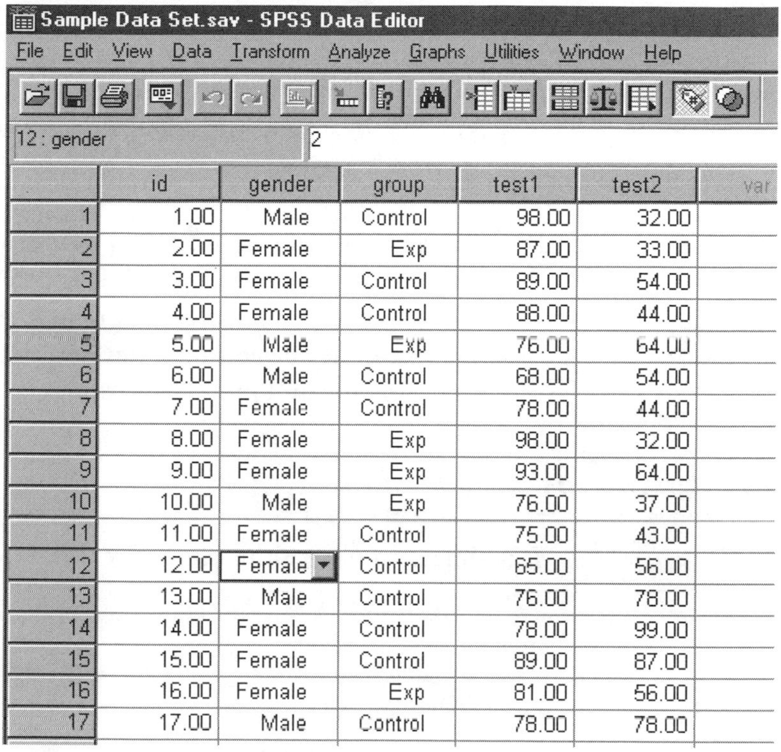

	id	gender	group	test1	test2	var
1	1.00	Male	Control	98.00	32.00	
2	2.00	Female	Exp	87.00	33.00	
3	3.00	Female	Control	89.00	54.00	
4	4.00	Female	Control	88.00	44.00	
5	5.00	Male	Exp	76.00	64.00	
6	6.00	Male	Control	68.00	54.00	
7	7.00	Female	Control	78.00	44.00	
8	8.00	Female	Exp	98.00	32.00	
9	9.00	Female	Exp	93.00	64.00	
10	10.00	Male	Exp	76.00	37.00	
11	11.00	Female	Control	75.00	43.00	
12	12.00	Female	Control	65.00	56.00	
13	13.00	Male	Control	76.00	78.00	
14	14.00	Female	Control	78.00	99.00	
15	15.00	Female	Control	89.00	87.00	
16	16.00	Female	Exp	81.00	56.00	
17	17.00	Male	Control	78.00	78.00	

Figure A12. Using Variable Labels

Opening a Data File

Once a file is saved, you have to open or retrieve it when you want to use it again. The steps are simple.

1. Click File → Open Data. You will see the Open Data File dialog box.
2. Find the data file you want to open, and highlight it.
3. Click OK.

A quick way to find and open an SPSS file is by clicking on Recently Used Data at the bottom of the File menu. SPSS lists the most recently used files there.

PRINTING WITH SPSS

Here comes information on the last thing you will do once a data file is created. Once you have created the data file you want or completed any type of analysis or chart, you probably will want to print out a hard copy for safekeeping or for inclusion in a report or paper. Then, when your SPSS document is printed and you want to stop working, it is time to exit SPSS.

Printing is almost as important a process as editing and saving data files. If you cannot print, you have nothing to take away from your work session. You can export data from an SPSS file to another application, but getting a hard copy directly from SPSS is often more timely and more important.

Printing an SPSS Data File

It is simple to print either an entire data file or a selection from one.

1. Be sure that the data file you want to print is the active window.
2. Click File → Print. When you do this, you will see the Print dialog box shown in Figure A13.

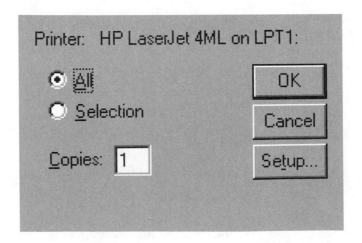

3. Click OK, and whatever is active will print.

Printing a Selection From an SPSS Data File

Printing a selection from a data file follows exactly the steps that we listed above for printing a data file, except that in the Data Editor window, you select what you want to print and click on the Selection option in the Print dialog box. The steps go like this.

1. Be sure that the data you want to print is selected.
2. Click File → Print.
3. Click Selection in the Print dialog box.
4. Click OK, and whatever you selected will be printed.

EXITING SPSS

To exit SPSS, follow this step.

1. Click File → Exit. SPSS will be sure that you get the chance to save any unsaved or edited windows and will then close.

CREATING AN SPSS CHART

A picture is worth a thousand words, and SPSS offers you just the features to create charts that bring the results of your analyses to life. In this part of Appendix A, we will go through the steps to create several different types of charts and provide examples of different charts. Then, we will show you how to modify a chart, including adding a chart title, labels to axes, modifying scales, working with patterns, fonts, and more. For whatever reason, SPSS uses the words *graphs* and *charts* interchangeably.

Creating a Simple Chart

The one thing that all charts have in common is that they are based on data. While you may import data to create a chart, in this example we will use the data from Appendix C to create a bar chart (like the one you saw in Figure A6 on page 307) of the number of males and females in each group.

Creating a Bar Chart

The steps for creating any chart are basically the same. You first enter the data you want to use in the chart, select the type of chart you want from the Graphs menu, define how the chart should appear, and then click OK.

1. Enter the data you want to use to create the chart.

2. Click Graphs → Bar. When you do this, you will see the Bar Charts dialog box shown in Figure A14.

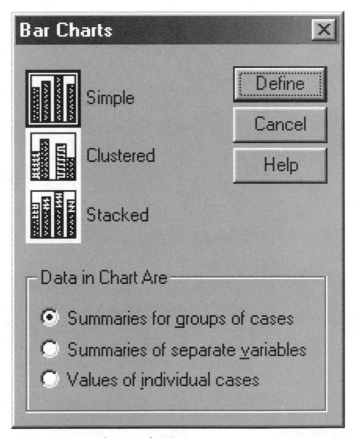

Figure A14. Bar Charts Dialog Box

3. Click Simple.

4. Click Summaries for groups of cases.

5. Click Define. When you do this, you will see the Define Simple Bar: Summaries for Groups of Cases dialog box.

6. Click Cum n of cases.

7. Click gender, then click ▶ to move the variable to the Category Axis area.

8. Click OK, and you see the results of the chart in Figure A6.

That's just the beginning of the chart, and to make any changes you have to use the chart editor tools.

Saving a Chart

A chart is only one component of the Viewer window. A chart is part of the output generated when you perform some type of analysis. The chart is not a separate entity that stands by itself, and it cannot be saved as such. To save a chart, you need to save the contents of the entire Viewer. Follow these steps to do that.

1. Click File → Save.

2. Provide a name for the Viewer window.

3. Click OK. The output is saved under the name that you provide with an .spo extension.

ENHANCING SPSS CHARTS

Once you create a chart as we showed you in the last section, you could finish the job by editing the chart to reflect exactly what you want to say. Color, shapes, scales, fonts, and more can be worked with. We will be working with the bar chart that was first shown to you in Figure A6.

Editing a Chart

The first step in editing a chart is to double-click on the chart, then click the maximize window button. You will see the entire chart in Figure A15 in the Chart Editor window.

Working With Titles and Subtitles

Our first task is to enter the title and a subtitle on the chart you see in Figure A15.

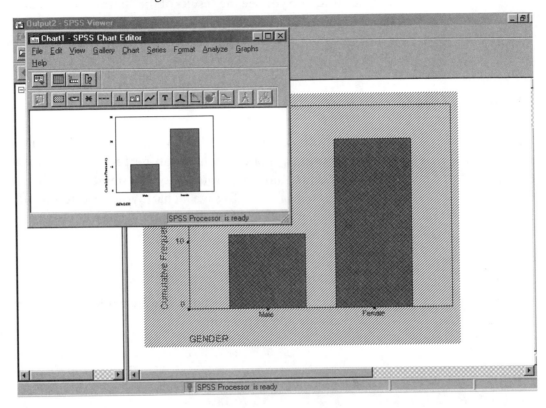

Figure A15. Chart Editor Window

1. Click Chart → Title. When you do this, you will see the Titles dialog box as shown in Figure A16.

2. Type Frequency of Gender in the Title 1 section.

3. Click Center from the drop-down menus for justification of the title and subtitle.

4. Press the Tab key to go to the Subtitle text box.

5. Type Draft Chart.

6. Click OK.

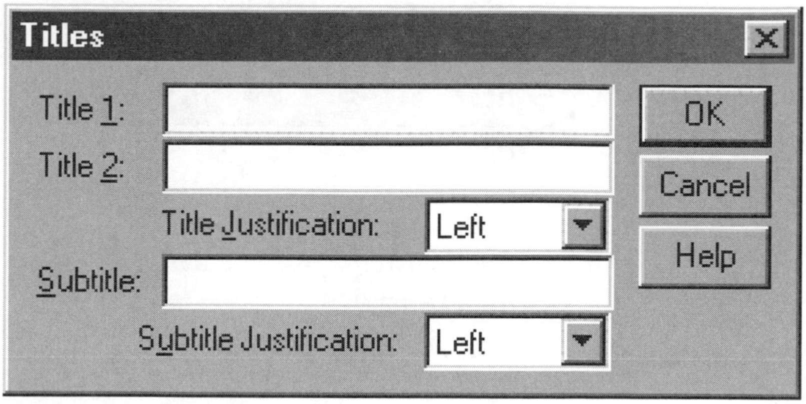

Figure A16. Titles Dialog Box

The title and subtitle should appear on the chart. If you want to edit a title or a subtitle, just be sure that the chart is active, then select Chart → Titles.

Working With Fonts

Now it is time to work with the font used to represent any of the text in the chart. You can do this one of two ways, with each way using the same dialog box.

1. Select the area of the chart containing the font you want to change. When you select text, it appears with a solid line around it.

2. To select a new font and size, you select Format → Text. You will see the Text Styles dialog box shown in Figure A17 on page 322.

3. Select the font and size you want to use.

4. Click Apply, and the font will change in the chart.

5. Click Close when all the changes are made.

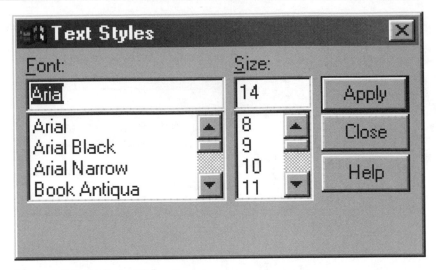

Figure A17. Text Styles Dialog Box

Working With Frames

SPSS, by default, places a frame around the top and right side of the chart, an inside frame. To include or exclude an inner or outer frame, select the option (Inner Frame or Outer Frame or both) from the Chart menu. We removed the inner frame for a less cluttered appearance.

Working With Axes

The x- and y-axes provide the calibration for the independent (usually the x-axis) variable and the dependent (usually the y-axis) variable. SPSS names the y-axis the Scale axis and the x-axis the Category axis. Each of these axes can be modified in a variety of ways. To modify either axis, double-click on the title of the axis.

How to Modify the Scale (y) Axis

For example, to modify the y-axis, follow these steps.

1. Double-click on the label of the y-axis. When you do this, you will see the Scale Axis dialog box as shown in Figure A18.

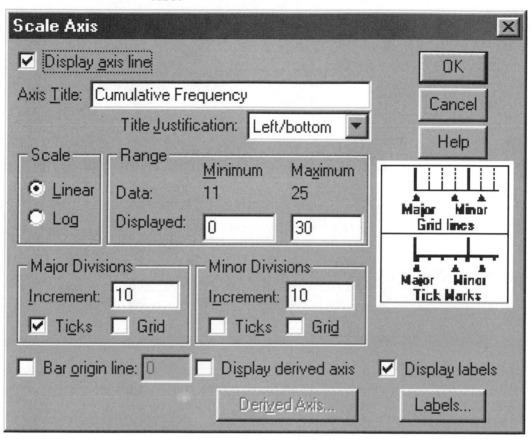

Figure A18. Scale Axis Dialog Box

2. Select the options you want from the Scale Axis dialog box.

We did the following:

Changed the label cumulative frequency to Number
Centered the axis title

3. Click OK.

We could have done several other things, such as changing the range of the scale and working with major divisions and minor divisions.

How to Modify the Category (x) Axis

Working with the x-axis is no more difficult than working with the y-axis.

Here is how the x-axis was modified.

1. Double-click on the label of the x-axis. The Category Axis dialog box opens. It is very similar to the Scale Axis dialog box you see in Figure A.18.
2. Select the options you want from the Category Axis dialog box. We did the following:

   Changed GENDER to Gender
   Centered the axis title

3. Click OK.

When you are done making changes, close the Chart Editor by double-clicking on the window icon or selecting File → Close.

DESCRIBING DATA

Now you have some idea about how data files and simple charts are created in SPSS. Let's move on to some examples of simple analysis.

Frequencies and Crosstab Tables

Frequencies simply compute the number of times that a particular value occurs. Crosstabs allow you to compute the number of times that a value occurs when categorized by one or more dimensions such as gender and age. Both frequencies and crosstabs are often reported first in research reports since they give the reader an overview of what the data look like. To compute frequencies, follow these steps. You should be in the Data Editor (Data View) window.

1. Click Analyze → Descriptive Statistics → Frequencies. When you do this, you will see the Frequencies dialog box as shown in Figure A19.

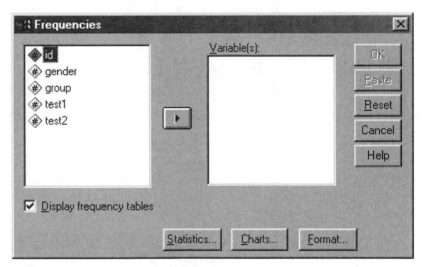

Figure A19. Frequencies Dialog Box

2. Double-click the variables for which you want frequencies computed. In this case, they are test1 and test2.

3. Click Statistics. You will see the Frequencies: Statistics dialog box as shown in Figure A20 on page 326.

Figure A20. Frequencies: Statistics Dialog Box

4. In the Dispersion area, click Std. deviation.

5. Under the Central Tendency area, click Mean.

6. Click Continue.

7. Click OK.

The output consists of a listing of the frequency of each value for test1 and test2 plus summary statistics (mean and standard deviation) for each as you see in Figure A21.

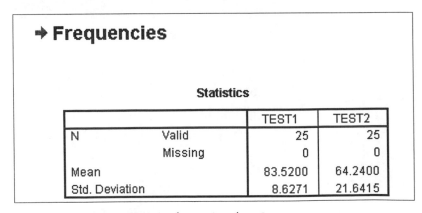

➡ **Frequencies**

Statistics

		TEST1	TEST2
N	Valid	25	25
	Missing	0	0
Mean		83.5200	64.2400
Std. Deviation		8.6271	21.6415

Figure A21. Summary Statistics for test1 and test2

Applying the Independent-Samples t Test

Independent-samples *t* tests are used to analyze data from a number of types of studies, including experimental, quasi-experimental, and field studies such as those shown in the following example where we test the hypothesis that there are differences between males and females in reading.

How to Conduct an Independent-Samples t Test

To conduct an independent-samples *t* test, follow these steps.

1. Click Analyze → Compare Means →, then click Independent-Samples T Test. When you do this, you will see the Independent-Samples T Test dialog box as shown in Figure A22.

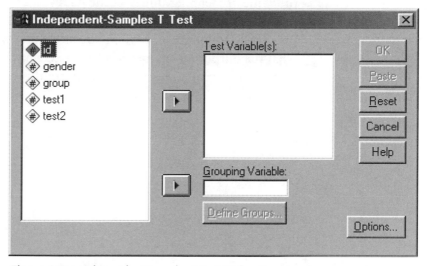

Figure A22. Independent-Samples *t* Test Dialog Box

On the left-hand side of the dialog box, you see a listing of all the variables that can be used in the analysis. What you now need to do is define the test and the grouping variable.

2. Click test1, then click ▶ in the Test Variables box to move it to the Test Variables(s) area.

3. Click group, then click ▶ to move it to the Grouping Variable area.

4. Click Define Groups.

5. In the Group 1 box, type 1.

6. In the Group 2 box, type 2.

7. Click Continue.

8. Click OK.

The output contains the means and standard deviations for each variable, plus the results of the *t* test as shown in Figure A23.

SUMMARY

We have just given you the briefest of introductions to SPSS, and certainly none of these skills means anything if you don't know the value or meaningfulness of the data you originally entered. So don't be impressed by yours or others' skills at using programs like SPSS. Be impressed when those other people can tell you what the output means and how it reflects on your original question. And be really impressed if you can do it!

Group Statistics

	GENDER	N	Mean	Std. Deviation	Std. Error Mean
TEST1	Male	11	82.5455	9.2343	2.7843
	Female	14	84.2857	8.3889	2.2420

Independent Samples Test

		Levene's Test for Equality of Variances		t-test for Equality of Means						
									95% Confidence Interval of the Difference	
		F	Sig.	t	df	Sig. (2-tailed)	Mean Difference	Std. Error Difference	Lower	Upper
TEST1	Equal variances assumed	.714	.407	-.493	23	.627	-1.7403	3.5321	-9.0470	5.5665
	Equal variances not assumed			-.487	20.532	.632	-1.7403	3.5747	-9.1847	5.7041

Figure A23. Results of the *t* Test

Appendix B
Tables

TABLE B1: AREAS BENEATH THE NORMAL CURVE

How to use this table:

1. Compute the z score based on the raw score and the mean of the sample.
2. Read to the right of the z score to determine the percentage of area underneath the normal curve or the area between the mean and computed z score.

Table B.1 Areas Beneath the Normal Curve

z Score	Area Between the Mean and the z Score	z Score	Area Between the Mean and the z Score	z Score	Area Between the Mean and the z Score	z Score	Area Between the Mean and the z Score	z Score	Area Between the Mean and the z Score	z Score	Area Between the Mean and the z Score	z Score	Area Between the Mean and the z Score	z Score	Area Between the Mean and the z Score
0.00	0.00	0.50	19.15	1.00	34.13	1.50	43.32	2.00	47.72	2.50	49.38	3.00	49.87	3.50	49.98
0.01	0.40	0.51	19.50	1.01	34.38	1.51	43.45	2.01	47.78	2.51	49.40	3.01	49.87	3.51	49.98
0.02	0.80	0.52	19.85	1.02	34.61	1.52	43.57	2.02	47.83	2.52	49.41	3.02	49.87	3.52	49.98
0.03	1.20	0.53	20.19	1.03	34.85	1.53	43.70	2.03	47.88	2.53	49.43	3.03	49.88	3.53	49.98
0.04	1.60	0.54	20.54	1.04	35.08	1.54	43.82	2.04	47.93	2.54	49.45	3.04	49.88	3.54	49.98
0.05	1.99	0.55	20.88	1.05	35.31	1.55	43.94	2.05	47.98	2.55	49.46	3.05	49.89	3.55	49.98
0.06	2.39	0.56	21.23	1.06	35.54	1.56	44.06	2.06	48.03	2.56	49.48	3.06	49.89	3.56	49.98
0.07	2.79	0.57	21.57	1.07	35.77	1.57	44.18	2.07	48.08	2.57	49.49	3.07	49.89	3.57	49.98
0.08	3.19	0.58	21.90	1.08	35.99	1.58	44.29	2.08	48.12	2.58	49.51	3.08	49.90	3.58	49.98
0.09	3.59	0.59	22.24	1.09	36.21	1.59	44.41	2.09	48.17	2.59	49.52	3.09	49.90	3.59	49.98
0.10	3.98	0.60	22.57	1.10	36.43	1.60	44.52	2.10	48.21	2.60	49.53	3.10	49.90	3.60	49.98
0.11	4.38	0.61	22.91	1.11	36.65	1.61	44.63	2.11	48.26	2.61	49.55	3.11	49.91	3.61	49.98
0.12	4.78	0.62	23.24	1.12	36.86	1.62	44.74	2.12	48.30	2.62	49.56	3.12	49.91	3.62	49.98
0.13	5.17	0.63	23.57	1.13	37.08	1.63	44.84	2.13	48.34	2.63	49.57	3.13	49.91	3.63	49.98
0.14	5.57	0.64	23.89	1.14	37.29	1.64	44.95	2.14	48.38	2.64	49.59	3.14	49.92	3.64	49.98
0.15	5.96	0.65	24.54	1.15	37.49	1.65	45.05	2.15	48.42	2.65	49.60	3.15	49.92	3.65	49.98
0.16	6.36	0.66	24.86	1.16	37.70	1.66	45.15	2.16	48.46	2.66	49.61	3.16	49.92	3.66	49.98
0.17	6.75	0.67	25.17	1.17	37.90	1.67	45.25	2.17	48.50	2.67	49.62	3.17	49.92	3.67	49.98
0.18	7.14	0.68	25.49	1.18	38.10	1.68	45.35	2.18	48.54	2.68	49.63	3.18	49.93	3.68	49.98
0.19	7.53	0.69	25.80	1.19	38.30	1.69	45.45	2.19	48.57	2.69	49.64	3.19	49.93	3.69	49.98
0.20	7.93	0.70	26.11	1.20	38.49	1.70	45.54	2.20	48.61	2.70	49.65	3.20	49.93	3.70	49.99
0.21	8.32	0.71	26.42	1.21	38.69	1.71	45.64	2.21	48.64	2.71	49.66	3.21	49.93	3.71	49.99

0.22	8.71	0.73	26.73	1.22	38.88	1.72	45.73	2.22	48.68	2.72	49.67	3.22	49.94	3.72	49.99
0.23	9.10	0.74	27.04	1.23	39.07	1.73	45.82	2.23	48.71	2.73	49.68	3.23	49.94	3.73	49.99
0.24	9.48	0.75	27.34	1.24	39.25	1.74	45.91	2.24	48.75	2.74	49.69	3.24	49.94	3.74	49.99
0.25	9.99	0.76	27.64	1.25	39.44	1.75	45.99	2.25	45.78	2.75	49.70	3.25	49.94	3.75	49.99
0.26	10.26	0.77	27.94	1.26	39.62	1.76	46.08	2.26	48.81	2.76	49.71	3.26	49.94	3.76	49.99
0.27	10.64	0.78	28.33	1.27	39.80	1.77	46.16	2.27	48.84	2.77	49.72	3.27	49.94	3.77	49.99
0.28	11.03	0.79	28.52	1.28	39.97	1.78	46.25	2.28	48.87	2.78	49.73	3.28	49.94	3.78	49.99
0.29	11.41	0.80	28.81	1.29	40.15	1.79	46.33	2.29	48.90	2.79	49.74	3.29	49.94	3.79	49.99
0.30	11.79	0.81	29.10	1.30	40.32	1.80	46.41	2.30	48.93	2.80	49.74	3.30	49.95	3.80	49.99
0.31	12.17	0.82	29.39	1.31	40.49	1.81	46.49	2.31	48.96	2.81	49.75	3.31	49.95	3.81	49.99
0.32	12.55	0.83	29.67	1.32	40.66	1.82	46.56	2.32	48.98	2.82	49.76	3.32	49.95	3.82	49.99
0.33	12.93	0.84	29.95	1.33	40.82	1.83	46.64	2.33	49.01	2.83	49.77	3.33	49.95	3.83	49.99
0.34	13.31	0.85	30.23	1.34	40.99	1.84	46.71	2.34	49.04	2.84	49.77	3.34	49.95	3.84	49.99
0.35	13.68	0.86	30.51	1.35	41.15	1.85	46.78	2.35	49.06	2.85	49.78	3.35	49.96	3.85	49.99
0.36	14.06	0.87	30.78	1.36	41.31	1.86	46.86	2.36	49.09	2.86	49.79	3.36	49.96	3.86	49.99
0.37	14.43	0.88	31.06	1.37	41.47	1.87	46.93	2.37	49.11	2.87	49.79	3.37	49.96	3.87	49.99
0.38	14.80	0.89	31.33	1.38	41.62	1.88	46.99	2.38	49.13	2.88	49.80	3.38	49.96	3.88	49.99
0.39	15.17	0.90	31.59	1.39	41.77	1.89	47.06	2.39	49.16	2.89	49.81	3.39	49.96	3.89	49.99
0.40	15.54	0.91	31.86	1.40	41.92	1.90	47.13	2.40	49.18	2.90	49.81	3.40	49.97	3.90	49.99
0.41	15.91	0.92	32.12	1.41	42.07	1.91	47.19	2.41	49.20	2.91	49.82	3.41	49.97	3.91	49.99
0.42	16.28	0.93	32.38	1.42	42.22	1.92	47.26	2.42	49.22	2.92	49.82	3.42	49.97	3.92	49.99
0.43	16.64	0.94	32.64	1.43	42.36	1.93	47.32	2.43	49.25	2.93	49.83	3.43	49.97	3.93	49.99
0.44	17.00	0.95	32.89	1.44	42.51	1.94	47.38	2.44	49.27	2.94	49.84	3.44	49.97	3.94	49.99
0.45	17.36	0.96	33.15	1.45	42.65	1.95	47.44	2.45	49.29	2.95	49.84	3.45	49.98	3.95	49.99
0.46	17.72	0.97	33.40	1.46	42.79	1.96	47.50	2.46	49.31	2.96	49.85	3.46	49.98	3.96	49.99
0.47	18.08	0.98	33.65	1.47	42.92	1.97	47.56	2.47	49.32	2.97	49.85	3.47	49.98	3.97	49.99
0.48	18.44	0.99	33.89	1.48	43.06	1.98	47.61	2.48	49.34	2.98	49.86	3.48	49.98	3.98	49.99
0.49	18.79	1.00	34.13	1.49	43.19	1.99	47.67	2.49	49.36	2.99	49.86	3.49	49.98	3.99	49.99

TABLE B2: T VALUES NEEDED FOR REJECTION OF THE NULL HYPOTHESIS

How to use this table:

1. Compute the t value test statistic.

2. Compare the obtained t value to the critical value listed in this table. Be sure you have calculated the number of degrees of freedom correctly and you have selected an appropriate level of significance.

3. If the obtained value is greater than the critical or tabled value, the null hypothesis (that the means are equal) is not the most attractive explanation for any observed differences.

4. If the obtained value is less than the critical or table value, the null hypothesis is the most attractive explanation for any observed differences.

Table B.2 T Values Needed for Rejection of the Null Hypothesis

	One-Tailed Test				Two-Tailed Test		
df	.10	.05	.01	df	.10	.05	.01
1	3.078	6.314	31.821	1	6.314	12.706	63.657
2	1.886	2.920	6.965	2	2.920	4.303	9.925
3	1.638	2.353	4.541	3	2.353	3.182	5.841
4	1.533	2.132	3.747	4	2.132	2.776	4.604
5	1.476	2.015	3.365	5	2.015	2.571	4.032
6	1.440	1.943	3.143	6	1.943	2.447	3.708
7	1.415	1.895	2.998	7	1.895	2.365	3.500
8	1.397	1.860	2.897	8	1.860	2.306	3.356
9	1.383	1.833	2.822	9	1.833	2.262	3.250
10	1.372	1.813	2.764	10	1.813	2.228	3.170
11	1.364	1.796	2.718	11	1.796	2.201	3.106
12	1.356	1.783	2.681	12	1.783	2.179	3.055
13	1.350	1.771	2.651	13	1.771	2.161	3.013
14	1.345	1.762	2.625	14	1.762	2.145	2.977
15	1.341	1.753	2.603	15	1.753	2.132	2.947
16	1.337	1.746	2.584	16	1.746	2.120	2.921
17	1.334	1.740	2.567	17	1.740	2.110	2.898
18	1.331	1.734	2.553	18	1.734	2.101	2.879
19	1.328	1.729	2.540	19	1.729	2.093	2.861
20	1.326	1.725	2.528	20	1.725	2.086	2.846
21	1.323	1.721	2.518	21	1.721	2.080	2.832
22	1.321	1.717	2.509	22	1.717	2.074	2.819

(continued)

Table B.2 Continued

df	One-Tailed Test			df	Two-Tailed Test		
	.10	.05	.01		.10	.05	.01
23	1.320	1.714	2.500	23	1.714	2.069	2.808
24	1.318	1.711	2.492	24	1.711	2.064	2.797
25	1.317	1.708	2.485	25	1.708	2.060	2.788
26	1.315	1.706	2.479	26	1.706	2.056	2.779
27	1.314	1.704	2.473	27	1.704	2.052	2.771
28	1.313	1.701	2.467	28	1.701	2.049	2.764
29	1.312	1.699	2.462	29	1.699	2.045	2.757
30	1.311	1.698	2.458	30	1.698	2.043	2.750
35	1.306	1.690	2.438	35	1.690	2.030	2.724
40	1.303	1.684	2.424	40	1.684	2.021	2.705
45	1.301	1.680	2.412	45	1.680	2.014	2.690
50	1.299	1.676	2.404	50	1.676	2.009	2.678
55	1.297	1.673	2.396	55	1.673	2.004	2.668
60	1.296	1.671	2.390	60	1.671	2.001	2.661
65	1.295	1.669	2.385	65	1.669	1.997	2.654
70	1.294	1.667	2.381	70	1.667	1.995	2.648
75	1.293	1.666	2.377	75	1.666	1.992	2.643
80	1.292	1.664	2.374	80	1.664	1.990	2.639
85	1.292	1.663	2.371	85	1.663	1.989	2.635
90	1.291	1.662	2.369	90	1.662	1.987	2.632
95	1.291	1.661	2.366	95	1.661	1.986	2.629
100	1.290	1.660	2.364	100	1.660	1.984	2.626
Infinity	1.282	1.645	2.327	Infinity	1.645	1.960	2.576

TABLE B3: CRITICAL VALUES FOR ANALYSIS OF VARIANCE OR F TEST

How to use this table:

1. Compute the F value.

2. Determine the number of degrees of freedom for the numerator $(k-1)$ and the number of degrees of freedom for the denominator $(n-k)$.

3. Locate the critical value by reading across to locate the degrees of freedom in the numerator and down to locate the degrees of freedom in the denominator. The critical value is at the intersection of this column and row.

4. If the obtained value is greater than the critical or tabled value, the null hypothesis (that the means are equal to one another) is not the most attractive explanation for any observed differences.

5. If the obtained value is less than the critical or tabled value, the null hypothesis is the most attractive explanation for any observed differences.

Table B.3   Critical Values for Analysis of Variance or *F* Test

df for the Denominator	Type I Error Rate	df for the Numerator					
1	.01	4052.00	5000.00	5404.00	5625.00	5764.00	5859.00
	.05	162.00	200.00	216.00	225.00	230.00	234.00
	.10	39.90	49.50	53.60	55.80	57.20	58.20
2	.01	98.50	99.00	99.17	99.25	99.30	99.33
	.05	18.51	19.00	19.17	19.25	19.30	19.33
	.10	8.53	9.00	9.16	9.24	9.29	9.33
3	.01	34.12	30.82	29.46	28.71	28.24	27.91
	.05	10.13	9.55	9.28	9.12	9.01	8.94
	.10	5.54	5.46	5.39	5.34	5.31	5.28
4	.01	21.20	18.00	16.70	15.98	15.52	15.21
	.05	7.71	6.95	6.59	6.39	6.26	6.16
	.10	4.55	4.33	4.19	4.11	4.05	4.01
5	.01	16.26	13.27	12.06	11.39	10.97	10.67
	.05	6.61	5.79	5.41	5.19	5.05	4.95
	.10	4.06	3.78	3.62	3.52	3.45	3.41
6	.01	13.75	10.93	9.78	9.15	8.75	8.47
	.05	5.99	5.14	4.76	4.53	4.39	4.28
	.10	3.78	3.46	3.29	3.18	3.11	3.06
7	.01	12.25	9.55	8.45	7.85	7.46	7.19
	.05	5.59	4.74	4.35	4.12	3.97	3.87
	.10	3.59	3.26	3.08	2.96	2.88	2.83
8	.01	11.26	8.65	7.59	7.01	6.63	6.37
	.05	5.32	4.46	4.07	3.84	3.69	3.58
	.10	3.46	3.11	2.92	2.81	2.73	2.67
9	.01	10.56	8.02	6.99	6.42	6.06	5.80
	.05	5.12	4.26	3.86	3.63	3.48	3.37
	.10	3.36	3.01	2.81	2.69	2.61	2.55
10	.01	10.05	7.56	6.55	6.00	5.64	5.39
	.05	4.97	4.10	3.71	3.48	3.33	3.22
	.10	3.29	2.93	2.73	2.61	2.52	2.46
11	.01	9.65	7.21	6.22	5.67	5.32	5.07
	.05	4.85	3.98	3.59	3.36	3.20	3.10
	.10	3.23	2.86	2.66	2.54	2.45	2.39
12	.01	9.33	6.93	5.95	5.41	5.07	4.82
	.05	4.75	3.89	3.49	3.26	3.11	3.00
	.10	3.18	2.81	2.61	2.48	2.40	2.33
13	.01	9.07	6.70	5.74	5.21	4.86	4.62
	.05	4.67	3.81	3.41	3.18	3.03	2.92
	.10	3.14	2.76	2.56	2.43	2.35	2.28
14	.01	8.86	6.52	5.56	5.04	4.70	4.46
	.05	4.60	3.74	3.34	3.11	2.96	2.85
	.10	3.10	2.73	2.52	2.40	2.31	2.24
15	.01	8.68	6.36	5.42	4.89	4.56	4.32
	.05	4.54	3.68	3.29	3.06	2.90	2.79
	.10	3.07	2.70	2.49	2.36	2.27	2.21
16	.01	8.53	6.23	5.29	4.77	4.44	4.20
	.05	4.49	3.63	3.24	3.01	2.85	2.74
	.10	3.05	2.67	2.46	2.33	2.24	2.18

Table B.3   Continued

| | | df for the Numerator | | | | | |
df for the Denominator	Type I Error Rate						
17	.01	8.40	6.11	5.19	4.67	4.34	4.10
	.05	4.45	3.59	3.20	2.97	2.81	2.70
	.10	3.03	2.65	2.44	2.31	2.22	2.15
18	.01	8.29	6.01	5.09	4.58	4.25	4.02
	.05	4.41	3.56	3.16	2.93	2.77	2.66
	.10	3.01	2.62	2.42	2.29	2.20	2.13
19	.01	8.19	5.93	5.01	4.50	4.17	3.94
	.05	4.38	3.52	3.13	2.90	2.74	2.63
	.10	2.99	2.61	2.40	2.27	2.18	2.11
20	.01	8.10	5.85	4.94	4.43	4.10	3.87
	.05	4.35	3.49	3.10	2.87	2.71	2.60
	.10	2.98	2.59	2.38	2.25	2.16	2.09
21	.01	8.02	5.78	4.88	4.37	4.04	3.81
	.05	4.33	3.47	3.07	2.84	2.69	2.57
	.10	2.96	2.58	2.37	2.23	2.14	2.08
22	.01	7.95	5.72	4.82	4.31	3.99	3.76
	.05	4.30	3.44	3.05	2.82	2.66	2.55
	.10	2.95	2.56	2.35	2.22	2.13	2.06
23	.01	7.88	5.66	4.77	4.26	3.94	3.71
	.05	4.28	3.42	3.03	2.80	2.64	2.53
	.10	2.94	2.55	2.34	2.21	2.12	2.05
24	.01	7.82	5.61	4.72	4.22	3.90	3.67
	.05	4.26	3.40	3.01	2.78	2.62	2.51
	.10	2.93	2.54	2.33	2.20	2.10	2.04
25	.01	7.77	5.57	4.68	4.18	3.86	3.63
	.05	4.24	3.39	2.99	2.76	2.60	2.49
	.10	2.92	2.53	2.32	2.19	2.09	2.03
26	.01	7.72	5.53	4.64	4.14	3.82	3.59
	.05	4.23	3.37	2.98	2.74	2.59	2.48
	.10	2.91	2.52	2.31	2.18	2.08	2.01
27	.01	7.68	5.49	4.60	4.11	3.79	3.56
	.05	4.21	3.36	2.96	2.73	2.57	2.46
	.10	2.90	2.51	2.30	2.17	2.07	2.01
28	.01	7.64	5.45	4.57	4.08	3.75	3.53
	.05	4.20	3.34	2.95	2.72	2.56	2.45
	.10	2.89	2.50	2.29	2.16	2.07	2.00
29	.01	7.60	5.42	4.54	4.05	3.73	3.50
	.05	4.18	3.33	2.94	2.70	2.55	2.43
	.10	2.89	2.50	2.28	2.15	2.06	1.99
30	.01	7.56	5.39	4.51	4.02	3.70	3.47
	.05	4.17	3.32	2.92	2.69	2.53	2.42
	.10	2.88	2.49	2.28	2.14	2.05	1.98
35	.01	7.42	5.27	4.40	3.91	3.59	3.37
	.05	4.12	3.27	2.88	2.64	2.49	2.37
	.10	2.86	2.46	2.25	2.14	2.02	1.95
40	.01	7.32	5.18	4.31	3.91	3.51	3.29
	.05	4.09	3.23	2.84	2.64	2.45	2.34
	.10	2.84	2.44	2.23	2.11	2.00	1.93

Table B.3 Continued

df for the Denominator	Type I Error Rate	df for the Numerator					
45	.01	7.23	5.11	4.25	3.83	3.46	3.23
	.05	4.06	3.21	2.81	2.61	2.42	2.31
	.10	2.82	2.43	2.21	2.09	1.98	1.91
50	.01	7.17	5.06	4.20	3.77	3.41	3.19
	.05	4.04	3.18	2.79	2.58	2.40	2.29
	.10	2.81	2.41	2.20	2.08	1.97	1.90
55	.01	7.12	5.01	4.16	3.72	3.37	3.15
	.05	4.02	3.17	2.77	2.56	2.38	2.27
	.10	2.80	2.40	2.19	2.06	1.96	1.89
60	.01	7.08	4.98	4.13	3.68	3.34	3.12
	.05	4.00	3.15	2.76	2.54	2.37	2.26
	.10	2.79	2.39	2.18	2.05	1.95	1.88
65	.01	7.04	4.95	4.10	3.65	3.31	3.09
	.05	3.99	3.14	2.75	2.53	2.36	2.24
	.10	2.79	2.39	2.17	2.04	1.94	1.87
70	.01	7.01	4.92	4.08	3.62	3.29	3.07
	.05	3.98	3.13	2.74	2.51	2.35	2.23
	.10	2.78	2.38	2.16	2.03	1.93	1.86
75	.01	6.99	4.90	4.06	3.60	3.27	3.05
	.05	3.97	3.12	2.73	2.50	2.34	2.22
	.10	2.77	2.38	2.16	2.03	1.93	1.86
80	.01	3.96	4.88	4.04	3.56	3.26	3.04
	.05	6.96	3.11	2.72	2.49	2.33	2.22
	.10	2.77	2.37	2.15	2.02	1.92	1.85
85	.01	6.94	4.86	4.02	3.55	3.24	3.02
	.05	3.95	3.10	2.71	2.48	2.32	2.21
	.10	2.77	2.37	2.15	2.01	1.92	1.85
90	.01	6.93	4.85	4.02	3.54	3.23	3.01
	.05	3.95	3.10	2.71	2.47	2.32	2.20
	.10	2.76	2.36	2.15	2.01	1.91	1.84
95	.01	6.91	4.84	4.00	3.52	3.22	3.00
	.05	3.94	3.09	2.70	2.47	2.31	2.20
	.10	2.76	2.36	2.14	2.01	1.91	1.84
100	.01	6.90	4.82	3.98	3.51	3.21	2.99
	.05	3.94	3.09	2.70	2.46	2.31	2.19
	.10	2.76	2.36	2.14	2.00	1.91	1.83
Infinity	.01	6.64	4.61	3.78	3.32	3.02	2.80
	.05	3.84	3.00	2.61	2.37	2.22	2.10
	.10	2.71	2.30	2.08	1.95	1.85	1.78

TABLE B4: VALUES OF THE CORRELATION COEFFICIENT NEEDED FOR REJECTION OF THE NULL HYPOTHESIS

How to use this table:

1. Compute the value of the correlation coefficient.

2. Compare the value of the correlation coefficient with the critical value listed in this table.

3. If the obtained value is greater than the critical or tabled value, the null hypothesis (that the correlation coefficient is equal to 0) is not the most attractive explanation for any observed differences.

4. If the obtained value is less than the critical or tabled value, the null hypothesis is the most attractive explanation for any observed differences.

Table B.4   Values of the Correlation Coefficient Needed for Rejection of the Null Hypothesis

	One-Tailed Test			Two-Tailed Test	
df	.05	.01	*df*	.05	.01
1	.9877	.9995	1	.9969	.9999
2	.9000	.9800	2	.9500	.9900
3	.8054	.9343	3	.8783	.9587
4	.7293	.8822	4	.8114	.9172
5	.6694	.8329	5	.7545	.8745
6	.6215	.7887	6	.7067	.8343
7	.5822	.7498	7	.6664	.7977
8	.5494	.7155	8	.6319	.7646
9	.5214	.6851	9	.6021	.7348
10	.4973	.6581	10	.5760	.7079
11	.4762	.6339	11	.5529	.6835
12	.4575	.6120	12	.5324	.6614
13	.4409	.5923	13	.5139	.6411
14	.4259	.5742	14	.4973	.6226
15	.4124	.5577	15	.4821	.6055
16	.4000	.5425	16	.4683	.5897
17	.3887	.5285	17	.4555	.5751
18	.3783	.5155	18	.4438	.5614
19	.3687	.5034	19	.4329	.5487
20	.3598	.4921	20	.4227	.5368
25	.3233	.4451	25	.3809	.4869
30	.2960	.4093	30	.3494	.4487
35	.2746	.3810	35	.3246	.4182
40	.2573	.3578	40	.3044	.3932
45	.2428	.3384	45	.2875	.3721
50	.2306	.3218	50	.2732	.3541
60	.2108	.2948	60	.2500	.3248
70	.1954	.2737	70	.2319	.3017
80	.1829	.2565	80	.2172	.2830
90	.1726	.2422	90	.2050	.2673
100	.1638	.2301	100	.1946	.2540

TABLE B5: CRITICAL VALUES FOR THE CHI-SQUARE TEST

How to use this table:

1. Compute the χ^2 value.

2. Determine the number of degrees of freedom for the rows $(R - 1)$ and the number of degrees of freedom for the columns $(C - 1)$. If it's a one-dimension table, then you have only columns.

3. Locate the critical value by locating the degrees of freedom in the titled (df) column, and under the appropriate column for level of significance, read across.

4. If the obtained value is greater than the critical or tabled value, the null hypothesis (that the frequencies are equal to one another) is not the most attractive explanation for any observed differences.

5. If the obtained value is less than the critical or tabled value, the null hypotheses is the most attractive explanation for any observed differences.

Table B.5   Critical Values for the Chi-Square Test

| | Level of Significance | | |
df	.10	.05	.01
1	2.71	3.84	6.64
2	4.00	5.99	9.21
3	6.25	7.82	11.34
4	7.78	9.49	13.28
5	9.24	11.07	15.09
6	10.64	12.59	16.81
7	12.02	14.07	18.48
8	13.36	15.51	20.09
9	14.68	16.92	21.67
10	16.99	18.31	23.21
11	17.28	19.68	24.72
12	18.65	21.03	26.22
13	19.81	22.36	27.69
14	21.06	23.68	29.14
15	22.31	25.00	30.58
16	23.54	26.30	32.00
17	24.77	27.60	33.41
18	25.99	28.87	34.80
19	27.20	30.14	36.19
20	28.41	31.41	37.57
21	29.62	32.67	38.93
22	30.81	33.92	40.29
23	32.01	35.17	41.64
24	33.20	36.42	42.98
25	34.38	37.65	44.81
26	35.56	38.88	45.64
27	36.74	40.11	46.96
28	37.92	41.34	48.28
29	39.09	42.56	49.59
30	40.26	43.77	50.89

Appendix C
Data Sets

This appendix contains the data sets that were used throughout this book. They are also available for downloading at the Sage Web site. Go to

www.sagepub.com

and search for

E-SalkindDataSets

then click on the book title.

Chapter 2 Data Set 1

	prej
1	87.00
2	99.00
3	87.00
4	87.00
5	67.00
6	87.00
7	77.00
8	89.00
9	99.00
10	96.00
11	76.00
12	55.00
13	64.00
14	81.00
15	94.00
16	81.00
17	82.00
18	99.00
19	93.00
20	94.00

Chapter 2 Data Set 2

	score1	score2	score3
1	3.00	34.00	154.00
2	7.00	54.00	167.00
3	5.00	17.00	132.00
4	4.00	26.00	145.00
5	5.00	34.00	154.00
6	6.00	25.00	145.00
7	7.00	14.00	113.00
8	8.00	24.00	156.00
9	6.00	25.00	154.00
10	5.00	23.00	123.00

Chapter 3 Data Set 1

	reac_tm
1	.40
2	.70
3	.40
4	.90
5	.80
6	.70
7	.30
8	1.90
9	1.20
10	2.80
11	.80
12	.90
13	1.10
14	1.30
15	.20
16	.60
17	.80
18	.70
19	.50
20	2.60
21	.50
22	2.10
23	2.30
24	.20
25	.50
26	.70
27	1.10
28	.90
29	.60
30	.20

Chapter 4 Data Set 1

	comp-sc
1	47.00
2	2.00
3	44.00
4	41.00
5	7.00
6	6.00
7	3.00
8	38.00
9	35.00
10	36.00
11	10.00
12	11.00
13	14.00
14	14.00
15	30.00
16	30.00
17	32.00
18	33.00
19	34.00
20	32.00
21	31.00
22	31.00
23	15.00
24	16.00
25	17.00
26	16.00
27	15.00
28	19.00
29	18.00
30	16.00
31	25.00
32	25.00
33	26.00
34	26.00
35	27.00
36	29.00
37	29.00
38	28.00
39	29.00
40	27.00
41	20.00
42	21.00
43	21.00
44	21.00
45	24.00
46	24.00
47	23.00
48	23.00
49	21.00
50	20.00

Chapter 5 Data Set 1

	income	educ
1	$36577	11
2	$54365	12
3	$33542	10
4	$65654	12
5	$45765	11
6	$24354	7
7	$43233	12
8	$44321	13
9	$23216	9
10	$43454	12
11	$64543	12
12	$43433	14
13	$34644	12
14	$33213	10
15	$55654	15
16	$76545	14
17	$21324	11
18	$17645	12
19	$23432	11
20	$44543	15

Chapter 5 Data Set 2

	correct	att
1	17.00	94.00
2	13.00	73.00
3	12.00	59.00
4	15.00	80.00
5	16.00	93.00
6	14.00	85.00
7	16.00	66.00
8	16.00	79.00
9	18.00	77.00
10	19.00	91.00

Chapter 6 Data Set 1

	training	injuries
1	12.00	8.00
2	3.00	7.00
3	22.00	2.00
4	12.00	5.00
5	11.00	4.00
6	31.00	1.00
7	27.00	5.00
8	31.00	1.00
9	8.00	2.00
10	16.00	2.00
11	14.00	7.00
12	26.00	2.00
13	36.00	2.00
14	26.00	2.00
15	15.00	6.00
16	11.00	5.00
17	16.00	7.00
18	14.00	8.00
19	15.00	3.00
20	16.00	7.00
21	22.00	3.00
22	24.00	8.00
23	26.00	8.00
24	31.00	2.00
25	12.00	2.00
26	24.00	3.00
27	33.00	3.00
28	21.00	5.00
29	12.00	7.00
30	36.00	3.00

Chapter 6 Data Set 2

	time	correct
1	14.50	5
2	13.40	7
3	12.70	6
4	16.40	2
5	21.00	4
6	13.90	3
7	17.30	12
8	12.50	5
9	16.70	4
10	22.70	3

Chapter 10 Data Set 1

	group	memtest
1	Group 1	7
2	Group 1	3
3	Group 1	3
4	Group 1	2
5	Group 1	3
6	Group 1	8
7	Group 1	8
8	Group 1	5
9	Group 1	8
10	Group 1	5
11	Group 1	5
12	Group 1	4
13	Group 1	6
14	Group 1	10
15	Group 1	10
16	Group 1	5
17	Group 1	1
18	Group 1	1
19	Group 1	4
20	Group 1	3
21	Group 1	5
22	Group 1	7
23	Group 1	1
24	Group 1	9
25	Group 1	2
26	Group 1	5
27	Group 1	2
28	Group 1	12
29	Group 1	15
30	Group 1	4
31	Group 2	5
32	Group 2	4
33	Group 2	4
34	Group 2	5
35	Group 2	5
36	Group 2	7
37	Group 2	8
38	Group 2	8
39	Group 2	9
40	Group 2	8
41	Group 2	3
42	Group 2	2
43	Group 2	5
44	Group 2	4
45	Group 2	4
46	Group 2	6
47	Group 2	7
48	Group 2	7
49	Group 2	5

(continued)

Chapter 10 Data Set 1 Continued

	group	memtest
50	Group 2	6
51	Group 2	4
52	Group 2	3
53	Group 2	2
54	Group 2	7
55	Group 2	6
56	Group 2	2
57	Group 2	8
58	Group 2	9
59	Group 2	7
60	Group 2	6

Chapter 10 Data Set 2

gender	hands_up
1.00	9.00
2.00	3.00
2.00	5.00
2.00	1.00
1.00	8.00
1.00	4.00
2.00	2.00
2.00	6.00
1.00	9.00
1.00	3.00
2.00	4.00
1.00	8.00
2.00	3.00
1.00	10.00
2.00	6.00
1.00	8.00
2.00	7.00
1.00	9.00
2.00	9.00
1.00	8.00
2.00	7.00
2.00	3.00
2.00	7.00
2.00	6.00
1.00	10.00
1.00	7.00
1.00	6.00
1.00	12.00
2.00	8.00
2.00	8.00

Chapter 10 Data Set 3

urban	rural
1.00	6.50
2.00	7.90
2.00	4.30
2.00	6.80
1.00	9.90
1.00	6.80
1.00	4.80
2.00	6.50
2.00	3.30
1.00	4.00
2.00	13.17
1.00	5.26
2.00	9.25
1.00	8.00
2.00	1.25
1.00	4.23
1.00	6.95
2.00	6.74
1.00	5.96
2.00	5.25
2.00	2.36
1.00	9.25
1.00	6.36
1.00	8.99
1.00	5.58
2.00	4.25
1.00	6.60
2.00	1.00
1.00	5.00
2.00	3.50

Chapter 11 Data Set 1

	pretest	posttest
1	3.00	7.00
2	5.00	8.00
3	4.00	6.00
4	6.00	7.00
5	5.00	8.00
6	5.00	9.00
7	4.00	6.00
8	5.00	6.00
9	3.00	7.00
10	6.00	8.00
11	7.00	8.00
12	8.00	7.00
13	7.00	9.00
14	6.00	10.00
15	7.00	9.00
16	8.00	9.00
17	8.00	8.00
18	9.00	8.00
19	9.00	4.00
20	8.00	4.00
21	7.00	5.00
22	7.00	6.00
23	6.00	9.00
24	7.00	8.00
25	8.00	12.00

Chapter 11 Data Set 2

	pretest	posttest
1	20.00	23.00
2	6.00	8.00
3	12.00	11.00
4	34.00	35.00
5	55.00	57.00
6	43.00	76.00
7	54.00	54.00
8	24.00	26.00
9	33.00	35.00
10	21.00	26.00
11	34.00	29.00
12	33.00	31.00
13	54.00	56.00
14	23.00	22.00
15	33.00	35.00
16	44.00	41.00
17	65.00	56.00
18	43.00	34.00
19	53.00	51.00
20	22.00	21.00
21	34.00	31.00
22	32.00	33.00
23	44.00	38.00
24	17.00	15.00
25	28.00	27.00

Chapter 11 Data Set 3

	before	after
1	1.30	6.50
2	2.50	8.70
3	2.30	9.80
4	4.10	10.20
5	3.60	7.90
6	4.70	6.50
7	6.20	8.70
8	5.20	7.90
9	4.40	8.70
10	4.00	9.10
11	53.20	8.40
12	4.50	6.40
13	4.50	7.20
14	1.10	5.80
15	3.10	6.90
16	5.10	5.90
17	3.70	7.60
18	3.20	7.80
19	5.60	7.30
20	5.20	4.60

Chapter 12 Data Set 1

	group	lang_sc
1	5 Hours	87.00
2	5 Hours	86.00
3	5 Hours	76.00
4	5 Hours	56.00
5	5 Hours	78.00
6	5 Hours	98.00
7	5 Hours	77.00
8	5 Hours	66.00
9	5 Hours	75.00
10	5 Hours	67.00
11	10 Hours	87.00
12	10 Hours	85.00
13	10 Hours	99.00
14	10 Hours	85.00
15	10 Hours	79.00
16	10 Hours	81.00
17	10 Hours	82.00
18	10 Hours	78.00
19	10 Hours	85.00
20	10 Hours	91.00
21	20 Hours	89.00
22	20 Hours	91.00
23	20 Hours	96.00
24	20 Hours	87.00
25	20 Hours	89.00
26	20 Hours	90.00
27	20 Hours	89.00
28	20 Hours	96.00
29	20 Hours	96.00
30	20 Hours	93.00

Chapter 12 Data Set 2

	prac	time
1	1.00	58.70
2	1.00	55.30
3	1.00	61.80
4	1.00	49.50
5	1.00	64.50
6	1.00	61.00
7	1.00	65.70
8	1.00	51.40
9	1.00	53.60
10	1.00	59.00
11	2.00	64.40
12	2.00	55.80
13	2.00	58.70
14	2.00	54.70
15	2.00	52.70
16	2.00	67.80
17	2.00	61.60
18	2.00	58.70
19	2.00	54.60
20	2.00	51.50
21	2.00	54.70
22	2.00	61.40
23	2.00	56.90
24	3.00	68.00
25	3.00	65.90
26	3.00	54.70
27	3.00	53.60
28	3.00	58.70
29	3.00	58.70
30	3.00	65.70
31	3.00	66.50
32	3.00	56.70
33	3.00	55.40
34	3.00	51.50
35	3.00	54.80
36	3.00	57.20

Chapter 13 Data Set 1

	qual_mar	qual_pc
1	76	43
2	81	33
3	78	23
4	76	34
5	76	31
6	78	51
7	76	56
8	78	43
9	98	44
10	88	45
11	76	32
12	66	33
13	44	28
14	67	39
15	65	31
16	59	38
17	87	21
18	77	27
19	79	43
20	85	46
21	68	41
22	76	41
23	77	48
24	98	56
25	99	55
26	98	45
27	87	68
28	67	54
29	78	33

Chapter 13 Data Set 2

	motiv	gpa
1	1	3.40
2	6	3.40
3	2	2.50
4	7	3.10
5	5	2.80
6	4	2.60
7	3	2.10
8	1	1.60
9	8	3.10
10	6	2.60
11	5	3.20
12	6	3.10
13	5	3.20
14	5	2.70
15	6	2.80
16	6	2.60
17	7	2.50
18	7	2.80
19	2	1.80
20	9	3.70
21	8	3.10
22	8	2.50
23	7	2.40
24	6	2.10
25	9	4.00
26	7	3.90
27	8	3.10
28	7	3.30
29	8	3.00
30	9	2.00

Chapter 14 Data Set 1

	voucher
1	For
2	For
3	For
4	For
5	For
6	For
7	For
8	For
9	For
10	For
11	For
12	For
13	For
14	For
15	For
16	For
17	For
18	For
19	For
20	For
21	For
22	For
23	For
24	Maybe
25	Maybe
26	Maybe
27	Maybe
28	Maybe
29	Maybe
30	Maybe
31	Maybe
32	Maybe
33	Maybe
34	Maybe
35	Maybe
36	Maybe
37	Maybe
38	Maybe
39	Maybe
40	Maybe
41	Against
42	Against
43	Against
44	Against
45	Against
46	Against
47	Against
48	Against
49	Against

	voucher
50	Against
51	Against
52	Against
53	Against
54	Against
55	Against
56	Against
57	Against
58	Against
59	Against
60	Against
61	Against
62	Against
63	Against
64	Against
65	Against
66	Against
67	Against
68	Against
69	Against
70	Against
71	Against
72	Against
73	Against
74	Against
75	Against
76	Against
77	Against
78	Against
79	Against
80	Against
81	Against
82	Against
83	Against
84	Against
85	Against
86	Against
87	Against
88	Against
89	Against
90	Against

Chapter 14 Data Set 2

	gender
1	Boys
2	Boys
3	Boys
4	Boys
5	Boys
6	Boys
7	Boys
8	Boys
9	Boys
10	Boys
11	Boys
12	Boys
13	Boys
14	Boys
15	Boys
16	Boys
17	Boys
18	Boys
19	Boys
20	Boys
21	Boys
22	Boys
23	Boys
24	Boys
25	Boys
26	Boys
27	Boys
28	Boys
29	Boys
30	Boys
31	Boys
32	Boys
33	Boys
34	Boys
35	Boys
36	Boys
37	Boys
38	Boys
39	Boys
40	Boys
41	Boys
42	Boys
43	Boys
44	Boys
45	Boys
46	Girls
47	Girls
48	Girls
49	Girls

	gender
50	Girls
51	Girls
52	Girls
53	Girls
54	Girls
55	Girls
56	Girls
57	Girls
58	Girls
59	Girls
60	Girls
61	Girls
62	Girls
63	Girls
64	Girls
65	Girls
66	Girls
67	Girls
68	Girls
69	Girls
70	Girls
71	Girls
72	Girls
73	Girls
74	Girls
75	Girls
76	Girls
77	Girls
78	Girls
79	Girls
80	Girls
81	Girls
82	Girls
83	Girls
84	Girls
85	Girls
86	Girls
87	Girls
88	Girls
89	Girls
90	Girls
91	Girls
92	Girls
93	Girls
94	Girls
95	Girls
96	Girls
97	Girls
98	Girls
99	Girls
100	Girls

Sample Data Set

	id	gender	group	test1	test2
1	1.00	Male	Control	98.00	32.00
2	2.00	Female	Exp	87.00	33.00
3	3.00	Female	Control	89.00	54.00
4	4.00	Female	Control	88.00	44.00
5	5.00	Male	Exp	76.00	64.00
6	6.00	Male	Control	68.00	54.00
7	7.00	Female	Control	78.00	44.00
8	8.00	Female	Exp	98.00	32.00
9	9.00	Female	Exp	93.00	64.00
10	10.00	Male	Exp	76.00	37.00
11	11.00	Female	Control	75.00	43.00
12	12.00	Female	Control	65.00	56.00
13	13.00	Male	Control	76.00	78.00
14	14.00	Female	Control	78.00	99.00
15	15.00	Female	Control	89.00	87.00
16	16.00	Female	Exp	81.00	56.00
17	17.00	Male	Control	78.00	78.00
18	18.00	Female	Control	83.00	56.00
19	19.00	Male	Control	88.00	67.00
20	20.00	Female	Control	90.00	88.00
21	21.00	Male	Control	93.00	81.00
22	22.00	Male	Exp	89.00	93.00
23	23.00	Female	Exp	86.00	87.00
24	24.00	Male	Control	77.00	80.00
25	25.00	Male	Control	89.00	99.00

GLOSSARY

Analysis of variance

A test for the difference between two or more means. A simple analysis of variance (or ANOVA) has only one independent variable, while a factorial analysis of variance tests the means of more than one independent variable. One-way analysis of variance looks for differences between the means of more than two groups.

Arithmetic mean

A measure of central tendency that sums all the scores in the data sets and divides by the number of scores.

Asymptotic

The quality of the normal curve such that the tails never touch.

Average

The most representative score in a set of scores.

Bell-shaped curve

A distribution of scores that is symmetrical about the mean, median, and mode and has asymptotic tails.

Class interval

The upper and lower boundary of a set of scores used in the creation of a frequency distribution.

Coefficient of alienation

The amount of variance unaccounted for in the relationship between two variables.

Coefficient of determination

The amount of variance accounted for in the relationship between two variables.

Coefficient of nondetermination

See coefficient of alienation

Correlation coefficient

A numerical index that reflects the relationship between two variables.

Correlation matrix

A set of correlation coefficients.

Criterion

Another term for the outcome variable.

Critical value

The value necessary for rejection (or nonacceptance) of the null hypothesis.

Cumulative frequency distribution

A frequency distribution that shows frequencies for class intervals along with the cumulative frequency for each.

Data

A record of an observation or an event such as a test score, a grade in math class, or response time.

Data point

An observation.

Data set

A set of data points.

Degrees of freedom

A value that is different for different statistical tests and approximates the sample size of number of individual cells in an experimental design.

Dependent variable

The outcome variable or the predicted variable in a regression equation.

Descriptive statistics

Values that describe the characteristics of a sample or population.

Direct correlation

A positive correlation where the values of both variables change in the same direction.

Directional research hypothesis

A research hypothesis that includes a statement of inequality.

Error in prediction

The difference between the actual score (Y) and the predicted score (Y').

Error of estimate

See error in prediction

Factorial design

A research design where there is more than one treatment variable.

Frequency distribution

A method for illustrating the distribution of scores within class intervals.

Frequency polygon

A graphical representation of a frequency distribution.

Histogram

A graphical representation of a frequency distribution.

Hypothesis

An if-then statement of conjecture that relates variables to one another.

Independent variable

The treatment variable that is manipulated or the predictor variable in a regression equation.

Indirect correlation

A negative correlation where the values of variables move in opposite direct ions.

Inferential statistics

Tools that are used to infer the results based on a sample to a population.

Kurtosis

The quality of a distribution such that it is flat or peaked.

Leptokurtic

The quality of a normal curve that defines its peakedness.

Line of best fit

The regression line that best fits the actual scores and minimizes the error in prediction.

Linear correlation

A correlation that is best expressed as a straight line.

Mean

A type of average where scores are summed and divided by the number of observations.

Mean deviation

The average deviation for all scores from the mean of a distribution.

Measures of central tendency

The mean, median, and mode.

Median

The point at which 50% of the cases in a distribution fall below and 50% fall above.

Midpoint

The central point in a class interval.

Mode

The most frequently occurring score in a distribution.

Multiple regression

A statistical technique where several variables are used to predict one.

Nondirectional research hypothesis

A hypothesis that posits no direction, but a difference.

Nonparametric statistics

Distribution-free statistics.

Normal curve

See bell-shaped curve

Null hypothesis

A statement of equality between a set of variables.

Obtained value

The value that results from the application of a statistical test.

Ogive

A visual representation of a cumulative frequency distribution.

One-tailed test

A directional test.

One-way analysis of variance

See analysis of variance

Outliers

Those scores in a distribution that are noticeably much more extreme than the majority of scores. Exactly what score is an outlier is usually an arbitrary decision made by the researcher.

Parametric statistics

Statistics used for the inference from a sample to a population.

Pearson product-moment correlation

See correlation coefficient

Percentile point

The point at or below a score appears.

Platykurtic

The quality of a normal curve that defines its flatness.

Population

All the possible subjects or cases of interest.

Post hoc

After the fact, referring to tests done to determine the true source of a difference between three or more groups.

Predictor

The variable that predicts an outcome.

Range

The highest minus the lowest score and a gross measure of variability. *Exclusive* range is the highest score minus the lowest score. *Inclusive* range is the highest score minus the lowest score plus 1.

Regression equation

The equation that defines the points and the line that are closest to the actual scores.

Regression line

The line drawn based on the values in the regression equation.

Research hypothesis

A statement of inequality between two variables.

Sample

A subset of a population.

Sampling error

The difference between sample and population values.

Scattergram, or scatterplot

A plot of paired data points.

Significance level

The risk set by the researcher for rejecting a null hypothesis when it is true.

Simple analysis of variance

See analysis of variance

Skew, or skewness

The quality of a distribution that defines the disproportionate frequency of certain scores. A longer right tail than left corresponds to a smaller number of occurrences at the high end of the distribution; this is a *positively* skewed distribution. A shorter right tail than left corresponds to a larger number of occurrences at the high end of the distribution; this is a *negatively* skewed distribution.

Standard deviation

The average deviation from the mean.

Standard error of estimate

A measure of accuracy in prediction.

Standard score

See z score

Statistical significance

See significance level

Statistics

A set of tools and techniques used to organize and interpret information.

Test statistic value

See obtained value

Two-tailed test

A test of a nondirectional hypothesis where the direction of the difference is of little importance.

Type I error

The probability of rejecting a null hypothesis when it is true.

Type II error

The probability of accepting a null hypothesis when it is false.

Unbiased estimate

A conservative estimate of a population parameter.

Variability

The amount of spread or dispersion in a set of scores.

Variance

The square of the standard deviation, and another measure of a distribution's spread or dispersion.

Y' or *Y* prime

The predicted *Y* value.

z score

A raw score that is adjusted for the mean and standard deviation of the distribution from which the raw score comes.

INDEX

ABOUT THE AUTHOR

NEIL J. SALKIND received his PhD in human development from the University of Maryland and has been teaching at the University of Kansas for 25 years. He has published over 70 professional papers and is the author of several college-level textbooks including *Child Development, Exploring Research,* and *Theories of Human Development*. He is also editor of *Child Development Abstracts and Bibliography,* published by the Society for Research in Child Development, and is also an active writer in the trade area. In the estimate of the author and his family, he was born to write *Statistics for People Who (Think They) Hate Statistics*. When Salkind showed the plan for the book to his daughter, she looked at him and said, "Finally, your true purpose for being on earth has been found."